James John Garth Wilkinson

The New Jerusalem and the Old Jerusalem

James John Garth Wilkinson

The New Jerusalem and the Old Jerusalem

ISBN/EAN: 9783337004385

Printed in Europe, USA, Canada, Australia, Japan

Cover: Foto ©ninafisch / pixelio.de

More available books at **www.hansebooks.com**

THE NEW JERUSALEM
AND THE OLD JERUSALEM

"*In that day shall there be a highway out of Egypt to Assyria, and the Assyrian shall come into Egypt, and the Egyptian into Assyria; and the Egyptians shall worship with the Assyrians. In that day shall Israel be the third with Egypt and with Assyria, a blessing in the midst of the earth: for that the Lord of hosts hath blessed them, saying, Blessed be Egypt my people, and Assyria the work of my hands, and Israel mine inheritance.*"

ISAIAH xix. 23–25.

THE NEW JERUSALEM

AND

THE OLD JERUSALEM

The Place and Service of the Jewish Church among the Æons of Revelation

WITH OTHER ESSAYS

BY

JAMES JOHN GARTH WILKINSON
FELLOW OF THE ROYAL GEOGRAPHICAL SOCIETY

JAMES SPEIRS
36 BLOOMSBURY STREET, LONDON
1894

CONTENTS.

		PAGE
DEDICATION,		ix
INTRODUCTION,		xi
I.	THE STRENGTH OF THE JEWS,	1
II.	THE PATIENCE OF THE JEWS,	4
III.	THE JEWS AND THE OLD TESTAMENT,	5
IV.	JUDAISM AND THE INCARNATION,	6
V.	WHY THIS PLANET WAS THE PLACE OF CHRIST'S REDEMPTIVE COMBATS,	8
VI.	THE FIRST ADVENT,	9
VII.	IMPLICIT ACCEPTANCE OF THE WORD DEMANDED,	11
VIII.	FALSITIES CAST OUT AND TRUTHS IMPLANTED,	13
IX.	THE VIRGIN MARY,	14
X.	THE MOTHER OF JESUS,	18
XI.	MARY BECOMES A DIVINE SYMBOL AS JOHN AND THE DISCIPLES WERE,	20
XII.	CHARACTER, NOT BLOOD-RELATIONSHIP, LIVES AND CONSOCIATES AFTER DEATH,	22
XIII.	THE REPRESENTATION OF A CHURCH BY THE JEWS,	24
XIV.	HOW A REPRESENTATIVE CAN ASCEND,	27
XV.	THE JEWISH CHARACTER WAS NOT ALTERED BUT MADE REPRESENTATIVE,	29
XV.	SIGNS PRECEDING JUDAISM,	33
XVI.	THE WORD VINDICATED,	38
XVII.	HUMAN NATURE NEEDS A REVELATION,	42

		PAGE
XVIII.	The Thick Darkness about God on Mount Sinai,	44
XIX.	Some Thoughts about Correspondence,	45
XX.	Jewish Freedom and Bondage,	48
XXI.	Saul and Samuel,	51
XXII.	Impossibilities were not asked of the Jews,	55
XXIII.	Ineradicable Polygamy, Jewish and Mahometan,	57
XXIV.	The Jewish Drama became more and more Ineffective,	59
XXV.	New Revelations,	61
XXVI.	The Mediumship of David and the Prophets,	62
XXVII.	The Immanence of Jehovah in the Mosaic Dispensation,	65
XXVIII.	The Messianic Promises,	70
XXIX.	The Expulsion of the Jews from Canaan,	76
XXX.	A Church must exist on Earth,	79
XXXI.	The Word, the conjoining Medium,	82
XXXII.	The Divine Value of the Letter,	86
XXXIII.	The Lord's Prayer,	89
XXXIV.	Goodness and Truth are the Two Sides of the Word,	94
XXXV.	The Keeping of the Jews fulfils Prophecy,	96
XXXVI.	The Food of the Jews Divinely Ordained and Limited,	99
XXXVII.	The Restoration of the Jews,	103
XXXVIII.	The Future of the Jews,	105
XXXIX.	Instances of Correspondences,	110
XL.	The Divine Natural,	129

CONTENTS.

vii

		PAGE
XLI. THE CANON OF THE WORD,	. .	141
XLII. THE FOUR GOSPELS,	. . .	142
XLIII. MARY MAGDALENE,	. . .	169
XLIV. RESIST NOT THE EVIL ONE,	. .	171
XLV. ESTIMATES OF THE BIBLE,	. .	176
XLVI. ETHNOLOGY,	. . . .	183
XLVII. ARCHÆOLOGY AND THE MONUMENTS,	.	184
XLVIII. THE BODY OF MAN,	. . .	199
XLIX. THE WELLS OF ABRAHAM,	. .	211
L. PERSONAL IDENTITY,	. . .	228
LI. THE CHANCES AND LIKELIHOODS OF SCIENCE,	. . . .	233
LII. SOME PRIVILEGES OF ATHEISM,	. .	241
LIII. THE FERTILIZATION OF FLOWERS BY INSECTS,	. . . .	246
LIV. DARWINISM CARRIED OUT,	. .	253
LV. SUN WORSHIP,	. . . .	257
LVI. THE HUMANE SUN,	. . .	262
LVII. SPACES AND NUMBERS IN THE WORD,	.	266
LVIII. THE ANIMAL KINGDOM AND THE EARTHLY BODY,	. . . . .	269
LIX. A PIECE OF MORAL PHYSIOLOGY,	.	274
LX. BREATH,	. . . . .	276
LXI. ASSYRIAN REASONINGS,	. . .	277
LXII. HEREDITIES,	. . . .	282
LXIII. DREAMS AND VISIONS,	. . .	286
LXIV. THE PLAGUES OF SCIENTISM,	. .	291
LXV. FUTURITY VERSUS IMMORTALITY,	.	298
LXVI. BEGINNINGS,	. . . .	300
LXVII. SPIRITUAL RULERS,	. . .	304
LXVIII. GOLD AS SOCIAL SUBSTANCE,	. .	305
LXIX. THE DIVINE CYCLE,	. . .	307

DEDICATION.

To JAMES SPILLING, Esq.

Dear Mr. Spilling,

I desire to inscribe to you the following pages because of the help and delight that I find in your Works. Peaceful and astir with life, doctrinal and not controversial, authoritative and humble, reverent and witty, they are warm with interests which the world little knows to exist in the opened Word of God. Your modest narratives burn and shine with its spiritual fire. And as Sagas of East Anglian Family Life they abound in touching episodes of the love and brotherhood which make true homes. Those who have lived with you AMID THE CORN and AMONG THE FLOWERS see how heaven in these sanctuaries prepares its transcendent and unspeakable dramas. In the lively pages of ME AND MINE, you enter the human form and its ancient realm by the Bible gate, and converse with its organs, seerwise, as their ministries are uplifted by Revelation: as the Rev. John Worcester in his PHYSIOLOGICAL CORRES-

PONDENCES travels through the peoples of the same organs in their provinces in the spiritual world.

In inaugurating so profoundly novel a literature adequate to these times, you are carrying the bread of the New Religion to every land where the English Language is spoken. And those who know you already will devoutly pray that your office may be greater and greater, and extend your genial hand to all the nations of the earth.—With heartfelt sympathy, yours,

JAMES JOHN GARTH WILKINSON.

June 2, 1894.

INTRODUCTION.

THE Christian world looks at the Old Bible through the New Testament, and is increasingly unable to do justice to the Jewish Dispensation as a Covenant of Jehovah with a peculiar people. Our purpose in this book is to show that both the Jewish and Christian Churches stand at this day under the light of a higher Revelation, into which it is necessary to enter, in order that the Word of God may be vindicated, and be seen and rationally acknowledged to be such : that both the Old and the New Testaments contain a divine sense, the admission and comprehension of which gives the Church of Christ a new understanding and a new life. Its first epoch, founded upon the mission and forthgoing of disciples and apostles, is terminated, and though there be no apparent pause in history, its end has come. The epoch which is its successor is founded upon an inward mission from the natural to the spiritual man. Let us now consider the evidences of the new divine beginning, and then of the human end.

Nation rises against nation, and kingdom against kingdom in the last days of the Æon or Church ; but this has been the case along the line of history; so that, looking from the outside or letter, we may say that the last days of the present epoch began with its beginning, and are in consummation only now.

Christ was born of a Jewess, and made His Humanity divine by putting off His motherhood and putting on His Fatherhood. Christianity was born of Judaism, and could not put the nature of the world's senility aside.

But now by miracle of judgment and providence a religion is inaugurated which can be redeemed from its origin, and the Lord, and not Judea, will be the Father of it, the Father in the heavens. And its Church will not pass away.

We have dwelt in the following pages on the divine and positive signs of the End, which are, *first*, the Second Coming of the Lord, in a doctrinal revelation to the highest reason of faith, and to the series of sciences internal in the soul of man. This embraces a divine assurance from the whole Word that He is God, and that whoso seeth, that is, understandeth Him, seeth the Father. The *second* sign of the End is, that the spiritual Word is now added to the natural Word; and the spiritual sense is again the Second Advent. The clouds of heaven are opened, and the glory of the Lord is revealed. The *third* sign is that the spiritual world is made known to mankind: that the Last Judgment on the first Christian Church has been witnessed and is testified to; that the first heaven and the first earth have passed away, and their sea is no more: also that the first resurrection has taken place, and the new heaven and the new earth have been visioned from the Patmos of celestial charity, by John, now Emanuel. A *fourth* sign of the End is, that the veil of the mind's Old Temple is rent in twain from the top to the bottom; and that Freedom and Rationality in quite new measure are given away by the Redeemer to all mankind. He maketh His Sun, the Spiritual Sun, whose heat is love, and its light wisdom, to shine upon all, the evil as well as the good; and faculties and powers unknown

INTRODUCTION. xiii

come forth into day from the new liberty of will on the new orb of intellect. These signs are mere powers until they are housed in a New Church. Yet they are testimonies the like of which no previous religion has had on the human side; for Christ is the Lord God Himself, and not a religion.

The negative testimonies to the consummation of the Æon are manifold. The Church is in almost undisputed possession of the world, and the world is uninfluenced by it so that the coming of the kingdom of God on earth is no aspiration of ecclesiastics, though it lies concealed in the heart of lay populations. The old theological ages might be geological in length, and no clerical expectation would arise that human nature can be changed or regenerated. The Atonement, promising salvation on loose terms, is chargeable with this breadth of death.

Note here that a single ruling falsity when a man persuades himself that it is a truth, so hinders the intellectual sight in that respect as to make revelation against the falsity impossible. The victim to such confirmation is spiritually blind. Such a falsity it is that Christ by the passion of the cross paid the penalty of the world's sins to the Father; and that faith in this transaction alters the final divine judgment on good and evil, right and wrong. A physical illustration of this fact, that one obstinately false position destroys a realm of truths, is furnished by those who still insist that the earth is the centre of the solar system. For them astronomy does not exist, excepting as so much raw sensuality. The dogma of the Churches concerning the Cross has been attacked from the side of irreligion; and is easily convicted of absurdity. The strong faith in it is the Red Dragon of the Apocalypse. Swedenborg in his commission has conquered this monster for us if we will, by revealing the true doctrine of the Incarnation, and teaching what it did for mankind, and what it enables every religious man to do for himself.

But without characterizing false dogmas further one by one, it may better be said broadly that the Old Christianity of the Churches and Sects is worn out. Its past literature is a dead sea, like that very sea that is no more. Full of excellent writings by good Churchmen, it succumbs to the fate of its time, and is in liquidation or consummation. The Human Will and Intellect, bankrupt by the all-pervading Atonement, in mercy will depart from its ways and thoughts, and must live in new adventures.

For now, looking at the case in a secular way, everything that literature and learning could do has been expended upon the elements and materials of this same old Christianity. No new lights come to it from age to age. Nothing new can be written on the letter of Scripture, the only Scripture that is believed in. No new statement of dogmas is to be expected. Those of orthodoxy are clearly defined, and are altered by no disputation. They are plainly the only flesh and bone of the Church, but have no testimony in the Bible.

The dissenting sects live in the same dogmas, only that with them these are not endorsed in thirty-nine articles. For that reason they are held more individually, and with some choice as to those which each mind prefers. But Dissent has nothing further to say about its creed, and cannot hope to add fresh confirmations to the literature and preaching it has already given forth.

The same may be said of Unitarianism. Its negative attitude to the Deity of Christ, modified by some belief in His Divinity, is a reasoned and settled produce of history, and its career as a fixed creed is made. The religion of it is good morality.

INTRODUCTION.

Thus the religious bodies have said their say, and for the most part abide in it. The place which the result occupies in their several brains is definite, and the influence established.

Among the orthodox, faith dominates reason, though not averse to welcome reasonings or likelihoods in favour of its dogmas.

There are, however, many protests against this core of fixed opinions. There are latitudinarians who think for themselves, and believe that their own minds are adequate to discern what is necessary to the formation of true opinions. Though they are free here, nothing original comes of it, and nothing impartible. There are Theists to whom the same remark applies. There are the people of the inner light accredited with the Holy Spirit, but no outer light unknown before comes of it.

There are the many-handed learned men who work at the "higher criticism," and vivisect the Bible to find out how and by whom it was made and put together. They establish for themselves that it is a patchwork of great and little fragments unscientifically pieced into one, and they are busy, and will be busy, in fitting the parts and members of their puzzle by another order into their proper places. Whatever novelty they attain will belong to themselves, and excite little interest in the minds of religious conservators.

Then there are the anti-supernaturalists, who love the "grand old book," but see at a glance that it is spoilt by myths, superstitions and fables; by spiritual pretences and delusions; by visions, prophecies, and miracles. These vitals they pluck out and cast away, to make the Bible tolerable and reasonable. There is no new universal endowment in casting out of the mind what your temperament dislikes.

Absence of novelty is our salient point here; though mere novelty has no claims. Strictly speaking there is nothing novel in religion from the first. From Adam to Swedenborg dispensation after dispensation is nothing but love to God and love to man proclaimed in each Æon with a different fresh authority. But the novelty comes in where this awful identity declares itself, and it is nothing less over the present mankind than their new behaviour commanded for a new heaven and a new earth.

Now where the same dry dead study in Church and Church, in Sect and Sect, in Freethinking and Criticism, in Theism and Atheism, leaves everything the same at the end of the day's work, the question we respectfully put to the several bodies and individuals mentioned, with exception of the Atheists, but most especially to our own National Church, is, how religious vitality can be kept when this fatiguing want of results is so manifest, and when no hope is shown anywhere of spiritual refreshment? Being under Christ, we are under the Way, the Truth, and the Life. Way in Him involves progress of our will to walk in it, willing the walk day by day; truth from Him is divine original guidance into newness of heart; life is action such as cannot be anticipated or dreamed of, in careers which He alone opens in the genius of the day's works.

There is none of this progress in the Church, and owing to its dogma of salvation by faith alone, there is no felt need of change of heart. Human nature is unregenerate, and is not summoned by the Church to confess to any need of regeneration, which is the only new thing that can come to man.

The Church is busied in its rituals as the Jews were in theirs, but without the Jewish authority. It sends missions to the ends of the earth, dogmatic missions to races incapable of dogmas. Its good work prints Bibles in all languages, which will be stores for a future time. But its own mind is such that it cannot open these Scriptures. So here its way comes literally to an end.

The Church is a useful almoner to the poor and needy, a minister to the sick; and benignantly associated with birth and death and wedlock. I reverence it as a visible testimony of this nation to Christ's religion, and as the keeper of great traditions. But what it lacks is religious movement, as totally distinct from social movement. The one is inward, the other is outward. The letter of the Word now pleaded as the Word of God cannot furnish religious movement. The Word must descend from heaven into the mind to give new conditions to human nature; and the Word in heaven is the Word which alone can come down from heaven. It is the Sun of Life. The natural sense of itself is the same every day, with outward variation according to the state of the reader. But, unless through knowledge, it never reaches the spiritual degree. The spiritual sense, when it is attained in a clean life, is never the same; but each text fills the reverent mind, and communicates, as we now know by revelation, with heaven after heaven, with one spiritual society and with another. And the more societies it communicates with, the more ample are the descending love and wisdom that dissipate the letter, and stand as the Word freshly spoken through the heavens by the Lord.

In talking of Newness, my dear Vicar, this is what I am aiming at. It seems that with such a fountain of living waters, the better side of the world would be gained to your ecclesia. If, as I believe, you, and other large bodies, according to the rule of *bonus textuarius bonus theologus*, have said and done all that is possible about the letter, what remains is that you walk to Emmaus with Him who opens eyes to *understand* the Scripture, whether in Moses, the Prophets, or the Psalms; and that you also continue the Way, Truth and Life, through His Commissioner, Swedenborg, in an onward course through the Four Gospels and the Apocalypse. It is not an easy course for an Old Churchman; but it is better than undeserved sleep. Like the Master, you must go down into Egypt, but with the young child *in* you, and remain there with him until your ruling Herod is no more.

In their present case, religious bodies are, in any higher sense than takes note of useful mundane institutions, mainly dull and uninteresting. We appreciate the good they do in parishing and public service, but when they stand by death-beds and graves, and we would fain have light from them about the life after death, and the reception of the parting soul, then they are identified with the dead body, and human interest is affronted. They are a case of what Professor Sayce calls the 'single instance'; for the Letter of the Word is such. Without the spirit it is dead and undivine, an unchecked lower house voting heresies. And the spirit of man sleeps in it as in the grave. The Church herself puts in the earth or dust that stops up the Wells of the Waters of Abraham. Ashes to ashes express sadly the dogma of dead resurrection.

It will be allowed by all public men, and eagerly endorsed by all private, that the first duty of prophets, teachers, churches, is to gain the ears of flocks by awakening *interest* in the subjects of discourse, and by making even rituals living; and this can only be done by the wallet of priest and preacher containing things new and old; the new being apparent, and giving young life to the old. And for clergy themselves, the new doctrinal and then spiritual life perpetually imparted *to them first*, is the most important of all, inasmuch as it eliminates monotony from their laborious lives, and makes every reading of the Word affecting from the inner love and light in it. The clergy are also companion friends to the tenderest affections of home. Every christening is a new Name in it. Every marriage is an aspiration to the marriage in heaven, where the bride and bridegroom of this altar are "no more twain but one flesh." Every good deathbed and funeral day is a declaration through sacred sorrow of a present or future heaven.

Throughout life, the whole mind of the laity has to be touched by the clergy with spiritual fire from the living Word: and truth must be insisted upon as truth only when it is applied to life and obeyed in conduct, or in other profound words, *made good*. That is the conjunction of truth with good in the character, and this conjunction is in each instance a piece of regeneration. To have done what you know you ought in the sight of God is the plain English of it.

It is easy to foresee immeasurable results from Archbishops, Bishops, Priests and Deacons devout to the living Word, and expounding it to willing Congregations; and Congregations in plenty would be willing enough. For the transmutation of the letter of the Word into the spirit is a perpetual miracle; a supernatural delight to heart and mind. The letter must die before the change can take place. At its deathbed you stand and watch its complete resurrection. And the form of the spirit was inconceivable before it was revealed to you. Here is perpetual newness indeed. The life after death is suggestively opened in every verse.

But now let me chronicle another negative testimony to the End of the Æon. Science is dead in it. It is spacious as astronomy can make it, and timelong as the avenues of history. It is active and aspiring, and aims to school both the world and the Church. But it is now mere Matter, and the froward newspapers and records of that potentate. God has disappeared out of it, and science has no conscience. The living God inhabits the living mind: the dead mind is the mind self-moved, as it were in the Lucretian right lines of its own wilful atoms. The drifts of such death are vivacious and masterful.

But how should science recognize God? How can it do this? Rather, how can it help doing it so? Things were not always thus, but the night of science has come on by degrees, and we are in its midnight now. The highest ground for science is man: he is its "proper study": and therefore it cannot pass over or escape the Human Form. But this form contains the mind organic within it, the spirit of the mind which is the man; and the immortal soul. If no God is discerned here, science about the body is dead, and function is without a purpose. Science is then the negation of everything but its own self-love and self-glorification. A sign of the end.

There is however a positive sign answering to this negative, and again confirming the End of the Æon. The Human Form is the rock on which the New Dispensation stands. It is a divine form, and our personality is in the image and likeness of God. How then should it be possible to banish Him from proper science when every fact and fibre in the creation of man tells of Him. This line of things has been abundantly treated of in the following pages.

And if Man, the Human Form, has God in a manner visible in him, every other form in nature, suns and systems, night and day, and all that is, lives and moves on our planet, is known only through this human form, its twain eyes, and double senses. It is part and property of these ministers.

INTRODUCTION. xxi

Thus it is an appanage to a true theology, an image-and-likeness theology down to the very sand, and is a permitted science about God. And it is studied not only at the peril of science, but to its destruction, if God be left out. For everything streams from Him, represents and corresponds to Him. And in it His divine form and our human form can meet and commune for our deepest knowledge. That is why Anatomy and Physiology as speaking hieroglyphs will become texts to future generations in the New Jerusalem.

In concluding we may hope and pray that the early miracles of conversion may be repeated in all our Churches and Chapels for the high truths now revealed by the Lord, the Redeemer. The troublous times assist the humiliation which is necessary to this end. For religion cannot die without leaving a gap which is instantly filled in a world of wilful pressures. The bodily love of dominion in politics, the prince now of the powers of the air, enters the vacant space. In its unclean heat Church and Dissent alike lose their best characteristics, and hate each other, and this is mutual destruction. To keep the higher plane undestroyed, let them apply themselves mutually to the spiritual sense of the Word. This English nation of which Swedenborg speaks as being of different genius from the other nations in Europe, and also as being in the centre of all Christians, can be interested by its betters in the openings and progressions of truth now afforded; especially as one characteristic of our nation, which accounts for its state is, that we are easily guided by those above us in name and station, and follow their lead. How easily then might our blind eyes be opened by clergy and ministers who themselves have made humble submission to spiritual truth, and who openly consent to be taught by the Lord Jesus.

One passage respecting our people seems to have lessons for godly Conservatism at the present hour.

"The best of the English nation are in the centre of all Christians, because they have interior intellectual light. This comes from their freedom of thinking, and of speaking and writing. The light, however, is not of itself active, but becomes so from others, especially from men of reputation and authority among them. When these men say anything, or when anything they approve of is read, that light shines forth; but rarely before. On this account they have leading men set over them in the spiritual world, and priests renowned for learning and ability are given them, to whose commands and admonitions from this their peculiar nature they listen and obey" (*True Christian Religion*, n. 807).

It may indeed be too late to save the Church from political extinction. But her very distress then will be a divine agent for what is to come, for resurrection and recovery. For when she is in the doctrines called the Holy City, public excitement will crouch before her, and the crusade in each man and woman against the interior evils and vices of life will settle, almost offhand, problems that have no solution now. With no loss of population, another race of people will be here. Wisdom and its will shall be born again. In short, heaven is to begin on earth; and the Church, instead of being reformed by Convocations, is to be regenerated in its individual members, and to be the mistress and inspiration of all sciences, a blessing in the midst of the land.

The Archbishop of Canterbury in his praiseworthy zeal for our Church expressed the opinion some days since that "geniuses" should be enlisted in its service; and he named Peter, Paul and Gregory as examples of the persons required, men of great and good rule. Of Peter we have experience in the canonical books of the New Testament. With these, Paul in his time was unacquainted. Dogmatically he *comes between* Christ and the divine inspiration of the Four Gospels and the Apocalypse, in which the Word is completed. He sowed the seed of the atonement in the earliest mind of Christianity; gave forth his Apostleship as coming directly from Jesus Christ and from God the Father; and his dogmas as 'the gospel of Christ.' Of this he says, 'though we, or an angel from heaven, preach any other gospel unto you than that which we have preached, let him be accursed. For I neither received it of man, nor was I taught, but by the revelation of Jesus Christ" (Galat. i.). Except Peter and James, he saw none of the Lord's Apostles. His inner light seems identical with that of the Quakers. The Four Gospels enable us to compare his theological system with the revealed Word. Both Peter and Paul as personal ideals and natural powers are worn out. John is he who is to remain till Christ comes again. John of the Apocalypse, who lay on his Lord's breast, and who is now representatively in the letter of the Word the Son of Mary. John represents salvation by good works, by a renewed life. This life, and these works, are the Lord's giving and doing, and we are His agents in reception and in deed. This is the sole end and outcome of every true Church.

Whatever judgment we have passed here on learned critics and theologians has no application to humble Christians, and to the simple in faith. These pious Bible readers receive their love of religion from heaven, and their catechisms from the tradition of their forefathers. They are founded in the good of the Word, and not intellectually confirmed in current dogmas. So they belong to the souls under the altar, that is, under divine protection, and they wait to be taken into the upper light when their time comes, for they are little children still, even though now in old age.

For continuing the line of thought in this book, I recommend the particular works of Swedenborg mentioned throughout: also Doughty's *Parable of Creation;* a clear exposition of the first Chapters of Genesis: the books mentioned in my Dedication: and especially to Churchmen, the works of the Rev. Augustus Clissold, *Paul and David*, *The Consummation of the Age*, *Sancta Cœna*, *The Divine Order of the Universe*, and *Illustrations of the End of the Church.* To those who are advanced in the knowledge of the doctrines, *Swedenborg and the Doctrines of the New Church*, by the late Rev. R. L. Tafel; a veritable mountain of light: and lastly, to all who wish on easy terms to see what the Writings are, *The Swedenborg Concordance* by the Rev. John Faulkner Potts; a digest which I apprehend has no parallel, in six quarto volumes, of which three are completed. All these works can be supplied by my Publisher.

THE NEW JERUSALEM
AND THE OLD JERUSALEM.

―――・―――

I.—THE STRENGTH OF THE JEWS.

IN a speculative material age with many obdurate elements to take account of, the Jew is a problem which interests our societies from his relation to money, and through that indispensable substance, to private property and its rights, and to the power which the genius for amassing gold, and guarding it, confers upon this exceptional race. His faculty of absorbing and retaining wealth in rich and poor lands alike, and, in the highest instances, of touching and stimulating the financial affairs of states, and controlling great undertakings of war and peace, is the feature by which the Jew is principally known in so-called Christian Nations. It is not an ideal but a real feature. It offends the demagogue and the Socialist in Western Countries, and the Capitalist, professional man and common proprietor in Russia, where also ecclesiastical rancour is awakened by the worldly success and ubiquity hitherto of these inconvertible primeval Antichrists. The question comes from many quarters, What shall be done with the Jew? From the curious and interested mind, What is the Future of the Jew? From the religionist mind, Has theology anything new to say to him? May we clear the ground for some approximate answers!

Secularly the Jews have a long future before them. They understand the natural mind of man, the *proprium* or selfhood as affecting property, better than any other race, and as usual their knowledge is power. They can attain relative affluence in the midst of poverty, and increase and multiply under the heel of persecution. They are turned out of one kingdom after another, out of England in the past, and now out of Russia, but the race bears local translation from Abraham downwards. Having now no country of their own, they cannot be expatriated. The Jew is not extinct or absorbed by the foreigner, but is still in land after land the evident, and so far as human nature permits, the complacent Jew. The Babylonish captivity left the Jewish captives unaltered; they absorbed from the nations, and annexed their mentality, as they do from the English to-day, but were not absorbed by them. Many of them also enjoyed Mesopotamia, and settled there for good.

Antisemitism is a creed with a propagandism in France as well as in Germany. Mons. Edouard Drumont ordains the proximate fate of the Jews in a few lines. "Antisemitism," says he, "has the advantage of not disturbing anybody. When the question is ripe, it will triumph without interrupting the circulation of the omnibuses. When the moment shall have come, when the officer with the resolution and good sense necessary for the work shall be found, then Antisemitism, which for some years will have educated public opinion, will have need of nothing more than one battalion of foot, and one company of well-chosen cavalry, to conduct the grand offenders to Mazas. All the world will then say, 'This has been talked about too long. It was due now to come to pass.'"

We ask here whether the love of acquiring wealth and keeping it, and making power out of it, is not innate in nearly every man, and whether anything short of altering or curing that love and will, can allow the conditions marked *when* and *then* in the last paragraph, to be easily realized without disturbing anybody? The passion is so hugely visible an object, so dominant and general in all

Christian lands, and in all classes, that to compass its extinction offhand, M. Drumont must rather be written Antihuman than Antisemite. It would take a jail as big as Paris to house the money-lust of Paris. However, he names Rothschild as the Capital to be attacked, perhaps thinking that if the fountain of evil is found in the Jew, and its gush stopped, the inundation will be at an end.

Supposing nominal capital, gold and representative paper abolished, and stomachs not abolished, bread and cheese will then be capital surviving, and will be a circulating medium. And thinking now again mainly of the Jews, their unimprisoned masses, more self-denying than the undervaluers and destroyers of property, will store their provender in their pockets, and have in Ghetto the biggest platefuls at last, and so will have something to sell. Of course service to the commune must be in the conditions of this barter, for barter would begin presently. Let it be equal all round. Still unless you can alter man's push, strength will help itself to more than weakness, cunning to more than stupidity, and audacity to more than timidity, and man will get more than woman. So hereditary sleight of mind and hand, ingrained love of possession and hoarding, the genius which an inveterate will, corporate and individual, means in worldly things, are a worm that never dies, and a fire that is not quenched. Property, most private, is its intimate and omnipotent god. On its own ground nothing is successful against it. Least of all, that unbred and bodiless thing, dogmatic Equality, not extant for many minutes even in chaotic revolution. The Jewish Will, a real naughty Old Testament from Abraham to Rothschild, upheaving mountains of inequality, is sleepless and practical in working; as it was before Abraham was thought of.

But if you could destroy, and then by social legislation prohibit, private property, where would the Jew be then? Would he not be checkmated? Well, no experiment has shown that success in that plan means in the long run anything else than the lower nomad state; Mesopotamia is covered with the ruins of public and private property, and shows the tombs of Nineveh and Babylon. Yet, Semites continue to wander there, and are not communists. And however low or brute the state, if Jews were surviving, they would still be usurers of the most convenient goods, if not of money; in which case, gold, which no antisemitism supposes to be annihilated or irrecoverable,—gold, the topmost representative of accumulation or private property,—would always be within hail, and Saviours of Society, Cæsars great or small, would be at hand to put their image and superscription upon it.

The Jewish race itself is now as remarkable for inequality as other races; it is also distinguished by a wide family charity, which embraces the whole people, and makes the inequality exemplary to other societies. Though it consists of the very rich and the very poor, the disgrace of want is not evident in the Jews as in the Christians. So the inequality is a way to racial permanence, by perpetuating a great community throughout its ramifications. Perhaps the tradition of the distribution of land among the tribes, and of its recovery to its first owners at certain intervals, may still influence the Jewish character.

II.—THE PATIENCE OF THE JEWS.

Not reckoning time, but *state of man*, human character, there is no future for the Jews, but an immanent monotonous present. A present, however, not of *ennui*, but outwardly various. They have no Way before them, and do not want one. Christ was proffered to them as the Way, the Truth, and the Life. They rejected Him in favour of the Messiah of the letter of the Word, who was to make them the ruling nation for all time. Against this interpretation, flattering to their self-love, and corrigible by no spiritual

AND THE OLD JERUSALEM. 5

insight, demonstration and History, and the woes and catastrophes of ages, are ineffectual. For the Jews are the Jews. Is this heroism, or is it something more mysterious? This hardness which makes a despised and at present a cowering race into the enduring anvil of the wrath of ages?

They had indeed temptation to a future almost after their own heart, but refused the way of it when it was offered. Mahometanism, in its early times, cast longing eyes upon the Jews, as wholesale possible converts. It held before them a prospect of in part fulfilling their own views of prophecy, of dominating the world under the Crescent, and of triumphing by some concessions to Christ at the expense of the Cross. Mahomet and his Successors would furnish temporal rulers in whom the victorious Israelites should believe. The Messiah would be an open promise dilated with hope, or Mahomet himself might in time be accepted as the crown of prophecy. A more absolute monotheism than the Jews liked was given in the Koran : Allah was not one of the Gods of the nations as Jehovah was for the Jews, but was God alone. Notwithstanding this drawback, if only mundane causes had been at work, a Mahometan Judaism might have been contracted. Islam without the Jews threatened Southern Europe from east to west, and like the Jews of the letter, intended universal dominion. It seemed from the Mahometan side as if a compromise could be made between the forecast of old Judaism, and the realization so nearly the same of young Mahometanism. See Gibbon in his record of Mahomet. There was, however, apart from the Jewish character, another cause at work, as we shall see presently, which overruled the issue.

III.—THE JEWS AND THE OLD TESTAMENT.

The Antisemites in France, the "Jew Haters" in Germany, and in general those who write and think about the modern

Jew in his social and political relations, take no notice of his lineage from the Old Testament. They may justify themselves in this, if they choose to consider him as a fact of the day,—this child of three thousand years. Those who disbelieve in the Word of God and the direct dealing of Jehovah with the Jews, ignore what is generally called the Jewish Church as furnishing the true light on the Jewish nature and character, and on the Use which he serves. But apart from the Jewish Dispensation taken in full faith into the account, the Jew cannot be understood. Apart from this preliminary fact of facts, the Divine Providence in its series of revelations from Adam to Noah, from Noah to Abraham, and from Abraham to Christ, cannot be rationally seen. The Mosaic dispensation was the end and remainder of what could be and exist before Christ came into the world. The Jew, up to this point, was the final instrument in the hand of Jehovah.

The legend of the Wandering Jew, if applied to the whole Jewish race since Christ, and seen spiritually, with the few details which it gives and the suggestions which it leaves, furnishes a true account of all we have to say concerning the Fate of the Jews. Wandering, dispersion, preservation until Christ's second coming, are foretold in it. After this, will the Wandering Jew disappear? The Second Coming has indeed taken place in the revelation of the spiritual sense of the Word, and of Christ the Lord therein as one God in one Person. But the New Church in which this Advent will be received and acknowledged, is yet in its Infancy. On this account the Jew is still here for important Ends, of which we treat in the sequel.

IV.—JUDAISM AND THE INCARNATION.

In the dealing of Jehovah with the Jews, two ends were successively accomplished: 1. The Jewish Church wa established ; and 2, the Incarnation was prepared. For the first purpose Jehovah laid hold of the Jewish nature, and with it commanded an external ecclesiasticism. Its self-love was the fundamental selfhood of that Æon, and had nothing below it. In other words, the Jews were the worst race on earth ; a religiosity was offered them ; and more readily than any other nation they laid the flattering unction to their souls that they were the best race on earth, and the chosen of Jehovah. So outward holiness clave to them by delusion of their own corrupt nature. The necessity of them in this regard was made Divine use of, without violating their free-will; it was of the Rock of Ages ; and was the Jewish Dispensation.

For the second purpose, an added Æon of iniquity was stored away, and, at the end, the race, more evil by the heredity of thousands of years, was again laid hold of by the mercy of Jehovah, the worst humanity being utterly indispensable here. The Lord Jesus Christ must come into the world ; must be born. He came to redeem mankind from below upwards ; and He could effect this only by coming through birth into Evil's own chief country and capital. So He was born from Jehovah God as His Father by the conception of a Jewish Virgin. Therefore she had in her the heredity or transmitted nature of the most sinful race then extant. Redemption, reaching in the fulness of time to the deepest recesses of finite man, and in the spiritual world to the abyss of the hells, depended upon Christ's taking upon Himself a worst human nature which could be tempted by the Devil and Satan ; that is to say, by the entire abyss. In vanquishing the empires of the Pit, He brought the Godhead into His natural humanity, as man in conquering his temptations to evil brings his religious conscience into his lower nature, and by his resistance makes conscience good there, and so far, by enduring to the end, regenerates his mind. Jesus Christ, by a process which our regeneration illustrates for us, made His Humanity divine ;

namely by leading a divine life in it. And now we actually see and know God as God-Man in Him. This is the Incarnation, in which the Eternal Word, the divine truth, became flesh, that is, became a divine natural human heart, and a Divine Natural Man. Before this, Jehovah was present to the race as God-Angel through the heavens. In and after the Incarnation, He was in His own acquired person an Infinite and Omniscient natural man, historically memorable in the Gospels: visible, apprehensible, and loveable to all who keep His Commandments, and acknowledge Him as the source of all our virtue in doing so.

V.—WHY THIS PLANET WAS THE PLACE OF CHRIST'S REDEMPTIVE COMBATS.

The same reason for which Christ took upon Him a representative form of the worst natural humanity in the Jews, namely that He might redeem us from the power of hell, and in the end save to the uttermost, caused Him also as the Creator and God of all universes to make this planet earth the theatre of His incarnation. For this earth is to the immense system of worlds what the Jews were to the nations and peoples of the earth; it is the worst of worlds. Nothing short of conquering the worst, and by resisting its temptations and allurements, subjugating it, and so rendering it powerless to destroy man without his own complicity, could be a divine Victory over Hell and Death. Respecting the truths in this paragraph, see Swedenborg's *Earths in the Universe*. He informs us that intelligence of the Incarnation which took place on our earth, was and is propagated by our inhabitants after death, consequently in the spiritual world, to all the planets of all the systems, and is thus known as Redemption and means of salvation to all universes. In the meantime, and always from creation, a divine influx gave to all mankind wherever born, an innate knowledge of God as a Divine Man. The Gospel therefore now is written for the entire universe. From not knowing this fact, eminent men have rejected Christianity as being a tiny local system. Redemption is, however, coextensive with creation, and the publication of it co-extensive. The reader is recommended to peruse *The Divine Order of the Universe as interpreted by Emanuel Swedenborg, with especial relation to Modern Astronomy*, by the Rev. Augustus Clissold.*

VI.—THE FIRST ADVENT.

Between the beginning and end of the Mosaic Dispensation, which was a state of perpetual decline towards evil, the deaths into the spiritual world had peopled its regions nearest to the earth with multitudes of evil spirits, who, when the Lord was born, were in dense masses between man and heaven, and of an influence so potent as to make allurements to wickedness irresistible, and to threaten Free Will with extinction. Such companionship has evil with evil here and hereafter. The pressure on personality was so overpowering that mankind was becoming a victim to demoniacal possession. These seductions, temptations, allurements, the Lord in His tempted Humanity confronted, beat them back, and trod them under His Divine feet; that is to say, under the new nature or *natural* which came down through the combats from the indwelling Divinity. This effected a Judgment in the spiritual world, and removed the obstructing sphere between heaven and man. It made new heavens and new hells, as Assizes on earth should make new security for order, and new imprisonment for disorder. Thus, by limiting the powers of evil to what sane mankind can resist if they choose, the Lord gave back Freewill to the race, emancipating it from Legion, and made man again one person under one God.

* London : Longman & Co., 1877.

This can be plainly understood by whoever studies it. There is nothing difficult about it, and nothing mysterious if you have full faith in an infinite Divine Man. And if you also know, which you easily may, that the heart of man is deceitful above all things and desperately wicked. A divine life led on earth makes a divine natural man, as a natural life so led makes a natural man, a sensual life a sensual man, and a spiritual life a spiritual man. To lead a divine life is impossible to a finite soul which comes from the seed of other men. The soul for this supreme experience must be God Himself, Deity Himself: the Seed, Divine Truth. "The Lord descended as the Divine Truth in Heaven." Divine Truth teaches what shall be divinely done. The field of personal evil is the place and plane of operation. This for the Soul; now for the body. The body must be conceived by a Mother who brings sinful humanity into the field of the battle. The Way is vastness of *temptation* for the one only surviving Man; namely, the Divine Man; temptation from the World, from the Universal Hells; and from the Universal Heavens: for the heavens are not pure in the sight of the Lord; and Swedenborg by divine instruction tells that the Lord's inmost and most subtle temptations were from the angelic heaven. See the *Arcana Cœlestia*, n. 4295. The passage says: "In order that the Lord might restore the universal heaven to celestial order, he even admitted into himself temptations from the angels, who, in so far as they were in their own proprium or selfhood, in so far were not in good and truth."

Think then of resistance to temptation in the supreme cases and meanings as the Redemption of the Whole World by the Lord in His veriest real presence, making His humanity divine. The subjugation of the then overruling hells gave back to mankind the personal freedom of the Will which they had lost; and when the new freedom is used to resist temptation to evil as the Lord in His infirm humanity resisted, then redemption finds its appointed end in salvation, or admission to heaven after death.

Whoever has resisted any evil delights to which he is prone, and fought against them, and persevered in resistance until they are no longer delightful but hateful, has in him the faculty of understanding from some experience how the better mind can come down into the seductive sensual, and become a new birth in it, exterminating the evil into circumferences at length beyond danger of recall. By this process the Lord wrought, and made faculty after faculty divine. He put on at length the Divine Sensual. He abolished in Himself the weight of the corporeal, and Death naturally disappeared,—divinely-naturally,—before Him.

Jesus was of Jewish race by Mary, and He longed to gather that race into His fold. He says of Jerusalem, "How often would I have gathered thy children together, even as a hen gathereth her chickens under her wings, and ye would not" (Matthew xxiii. 37). The Jews who rejected Him have now no part in His genealogy. He exterminated whatever was derived from the Virgin Mother; nay, He put off the heredity of the human race in his Resurrection and Glorification. He was not only no Jew, but no finite man in His ascension and union with Jehovah the Father, but one God in one adorable Person; practically adorable because comprehensible. His life on earth gave the human race for all worlds a finited image of Him, while the Word, which is the divine truth, gives the doctrinal verity of the Infinite Father indwelling in this approachable Son. So in His alone wisdom and mercy we can know Him as Friend and Brother, and adore Him as our one only God.

VII.—IMPLICIT ACCEPTANCE OF THE WORD DEMANDED.

This Revelation most literally taken and gathered from the whole letter of the Word, the written Logos, is a sun and a shield to future Epochs or Æons. It is simply the body of the letter accepted utterly, whether its stated facts jar with our denominational minds, or not, and a revealed soul of truth and love from Christ Himself informing and glorifying it. If you do not agree to this, you discard the letter, and make it fraudulent: if you strike out what you do not like, for instance, the supernatural, from the narrative, you claim a right of intellect which puts yourself in question. The whole Word together is supernatural, and miracle is its means. Accept it if you will with no ecclesiastical glosses or words of Councils. The spiritual sense revealed by the Lord through a man, in no way enslaves you *in Verba Magistri*, or as imprisoned in Swedenborg in the way in which the orthodox are imprisoned in the dogmas of the old churches. It is indeed learnt from Swedenborg and stored in the rational mind; but it reveals itself to the reverent reader from that stem in wonderful clusters on the vine of life, and in harvests of fruit on the Mount of Olives. The language of Correspondence in which the Word is written is given to us by the same good Servant as in a dictionary. We refer to the dictionary to read the language when we require its aid. But the dictionary is not our Master or our Aristotle, but the Lord is our Master, and teaches us daily proficiency as we read His Word. As well be charged with undue minority under Rawlinson or Norris, Champollion or Sayce, in studying Hieroglyphics, Cuneiform, or Accadian, because we make use of their knowledge to continue our own, as with abolishing our minds in favour of the dicta of Swedenborg. The dogmas of the old Church which have no spiritual life or sense in them are indeed infringements of the rule, "Call no man your Father upon the earth, for one is your Father which is in heaven. Neither be ye called Masters, for one is your Master, even the Christ. But he that is greatest among you shall be your Servant." Swedenborg, Emanuel, prepared to reveal the spiritual sense, as the greatest among us is our servant, and while dogmas close the Word and imprison us, the true doctrines which he has brought make us free.

VIII.—FALSITIES CAST OUT AND TRUTHS IMPLANTED.

In the Revelation here made we have a divine Trinity in Unity, One God and Lord, Father, Son, and Holy Spirit. These are the divine love, the divine wisdom, and the divine providence, all in the *person of Christ. The three Gods of Christendom vanish as polytheism from a New Church and a true Christian Religion. The Atonement disappears with the Tripersonality in the identity of the Son and the Father. The cross disappears as payment for the sins of the world : but it is seen in our intellectual sky as the last temptation and the crowning victory over the hells ; the "*It is finished*" of a Life of Divine Victories. Justification by Faith vanishes before Christ to whom Judgment belongs ; for by fulfilling the Word He became Divine Justice; and He exacts life according to His Commandments, and admits no justification for man ; but demands repentance, and a new life according to it, and then grants remission of sins. If we consider the dogma of three Persons, or three Gods, it is remarkable how their attributes are apportioned. The Father represents wrath implacable save by a divine and infinite sacrifice for human and finite sin : whereas Christ says, the Father Himself loveth you. Christ on the other hand is put as the God of soft mercy, whereas He Himself says, The Father has committed all judgment to the Son. With regard to the Holy Spirit, the sphere of Christ, the Gospel says "*it was not yet, because Christ was not yet glorified.*" The Spirit of God in the Old Testament is the divine spiritual sphere proceeding from Jehovah through the heavens. The Holy Spirit is the divine natural sphere pervading the true Church wherever it is, and is the Paraclete or Comforter proceeding from the divine humanity. It had no existence until Christ's Coming; nor actually till His Glorification.

The spiritual sense of the Word within the Letter contains, or rather consists in, the true doctrines here shadowed forth, —contains them in infinite detail and expansion; for indeed they are virtue and they are heaven. That sense may also be called scientifically the theory of the Letter. In another statement it is the Second Coming of Christ in which He comes as the One only God and Lord. It heralds the Second Coming of mankind when from age to age they come as individuals, as Sons of God in Regeneration. Such considerations grow in the mind when the climate of the Divine Overshadowing and the maternal Conception is around us.

IX.—THE VIRGIN MARY.

In continuation of the same thoughts, we may ask ourselves how the Incarnation took place in the worst nation on our planet, that Christ by nativity might be exposed to all the assaults and contagions of evil in order to conquer them, and yet that He was born of Blessed Mary. Was she then vile in this sinful race? The question was crucial to Pius IX., and caused him to decree the immaculate conception of the Virgin, who according to Roman Catholic and also Anglican Theogony is the Mother of God. The Infallibility of His Holiness was at the same Council placed on the like certainty with the immaculateness of Mary. He admitted the depravity of the Jewish nature in thus breaking with it. But he made the Incarnation of none effect in decreeing that Christ did not take upon Himself our infirm Humanity. The good Pius IX. has the credit of seeing that some explanation was needed, and he, being self-made infallible, could vote one. *Stet pro ratione voluntas* is a gagging power. To the Romanist, even to Cardinal Newman, nothing more can be said. But Protestantism has made thinking allowable, and made truth ashamed of being decreed. The bringing the Word out of its sepulchre was the chief use of the Reformation, and supplied the opportunity for a new foundation of heavenly doctrine. What then might be an alternative thought with regard to the Virgin? I write in all humility here, for I cannot quote literal authority, but draw conclusions as inferences from admitted verities. For convenience, however, I put the case so far as I see it positively.

Now the alternative is that Blessed Mary was not the worst but the divinely accommodate correspondent best of the Jewish nation. Pius IX. might have been satisfied with this if he had read the divine letter as the Word in supreme authority over every Church. This fitness of Mary meets the case of Jehovah assuming through her a Humanity open to the temptations of all the hells, of all the earths, and of all the heavens. Had she been immaculate, she had been a fourth person in the Christian Mythology, in fact, a Goddess, and could have conceived no son with an infirm humanity to be tempted. Had she been among the vilest of her race, her progeny of the body could have furnished no plane for deep temptations. A debased humanity could not be mother to one who was to be tempted by the most superb ecclesiastical and imperial ambitions, who was offered when the Devil transported Him to the pinnacle of the Temple, the Popedom of the future Church; and from the top of an exceeding high mountain to which Satan raised Him, the sovereignty and glory of the kingdoms of the world. A self-love supreme must have been innate in the material heredity which could be exposed to such temptations. Think also of his Fast of Forty Days in the Wilderness. Nothing of this openness to evil spirits appeared in Mary. She knew nothing of His Temptations, and was not capable of them. Whatever we read of her reveals a character beautiful in natural love. Humility under divine Proposition and condescension, faith in its Angelic Annunciation, obedience to the motherhood of her future Redeemer, heart-service to Him from the manger to the cross, and one of the first to be told of His Resurrection. We may well say in our human parlance that Mary was an immaculate mother. But the Jewish nature was in her, and to be revealed by the future Event, by the Birth of Christ, and His exposure to the Devil and Satan. We know by common experience, and by striking instances in history, what powers and great qualities men owe to good and true mothers who have to our eyes none of the characteristics of such greatness. The ground does not know what the seed will grow to. And almost all greatness is susceptible of abuse and temptation and heavy fall until regeneration surpasses it. So the letter shows, and we accept verbally, literally, implicitly, that the Lord inherited the greatest Jewish qualities from Blessed Mary, and that they were all of them when first given, untried, unregenerate; as inherited qualities, genius, talents, ambitions, loves, hopes, aspirations, likes and dislikes, are in every man.

And to speak now psychologically, inasmuch as conception on the Mother's part is called forth by seed from the Father, and inasmuch as the Father chose Mary; and also as the Divine Truth as the body of the Lord Who is Heaven descended into Mary, so the *nature* of the Child born must have been stupendous in faculties; in fact equal and able to be co-extensive, and ultimately in conflict, with all created mind, in the ancient Churches and in the Jewish Church, in the heavens over them and in the hells underneath them. There was, however, no evil in any of these merely natural faculties, for evil comes from prostituting the faculties by the abuse of free-will. Still they were of Jewish nature, with its *tendencies to evil*, but which like every nature is at first neutral before will has wrought in it. But in the Lord the mother faculties remained sinless, because He resisted all temptations to sin, and glorifying His natural faculties thereby, put on the Divine in them. The vast faculties inherited, and the tendencies to evil, are the openness of Jesus Christ to temptation; and at the same time suggest, that the consummate flower and pearl of Jewish womanhood was the medium of the appearance of the world's Redeemer in the world.

The Devil here always means the lusts of evil in their entirety, and Satan the loves of falsity. These collectively and organically are two mighty empires: they are hell. Foot to foot they are antipodean, opposite to the grand humanity, which being inspired with goodness and truth is the kingdom of heaven. So both the Devil and Satan are personal; being monstrous though still human forms and organizations of all the bad men and women who have lived on earth since the beginning of creation. These belong, spirit to spirit, by affinity, to our evil tendencies, and are continually near our natures; and in the degree that we will and do the evil which is in us, and which corresponds to one or many of them, they conjoin with us in most particular league, and add us to their company. After this, no justification by faith condones our sin, but only repentance, resisting the sin thenceforth, and continuing through life to resist it, and so casting out our devils and satans: the end of which when the life ends is regeneration and Salvation; as was said before.

Mary's nature is the supreme case of what the Word calls REMAINS. When races are dying out spiritually, the poor in spirit, the mourners, the meek, those who hunger and thirst after righteousness, the merciful, the pure in heart, the peacemakers, those who are persecuted for righteousness' sake, are bespoken from the Mount in the last days of an Old Church and the first days of a New Church. They are the humble and the simple, and are waiting and willing for they know not what, but for the Lord to come and help them. In their troubled lowliness a new Revelation can be made to them, and the race of man be thus perpetuated. These Remains, needy and naked, contain the old heredity still, but the Lord's gift of virtue with it; a fortune of natural good counterpoising the ancestral nature; making infancy what it is, and simplicity what it is ; and reigning while these states last; afterwards vanishing, but stored away for moments of awakened conscience, " Like wine put by at birth for days of age."

X.—THE MOTHER OF JESUS.

Without impiety if without strict authority, we may indulge the personal mind in dwelling a little longer on this Jewess who has been the delight in good ages of the earlier Church. We read in the Word that she was espoused to Joseph, but before they came together she was found with child of the Holy Spirit. That the angel of the Lord appeared to Joseph in a dream, saying, Joseph, thou son of David, fear not to take unto thee Mary thy wife : for that which is conceived in her is of the Holy Spirit. That Joseph being raised from sleep did as the Angel of the Lord had bidden him, and took unto him his wife. And knew her not till she had brought forth her firstborn son ; and he called His name JESUS. That when Mary came to Elizabeth the wife of Zacharias, Elizabeth was filled with the Holy Spirit, and lifted up her voice with a loud cry and said, Blessed thou among women, and blessed the fruit of thy womb. And whence is this to me, that the Mother of my Lord should come unto me? For behold when the voice of thy salutation came into mine ears, the babe leaped in my womb for joy. Elizabeth had conceived in her old age ; and when they called her son, Zacharias, after the name of his Father, she said, Not so, but he shall be called John. Of Zacharias and Elizabeth it is said that they were both righteous before God, walking in all the commandments and ordinances of the Lord blameless. Perhaps they were also Remains of the ancient church in the Jewish, and they were a blameless Jewish pair. And here we may recall the beginning of the ancient Church by which the race of man was preserved in that day:—And

Noah, who was a righteous man, perfect in his generations; Noah who walked with God. We also think of Sarah ninety years old, and of Abraham a hundred, and of the coincidence that Abraham, the Father of the faithful, could not believe that Sara could bring him Isaac; and that Zacharias, wanting evidence, and cross-questioning the Angel who is then declared as Gabriel, as to how he should know that his wife stricken in years should bring him John, because he believed not, had for evidence that he should be dumb and not able to speak until the birth of his son. Mary also, as in her own right, seeing she knew not a man, asked Gabriel how her conception could be? And the angel satisfied her enquiry: and she said, Behold the handmaid of the Lord; be it unto me according to thy Word. Then she said, My soul doth magnify the Lord, my spirit hath rejoiced in God my Saviour. For He hath regarded the low estate of His handmaiden: for behold from henceforth all generations shall call me blessed. In her faith she carried to her Lord His promise of presence which He made to Abraham and to a thousand generations. All this confirms the great inheritance which the Lord condescended to assume in the infirm maternal humanity, which is thus attested by the Word. In the ordinary sense the Virgin Mary ceases after the first conception, but in that conception there is a divine declaration of her Virginity. After Jesus came into His own country and taught them in their synagogues, they were astonished and said, Whence hath this man this wisdom and these powers? Is not this the carpenter's son? Is not his mother called Mary? And his brothers, James, and Joses, and Simon, and Judas? And his sisters, are they not all with us? It is clear then from personal testimony in the Word that Mary after her declared virginity was the wife of Joseph and the mother of Joseph's numerous children. Also that all generations shall call her blessed, as she, inspired, herself said; and that she is blessed among women, as inspired Elizabeth said. But the phrase

Blessed Virgin, has no Scripture for it. Holy Virgin cannot be thought of in any Church where the Word lies open. God alone is holy. Virgin may however be used of Mary in another sense sanctioned by the divine letter. We meet this in the Apocalypse: "These are they which were not defiled with women; for they are virgins. These are they which follow the Lamb whithersoever he goeth," xiv. 4. Swedenborg also instructs us that "Virgin denotes the Kingdom of the Lord, and the church properly celestial; also the spiritual church; and that the members are called Virgins from conjugial love, thus from innocence." (*Arcana Cœlestia*, n. 3081).

XI.—MARY BECOMES A DIVINE SYMBOL AS JOHN AND THE DISCIPLES WERE.

"When Jesus on the cross saw His mother, and the disciple standing by, whom Jesus loved, He said unto His mother, Woman, behold thy son! Then saith He to the disciple, Behold thy mother! and from that hour that disciple took her unto his own." Mary here in the divine letter, in its correspondential symbolism, is lifted above our humanity; but for us natural men and women she is for these moments the most pathetic of human souls: no other situation has approached it; she loses her Lord as a Son not by His death only, but by His recognized divinity, and she has a son given to her by her Lord, another son when the first must disown her. But we may not weep, for she had an infinite Redeemer and Comforter: but let us follow the Correspondence which she also is. May we conjecture that not as a Jewish representation, which was merely external without an internal, and ritual without an understanding of it, she truly and worthily personifies and so signifies and represents the great Jewish beginning of the Christian Church. John in the spiritual sense signifies what has been revealed by the Lord through heaven to those who from charity and its faith are in the good of life. Each disciple represented a quality or characteristic of the Church : the twelve its whole spirit, soul, will and understanding. John who lay on the Lord's breast, represents good works which are the good of life—*bonum vitæ*. Peter denotes faith, James charity, and John the good of charity, or charity active in life. Mary, therefore, instead of being the mother of God, is,—not was,—representatively the Mother of the embryo Church before it was a Church, as Noah representatively is the beginning of the Ancient Church but not the Ancient Church itself. Here we no longer dwell on the Mary of the letter, the BLESSED MARY for every good man and woman who can read the Bible. The Lord was no longer the Son of that Mary. He had rejected the human derived from her, and had put off the old garment of the Jewish nature. Thenceforth, and even before by divine anticipation He comes to the Universal Church, to the First Christian Church, and to the New Church, consisting of those who hear the Word of God and do it, and whom He says are His Mother and His brethren. As the Church is the presence of the Lord on earth, and as all that is genuine in it, that is good and true, and of the Word, is Himself, so these relations are also Himself, divine and infinite ; and His mercy attributes them to men and angels that human love in heaven and on earth may claim affiliation and conjunction with the Father of souls. In those who are His disciples His words are for ever, Behold my Mother and my Brethren ; for whosoever shall do the will of my Father which is in Heaven, he is my brother, and sister and mother.

XII.—CHARACTER, NOT BLOOD-RELATIONSHIP, LIVES AND CONSOCIATES AFTER DEATH.

A sundering of all merely natural blood-relationships at the death of the body, is here pointed out in the internal Word. Nothing founded upon birth alone, survives. The families of the spiritual world, to which we are all hastening, are families indeed; goodness and truth in their consanguinities are the great family of Maximus Homo above : evil and falsity, in exact lineages of monstrosity and perversion, are the opposite broods below. Each man and woman becomes a substantial organization of affections for Right or Wrong in their indefinitely multiplied forms. And now something of the vanishing of mortal and terrestrial relationships is taught to us in this supreme instance of Mary, who even in this world is warned to part from her still apparent Son. "Simeon said unto Mary his mother : Behold, this child is set for the fall and rising of many in Israel ; and for a sign which shall be spoken against. Yea, a sword shall pierce through thine own soul also, that the thoughts of many hearts may be revealed" (Luke ii. 34, 35). This distinction between the spiritual and natural worlds is a sign which is spoken against, unwelcome news to the natural side. Its sharp iron, a sword, pierced through Mary's soul; for iron signifies natural truth, here instructed towards spiritual ; the sword of the Spirit. It tries human love at first in revealing its origin in bloods and relationships. So it lays bare the thoughts of many hearts; and explains the dissolution of family ties on earth ; a lesson and anticipation of disjunctions and new conjunctions and unions after death.

Jesus Christ extirpated or lived down the maternal *proprium* or individual selfhood which He inherited, and the God in Him which did this, in every ultimate act came to the front, and stood there as a Divine *Proprium.* So He made His Human divine. In us there is a corresponding process when regeneration is going on. When bad ways are resisted and evils shunned as sins against the Lord, the heart is softened to His influx, the evil with its delights is rejected to the circumferences, and higher degrees in the mind through which the opposite good comes down, and where it can abide, are opened. Tiers of being are added to the man which practically do not exist before; for they are not his till then; but are in waiting at the door, opportune for him to open it. He is rejecting his hereditary character and his own previous life, and putting on a new nature. But yet he never can reject his proprium or evil selfhood as the Lord did, but only banish it from the centre to the circumference of his nature; from his delight to his aversion; from the warmth of his tropics to cold and congelation. It is kept in frost by God, but is indestructible, and sometimes a little of it is allowed to melt by the man's lapsing and compliance, to show him what he is, and to lead him back to greater humility and more complete acknowledgment of his unworthiness. But his evil proprium, though dormant at length and buried below his consciousness, and in heaven far below his conscience, is indestructible; and being fixed by birth in the natural world, is the basis of his immortality; of his everlasting Ego. Some permanent memory of his natural man, upon which the spiritual man is founded, extends upward through his spiritual faculties, and so the foothold of natural law is still under him as a plane giving the last substance and appearance to his life.

We make the Incarnation prefatory before coming more closely to the Jewish Church, because this order leads directly to the consideration of the former Churches, and the human faculties made use of in them; without which the Mosaic Dispensation cannot be understood. For it was not a religion, but an interregnum, a Theocracy between the Ancient and the Christian Churches. A moving Penitentiary of an imprisoned, not a privileged race. The coming of Christ when Judaism failed, sets the series and scale of Divine interpositions in a broad daylight, and makes the past and the future into an evident chain. The Incarnation itself, however, requires to be understood through the doctrines of the New Jerusalem, according to which we attempt to bring it before the reader.

XIII.—THE REPRESENTATION OF A CHURCH BY THE JEWS.

The Church with the Jews was the third inauguration of a Church with a Revelation to guide it, of which Jehovah God was the author. The first Church, called in Genesis, Adam, was from the creation,—the Adamic Church,— which passed through many variations signalized by names of persons, and became extinct in the race before the Flood. The second was the Church called the Noahtic, which, with many changes, held the human race from Noah to Abraham. This second Church became extinct in Asia, and in Africa when the hosts of Pharaoh were drowned in the Red Sea. The third Church was with the Jews and Israelites until the dispersion of the Jews, and the destruction of the temple at Jerusalem.

Each of these religious epochs or ages, had a distinct character, by reason of the spiritual elements extant in the Æon to which it belonged. Love was the soul of the Adamic Church, and perception from love was its mind. This was the most ancient or celestial Church. After its consummation, the Lord raised up a new church, and Faith with conscience in which a new will was formed, became the life of the Noahtic, ancient or spiritual Church. On the extinction of this Church, no further dispensation could be founded; for the resources in human nature were at an end. Yet a church with God present, and revealing Himself, is indispensable for the preservation of man. Accordingly, a Church was instituted *with* the Jews, but not *in* them, and God Himself became the upholder of the Jewish dispensation. It was not a Church, but it was the representation of a Church. Its virtue lay in implicit unhesitating obedience to external divine commands, attested by perpetual miracle, and reinforced by mortal fears and sublunary hopes.

Here was a third pause in History. Consider it carefully, because upon a comprehension of the three crises above mentioned, the understanding of everything in the Church *with* the Jews depends. The Love Ages, the primeval will, had passed away in the impure senility of the Adamic Church; and with the lusts which alone survived, the central intellect in the heart was turned into "direful persuasions."* So the *likeness of God* in man had perished: the inward Sun of goodwill had set. The age of instruction laying hold of the remains of the primeval integrity, and built into a second will as a new human faculty,—a conscience,—had in like manner run its course; and the Noahtic Church was consummated in Egypt, Babylon and Assyria. So the *image of God* in man was darkened; and the Æon of Divine Truth communicated by God from without had come to an end. Bear in mind that these two great faculties or Churches were not of the nature of man, but were superadded gifts and endowments conferred upon him, and when he refused to continue to receive them, they were no more, and like Astrea they had left the earth. A world of idolatry and superstition was left, and no revival was possible; for the depravity of mankind was complete. The magnetism of love had grown poisonous, and the voice of warning truth was drowned in a triple dominion of evil and falsity, embodied in Egypt, Assyria and Babylon.

* See my work, *Oannes according to Berosus*, where the last state of this Church is described from its autopsy by Swedenborg, as well as from Chaldean tradition.

Such a dreg and residue of humanity could only be compelled, not attracted or instructed, into the service of heaven. Nothing internal was left. Self-love was left, and its lust and pride of place. It was eminent in the Jews more than in other races. They alternately accepted and rejected Jehovah, and still would be His chosen people. They brought a measured and frail obedience to the compact. Compliance, not from Conscience, not from Love, was in their bond. They could not become a Representative Church, but the Representation of a Church. Thus the depravity and selfishness of the world was the instrument at God's disposal wherewith to found an ultimatum on which heaven could rest, and be connected with mankind. Without such connection in a church or the mechanism of a church, the natural man who is the seminary of heaven, and the natural universe which exists as his foothold, would perish: it would perish not by fire, or day of judgment, but by uselessness which is uncreation. Jehovah did not make the world evil, but found it so: and made it representative of good by events, by combats, and by religious rites and ceremonies; and first of all by the Ten Commandments directly forbidding evils; and then by Laws of order containing correspondences of the order of heaven. A Jewish Word was written by chosen men: by Lawgivers and Prophets, and by King David. In this Word direct verbal inspiration superseded the Jewish writer, and made him into the scribe and pen of Jehovah. This Word in its spiritual morality went utterly away from Judaism, and had the Gospel shining through it; and also was so accommodated to the Jewish character, that it accepted its peculiar self-love, and spoke according to it, allowing to it its naturalism, and not unveiling what was hidden and internal. In an evil world " it would not be difficult to enlist any nation in the service of representing religion provided it had holy externals of worship, and worshipped almost idolatrously; and it was the genius of the Jews more than any other nation completely

AND THE OLD JERUSALEM. 27

to worship external things as holy and divine apart from anything internal: for instance, to adore their fathers, Abraham, Isaac and Jacob, and afterwards Moses and David, as deities; and also to hold as holy and divine every piece of stone and wood which had been inaugurated into their divine worship; as the ark, the tables there, the lamp, the altar, the garments of Aaron, the Urim and Thummim, and afterwards the Temple. *By such things the communication of angels with man was brought to pass.* It was effected thus. Their external worship was communicated to angelic spirits of simple character, who do not reflect upon internal things, but who are interiorly good. Such are those who correspond to the layers of the skin in the Maximus Homo. In these simple spirits the interior Angels of Heaven saw the things which were represented, consequently the heavenly and divine things which corresponded. So the Holy of worship was miraculously elevated into heaven, leaving the Jews outside in the process" (*Arcana Cœlestia*, n. 8588).

Again, Swedenborg says: "As the representative of the celestial kingdom began to perish when the Jews asked for a king, therefore in order that the representation of the Lord's kingdom in the heavens might still be continued on earth, the Jews were separated from the Israelites; and the Lord's celestial kingdom was represented by the Jewish kingdom, and His spiritual kingdom by the Israelitish kingdom" (*Ibid.* n. 8770).

What a marrow of divine-human history, from the beginning of the world to the ends of it, these revelations open in thus opening the Word.

XIV.—HOW A REPRESENTATIVE CAN ASCEND.

Before proceeding further, an easy instance may help writer and reader to begin to understand this difficult matter, of spirits receiving the representatives of Jewish Worship, and leaving out the unholy Jewish interpretation of them, and thus rendering them fit to be presences in the heavens; so ensuring a sure communication of heaven with man from the basis of impure expressions, which become unnoticed dregs. Childhood sometimes shames grown men with this kind of angelry. Now regard Psalm cix. It is chiefly occupied in the Jewish letter with a prayer against the wicked who have spoken against the Psalmist with a lying tongue; have rewarded him evil for good, and hatred for love. If a Christian prayed it in the Jewish sense, it were an evil prayer. "Set thou a wicked man over him, and let Satan stand at his right hand. Let his prayers become sin. As he clothed himself with cursing as with his garment, so let it come into his bowels like water, and like oil into his bones. Let it be unto him as the garment covereth him, and for a girdle wherewith he is girded continually." The whole Psalm of which this is a small part is a prayer for curses upon an adversary, upon his children and posterity, upon his fathers, and upon his mother. It is a complete commination. To the Psalmist it was a series of ardent wishes addressed as prayers to the Lord. Good simple Christians dislike the Psalm, do not read it, and so are rid of the Jewish nature in it. But those who understand the spiritual sense of it all, know that the adversary against whom we pray is our own selfishness, and no person or persons outside of us; that the curses are specific prayers against those evils which curse us, and which are our deadly enemies; and also which stand in all the relationships which are correspondentially signified by the adversary himself, by his children, his fathers, and his mother. So in praying this prayer, it goes to heaven with no memory of Jewish meaning; it undergoes an apotheosis, and refuses to have external enemies. So also when it is said of the daughter of Babylon, "Happy shall he be that taketh and dasheth thy little ones against the rock" (Psalm cxxxvii. 9), the Jewish sense dies into the Angelic sense; the daughter of Babylon is the affection of our own love of dominion over the counsels of heaven; and the little ones are the intimate desires born of that affection; the rock of Divine truth recognized is that which these affections assail, and by which they perish. So the Jewish sense remains with the Jews, is ignored by the Christians, and is perceived as the road to heaven in the New Jerusalem.

XV.—THE JEWISH CHARACTER WAS NOT ALTERED BUT MADE REPRESENTATIVE.

The severe ritual given through Moses in no way infringed the Jewish Character; the commanded sacrifices prevented the sacrifices of sons and daughters which were practised among the nations. The idea of human sacrifice was so ingrained in the world in the ruin of the Ancient or Noahtic Church, and descended so lustfully upon the Jews, that they continually fell back into the practice; and they were permitted to sacrifice cattle, sheep, lambs, goats, kids, pigeons and doves, to divert their propensity, and also, from the correspondence of the animals, to present and represent the approach to heaven by good affections, the fruits of *self-sacrifice*, and by worship from these. A cruel nation had appetite for cruelty, as the Romans for gladiatorial murders, and lions and tigers at play with human life. The Jewish cruelty, ready to hand, was laid hold of by Him Who was to come in the Redeemer, and made into a link in the chain that bound mankind to heaven. We may say that the butcher's craft was consecrated. If Jehovah had made the Jews, unlimited sacrifice would have been in character, but the Jews, like all obdurately natural men, made themselves; and He curtailed them, and made Divine use of them.

If we grant as a fundamental postulate the mere Drama or Representation of a Church, in which the Characters were in costume, and in artistry other than the Realities they stood or spoke for; and in which their implicit obedience to their parts and prompters was inexorably necessary; and if we always remember that a divine Church commanded the situation, and that its existence was imperative, we then find that every circumstance recorded of the Jews in the Word puts on a new Justice and Judgment. The events of Jewish history are spiritual things: the forty years in the wilderness are the long trials and circuits of self-love, doubling upon itself, and getting no nearer to the promised land. Yet every day, notwithstanding its sins and punishments, the vague moving host is exactly guided to a representative end. The representation of a Church still subsists in spite of the actors. The Battles of the Jews, and the extermination of the nations before Canaan was reached, and in Caanan, if I do not mistake are always provoked, often by some excusable cause on the part of the nations. The massacres which followed Jewish victories, or Jehovah victories, the slaughters of men, women and children, were a part of the *regime* of the then world. Cæsar did thus in Belgium and Gaul, and Vercingetorix, like Agag in his country, was murdered in Cæsar's triumph, after the Gallic victories, in Rome. There was nothing remarkable in these events; they were ordinary human ways and games. Two things may strike us. The Jewish Warrior *minus* Jehovah does not seem a redoubtable man. But the wonder is that Jehovah commanded the massacres after Victory. That Samuel, the good high Priest, hewed Agag in pieces before the Lord. That Saul appeared to be more merciful than Jehovah: that on the vote of his people, which he dared not disobey, for he feared the people and obeyed their voice, he allowed them to take to themselves the best of the spoil, sheep and oxen, the chief of the things which should have been utterly destroyed, to sacrifice unto the Lord his God in Gilgal. And then Samuel said, " Hath the Lord delight in burnt-offerings and sacrifices as in obeying the voice of the Lord? Behold to obey is better than sacrifice, and to hearken than the fat of rams. For rebellion is the sin of witchcraft, and stubbornness is iniquity and idolatry. Because thou hast rejected the word of the Lord, He hath also rejected thee as King." Here obedience to literal command is declared as the keynote of the Jewish dispensation, and disobedience as fatal to it, and to those who disobeyed. The Amalekites represented sinners, while the Jews represented the righteous rejecting their sins, and in terrible drama they had to kill those whom Jehovah had vanquished. In this series, with its awful logic, the Lord of hosts had commanded Saul to go and smite Amalek, and utterly destroy all that they have, and spare them not, but slay both man and woman, infant and suckling, ox and sheep, camel and ass. This was because all the personalty and property of Amalek partook of his representation : his women stood for mothers of evil, his infants and sucklings for evil seed and its increase, his oxen for bad affections, his sheep for shameless pleas of innocence, his camels for general ways of wickedness, and his asses for every man's private inventions. Exactly the opposite of what the precious beasts signify in a series which begins with a good dominant. In the real life of a regenerate community the slaughter of the women and children were obviously heinous ; in the representation of such a life by the Divine Dramatist, where the reality takes the lowest form of actuality, the slaughter of these perhaps innocent women, and most innocent babes and sucklings, oxen and sheep, was done on earth that it might be translated in heaven as the victory of good, and the extermination of evil. It is indeed a difficult train to keep steadily in the mind, and will convince but few ; but the Scripture facts are there to be explained ; and the compulsory Representation of a Church where there was no Church, not in the ideas and imaginations, but in the flesh and blood and bones and bowels of the Jews and the Nations and Peoples extant from Abraham to Christ,—this is the Keynote of a consistent solution of this class of difficulties in the Old Testament.

The most obnoxious example of a man "after God's own heart" is King David.* Many of the deeds written in his history were by no means according to our reading of the Ten Commandments, or to the direct appointments of Jehovah. For his private ends he slew two hundred of the Philistines, and brought their spoil to Saul, to earn Michal, Saul's daughter, to wife; when Saul, not God, had desired him to slay one hundred. He was inventively ruthless in war, and pounded his captives in iron mortars. He committed adultery with Bathsheba, the wife of Uriah the Hittite, and compassed Uriah's death by treachery, that he might have Bathsheba to wife. She bore him a son who died for David's sin, stricken by the Lord. Afterwards Bathsheba bore a second son, Solomon, and "the Lord loved him." In the same chapter, with David's repentance to Nathan the Prophet, who comforted him by the assurance, Thou shalt not die, he took Rabbah the City of Waters. "And he brought forth the people that were therein, and put them under saws, and under harrows of iron, and under axes of iron, and made them pass through the brick kiln: and thus did he unto all the cities of the children of Ammon. So David and all the people returned unto Jerusalem." (2 Sam. xii. 31.) David's death-bed also was alive with his revenge and perfidy: he had Joab murdered, and in ordering his death said, "Let not his hoar head go down to the grave in peace. To Gera he had sworn by the Lord saying, I will not put thee to death with the sword. But now with his last breath he said to Solomon, Hold him not guiltless; for thou, a wise man, knowest what thou oughtest to do unto him. But his hoar head bring thou down to the grave with blood. So David slept with his fathers, and was buried in the city of David" (1 Kings ii. 5–10).

* The reader is especially advised to see on this subject, *Paul and David, or the Relation between Personal Character and the Apostolic and Prophetic Offices.* By Rev. A. Clissold. London: Speirs. 1873.

XV.—SIGNS PRECEDING JUDAISM.

We read in the internal sense of the Word that Jehovah in the call of Abraham, and up to the time of Moses, designed to institute a representative Church in the Jewish nation, but that the character of that nation made it impossible to carry out this end; and that therefore a representation of a Church was established. The difference between these two institutions has been abundantly shown above. This *apparent* change of purpose is correspondent to the dealing of God with individuals. He knows all men from the beginning, and creates every man for heaven and its happiness. But as the man is an independent freewill, he himself settles his own future, whether it is to be providential, or fatal. The divine knowledge in no way influences the result. In the case of an evil end, it does provide a true and safe administration of it. So Jehovah dealt with the Jews. He gave them all opportunity; so that neither they, nor the succeeding Æon of Christianity, nor the higher rationality of the New Jerusalem, can accuse the Creator of injustice to the creature. He showed His Love and Mercy in approaching them as if they could be the medium of a Representative Church; but His divine Wisdom in obedience to the truth that they were not fit for this holy office. The opportunity of it demonstrated that by their own act and deed they rejected the proffered dispensation.

This mode of thought, however, is of "the internal historical sense," and it is difficult not to fall into it when we think of the omniscience of God from time as foreknowledge. It is not of the spiritual sense. That sense saves us from attributing change of purpose to God, by the reverse process of attributing to man what belongs to him. His lust which pressed him into a dispensation under Jehovah is the account of it. At first from the call of Abraham he had remains which might be raised into a representative Church; and

C

these were not extinct until Zipporah's day, when the Jewish nation had become fixed in that external state which has been described throughout. This Church of the Patriarchs being consummated, the sternness of Judaism commenced in the circumcision of Zipporah's son; circumcision being a sign of purity. So there is no change in the Sun of Righteousness, but in the Jewish Earth, turning its face away from the day into the night. This thought, being spiritual, is easier than that on which Belial and his debating society were engaged, concerning "fixed fate, freewill, foreknowledge absolute, and found no end in wandering mazes lost," as told by Milton. Yet both lines meet practically in this, that man changes, and God makes the best for the good, and for the evil too their best in the to them painful process of preventing them from growing worse.

The record of this is a history of marvels in the Letter, and traverses the Jewish character. It began by signs and degrees in the time of the patriarchs. From the beginning they were alien to constituting a Church. Abram had to be changed into Abraham, and Sarai into Sarah to represent outwardly a portended support to his call. Jacob met a man and wrestled with him all night, a man who would not tell his name; but Jacob, not overthrown by him, would not let him go, but demanded his blessing, and the Man gave him the name of Israel, and Jacob acknowledged him for "God whom he had seen face to face." There is pressure here into a divine office, and a claim on Jacob's part to have wrestled with God. The change of name is to be noted as an *alias*, again involving some necessity of the supersession and hiding of the Jew, Jacob, as a representative member; and the underpropping of the man by a spiritual foundation which made him into the *persona* of a Church, that is, into the actor of it, and not into a religious agent in it. Mere correspondences were evidently put in operation to stand as external denominators when internal goodness and truth were absent. The name of Jacob was at first the symbol of the natural man, the name, Israel, signified the spiritual man and the spiritual Church. These were not instituted but were represented.

Further on in the Divine Letter, Moses is commanded by Jehovah to leave his father-in-law, Jethro, and to go down into Egypt, to his oppressed people, with a message of deliverance from their bondage. On the instituted way, "Jehovah sought to slay him." This loudly contains a divine mystery. God, the maker of all worlds and all men, sought to slay him! There is divine humour here; the Psalms speak of laughter and derision on the part of the Creator; and how except in such figures should the Omnipotent seek to slay Moses without effecting it! But it is in the same class of Word as when "it repented the Lord that He had made man on the earth, and it grieved Him at His heart," and as when He conversed with Abraham who interceded for Sodom. These things are to be held up to spiritual light, and then the shell becomes translucent, and divine wisdom is revealed under the strangeness of the previously opaque external. They are parturient with truth and good which could not otherwise be brought forth, and uncovering the internal fruit is a felicity to the spiritual mind.

Moses here, on account of the context, represents the Jewish nature and nation. He had just shown unwillingness to receive the command of Jehovah to expostulate with Pharaoh, because he was not a man of speech, but Jehovah told him that He who gave the command had also created the mouth to obey it. Nevertheless the command was set aside, and Aaron was appointed to be spokesman, and Moses to be his God. Was this a stage in what was to follow? Moses was in the way in an inn, and Jehovah met him, and sought to kill him. In the way signifies Institution. In an inn,—mark the series of meaning from Moses as its dominant,—the external sensual mind separate from the internal mind. And Jehovah met him, signifies opposition; namely, his opposition to Jehovah. And sought to kill him, signifies that amongst that posterity a representative church could not be established: in other words, that that nation could not be received or chosen. Zipporah, the daughter of the Priest of Midian, was Moses' wife. Zipporah now denotes the representative church. Moses opposing Jehovah was menaced in himself with a defect of all representation which was equivalent to his extinction. Zipporah took a flint stone, signifies quality manifested by that church by truth [operating upon it]: The flint stone signifies the truth of faith. And cut off the foreskin of her son, signifies the removal of unclean loves, and thereby the laying bare of the internal. And made it touch his feet, signifies, shewing the quality of that nation interiorly, which appears when the external is removed. To touch his feet = to exhibit his nature. And she said, thou [Moses] art a bridegroom of bloods to me, signifies that it was full of all violence and hostility against truth and good. And He [Jehovah] ceased from him, signifies that it was permitted that the Jewish nation should represent; for by Jehovah seeking to slay him was signified that a representative church could not be established among that nation; so when it is now said that He ceased from him, it signifies that it was permitted that they should represent; that is, that the representative of a Church should be established, but not a Church. The evil can represent a Church, but none except the good can be a Church, for to represent a Church is a mere external thing. "Those things which are of the Church, and are holy, can be represented even by the evil, for a representative does not respect the person, but the thing."

Then she said, "A bridegroom of bloods for circumcisions." This signifies that although the internal was full of violence and hostility against truth and good, still circumcision should be received for a sign representative of purification from unclean loves. This is said by Zipporah because now it was permitted to that nation to represent the Church, which is denoted by ceasing from killing him. When the internal is not at all attended to, as was the case with the nation which was in externals without an internal, there then remains the signification of circumcision as denoting the removal of unclean loves; thus purification; so that it could serve as a representative sign.

Note that Moses is called by his wife, Zipporah, who had born to him his son, a bridegroom, and a bridegroom of bloods, but not a husband; for she denotes a representative Church, and he, the representation of a Church.

This is transcribed, but abridged, from the *Arcana Cœlestia*, n. 7040-7049. It is hard reading to those who are unaccustomed to the spiritual *sense*, with its mere elements of good and evil, truth and falsity, living through their endless variety in the Word. But although difficult, and alien to the natural man, to whom the first view of such spiritual things is repulsive, and from the immediate sense of darkness, even awful; yet if the same interest can gradually be felt in it, and the same pains given, as in the deciphering of the hieroglyphics, and then gathering up and distilling their meaning, the readers will here find definite knowledge, brilliant representation, and spiritual light founded upon light scientific: in fact, underlying Divine Testimony; just as they find important human elements which still have some scent and flavour of great scientific verities long passed away in Egyptology and its strange language.

We conclude this subject with that typical instance of the Jewish and Israelitish nature when Moses being delayed on Sinai, a further change was enacted by Jehovah to suit the lapse of those two nations. It is a speaking illustration of God's policy in managing the Jewish Drama. The Ten Commandments, and the Old Word, were changed on account of the quality of the posterity of Jacob. When Moses came down after Forty Days with Jehovah from Mount Sinai, and learned from Aaron of the golden calf, he broke the tables of stone prepared and written on by

Jehovah, and another set of tables hewn by Moses himself were then written upon, and became the Commandments. A lower Word was thus given organic to the Jewish Character; a Word full of those abnormal and barbarous things which are stumbling-blocks to the present religious mind. Jewish externality when commanded to exterminate enemies, could not conceive that they were of his own household, and in his own bosom; and so his dispensation fell upon men, women and children, and his morals were slaughters. Yet were they perceived in heaven as wars in the heart only, and exterminations of evils there. As shown above, such was this astonishing "Representation of a Church."

XVI.—THE WORD VINDICATED.

Theologians account for the apparent discords of Holy Scripture, and their obvious contrariety to the Divine Being, by the formula that the Bible has a human element in it mixed with the Divine element; and that the human is chargeable with the dross which modifies all human things. If there is a really divine life, and a human imperfection written with it, the task of divaricating the one from the other is superhuman, and no born intellect can be impartial and adequate to it. Each man will throw away what does not suit his temperament, or please his character, or condone his sins. The breakers of commandments will each rule out of Court the Commandment which should be his executioner; as Bacon in his Jest Book shows a criminal on a capital charge, who says to the Court: Police,—pointing to the Judge,—"take that man away, for I go in fear of my life because of him." So also all things concerning Immortality, and heaven, and hell, will be ruled out as human elements by the wicked who have no bonds in their death. This will happen surely when the divine and human elements, which natural chemistry has to separate, are still two substances, and merely mixed. Those also who deny and perhaps deride the miraculous and supernatural, will unscrupulously exterminate it from the whole Word, as being the absurd human, while their own dust and ashes remaining is the sublime divine.

But when, and moreover, instead of this, the Scripture has, according to a more common formula of the learned, been given *through* men's minds, with self-love and human character generally as the recipient organism of it, then the analysis of it into divine and human is superfluous, and we must say that it is wholly human ; whether leavened or not by any unaccountable divinity or insane enthusiasm. It were as easy to think of a theology arising from it, as to expect to elicit sunbeams out of cucumbers. It would be a Word of man after Professor Clifford's heart ; and indeed we have myriads of such words of man in Literature already.

The Word of God comes by a different way to this. It comes neither partly through man, and partly to him ; as perhaps the thought is in the first formula ; nor wholly through man, as in the second. *It comes to man ; it does not come through him.* The prerogative of a Word that comes *to* man and *not through* him is to be exactly conformable to his state, to fit him in his whole mind, in every spherule and rolling convolution of his brain, in the recesses of his heart, in the inmost penetralia of his memory, and in every crack and cranny of his individuality. And withal, being conformable to him, to be utterly independent of him. A word that comes through him is himself over again, and he rebukes such a Word if ever it is inconvenient to his evils, as it will rarely be ; he drenches it with his own drugs, and stifles its warning. An external Word impinging with its truths on the religious and moral skin from without, may be rejected, but stands back in protest, as a living mirror, sculptured cast, and legible imprint of the sinner. It cannot be smothered internally. It fits and will fit ; it smites and will smite.

An external Word, or Revelation from God to man,

follows the state of man to converse with him. It was indeed *in* Man, and not external, except that man knew that the voice of God was not his own voice, but Jehovah's, in the Adamic Church; for man was sympathetic to the penetration of his Father and Creator, and from his heart of hearts loved the Advent into his soul's soul. But in the Noahtic Church the Word as the divine truth was an external instruction and appeal, seminal with Enoch tradition : a high Revelation. In the Jewish Church a low Revelation. In the Gospels, the Word made flesh and shining as the life of men : in the New Church, the Second Coming ; the Word made spiritual for Mankind, and Divine-celestial in the Lord. So the Word is diverse, and God appears to every man according to the state of each, and He has also a different name of Divine quality in each different heaven.

But now mark. Were the Word to come *through* man, through hearts deceitful above all things and desperately wicked, unless it destroyed its subject, it would partake of his quality and be debased to it. When it comes *to* man it does partake of his quality, and its divine truth and purity are not affected by it. In order to accompany us on the way the Word speaks by appearances and by Correspondences. To the men of evil passions, Jehovah has human passions. Wrath, revenge, delight in the destruction of enemies, are what our nature sees of God while evil reigns in ourselves. Our fixed literality is the gauge and meter of our character. But because the Word is not written through us its Divinity is reserved, and "God is His Own Interpreter ;" and revealing the Divine Spiritual Sense, we know by slow degrees of faith that our Father is never wrath, but loves His enemies, and is the Friend of sinners. Yet the sternness of Divine Truth remains, and is our way, truth and life. The evil look of the Word, say here, the Jewish Word, is our own evil upon which the letter is necessarily *moulded.* When the science of correspondences is applied to that Word, and reveals its spiritual sense, the letter perishes, and the heavenly fills the vessels of the earthly.

In closing these remarks, all bearing upon the Mystery of the Jews, and upon the problem of the cause and manner of the Representation of a Church, it seems reasonable to think that the wonderful means employed by Jehovah are also in accord and series with His general Government of the World. Without being peopled by Jews, is not the world in 1894 mainly darkened with the shadow of Judaism? And as Judaism was propped by a Theocracy, and the heavens were supported by that divine Atlas-work, is not the same work as a necessity continued with providential variation wherever divine support is needed. It does not now institute or build a compulsory religion, because a New Church, a New Religion, and a New Revelation are presently in the world, and respect human freedom as no previous dispensation has respected it: in fact, re-create it. Moreover, the tiny heart and lungs of this Infant Religion give the New Heavens a basis; a new earth and plane for the descent of the New Jerusalem; and for the pulse and breath of it to move human nature in all its organs and members and climates. A Theocracy which can never be absent takes charge of more external things, as it did in Judea, and by constant events no longer recognised as divine; by rewards and punishments, by the rise and fall of states and nations, by wars, pestilences, and famines; by shakings of the dead cosmos; by signs of the times, the Creator and Upholder overrules the days of evil, and secures a place from the wrath of man in which as in another Holy Land the descending City and the new Humanity may be established.

Judaism in the Word, the Jews also, have universal signification. In the spiritual sense, which does not belong to persons or nations, Jews are all those who have the quality of representing a holy internal without having a holy internal themselves. The Word is implied in a good sense spiritually in the Apocalypse, where it speaks of those who say they are Jews, but are not, but are of the Synagogue of Satan, ii. 9, iii. 9. The like holds of other names in the Word: they are not local or national or individual in the internal sense. So Babylon, which signifies the love of dominion over the souls of men, pre-eminently denotes the Church of Rome, but also all other churches, institutions and persons where this love is an essential quality. Thus Judaism, like Babylon, exists wherever its quality is, whether in the Jews, or in any other denomination.

XVII.—HUMAN NATURE NEEDS A REVELATION.

From the *Arcana Cœlestia*, where a divine imprint shines from every page, the following is commended to the reader as bread for the day :—

"Man, without a revelation from the Divine cannot know anything about eternal life nor even anything about God, and still less about love and faith to Him. For man is born into mere ignorance; and must after birth learn everything from worldly experiences, from which he must form his understanding. He is also born by inheritance into all the evil of self-love and love of the world. The delights derived from these two loves are continually prevalent, and their suggestions are diametrically opposite to the Divine. Hence now it is that Man of himself knows nothing about eternal life. Therefore there must be a Revelation to communicate such knowledge."

"That the evils of the love of self and the world induce such ignorance concerning those things that relate to eternal life, is very manifest from those within the Church, who, although they know from revelation that there is a God, that there is a heaven and a hell, that there is an eternal life, and that that life is to be gained by the good of love and faith, still fall into denial about these things ; as well the learned as the unlearned. Hence it is further evident what great ignorance would prevail if there were no revelation."

" Since then man lives after death, and in such case, to eternity, and a life awaits him according to his love and faith, it follows that the Divine, out of love towards the human race, revealed such things as may lead to that life, and conduce to man's salvation. What the Divine has revealed with us is the Word."

" The Word, as a Revelation from the Divine, is divine in all things and in everything. What is from the Divine cannot be otherwise."

" What is from the Divine descends through the heavens down to man. In the heavens therefore it is accommodated to the wisdom of the Angels who are there, and on earth to the apprehension of the men who are there. Thus in the Word there is an internal sense which is spiritual for the angels, and an external sense which is natural for men. Hence it is that conjunction of heaven with man is effected by the Word."

" The genuine sense of the Word is apprehended by none but those who are illuminated or enlightened, and they alone are enlightened who are in love and faith to the Lord, for the interiors of such are elevated by the Lord into the very light of heaven."

" The Word in the letter cannot be apprehended except by doctrine derived from the Word by one who is enlightened. The sense of the letter is accommodated to the apprehension of men, even of the simple. Therefore doctrine derived from the Word must be to them for a lamp."

" The Books of the Word are all those which have an internal sense ; those which have not are not the Word. The Books of the Word in the Old Testament are the Five Books of Moses, the Book of Joshua, the Book of

Judges, the two Books of Samuel, the two Books of Kings, the Psalms of David; the Prophets Isaiah, Jeremiah, the Lamentations, Ezekiel, Daniel, Hosea, Joel, Amos, Obadiah, Jonah, Micah, Nahum, Habakkuk, Zephaniah, Haggai, Zechariah, Malachi; and in the New Testament, the four Evangelists, Matthew, Mark, Luke, John; and the Apocalypse" (n. 10318-10325).

XVIII.—THE THICK DARKNESS ABOUT GOD ON MOUNT SINAI.

The cruelties mentioned in Section XVI., though apparent commands of Jehovah, yet come by reflex action from the Jews. But they exist in the Divine Word, and infernal as they are, they have heavenly opposites and correspondences, and they show the bed or nidus in which the Jewish Dispensation was born. The very womb of it was Sinai, of which it is written, " And Mount Sinai was altogether on a smoke, because the Lord descended upon it in fire; and the smoke thereof ascended as the smoke of a furnace; and the whole mount quaked greatly. And after the commandments were delivered, All the people saw the thunderings, and the lightnings, and the noise of the trumpet, and the mountain smoking; and when the people saw, they removed, and stood afar off. . . And the people stood afar off, and Moses drew near unto the thick darkness about God." In the spiritual sense, which we now possess more indestructibly than we possess the English Language, and from the same Lord God who spoke the Ten Commandments from Sinai, these terrible appearings were far off from Jehovah Himself, but were the project of the human nature opposed to Him, and reacting against His Divinity: they denoted the self-love of the Jews about to receive the last word and dispensation which was then possible; and about to reject and destroy it. The thick darkness about God was the nature of that race. The obverse love and truth which alone are the Father was shown in condescension of Glory when other Jews were blessed by Christ, and it came to pass while He blessed them, He was parted from them, and carried up into Heaven. God appears to every man, and to all bodies collectively, differently according to the state of each, which we shall be pardoned for repeating.

Also compare the overshadowing of the Virgin by Jehovah the Lord, and the Heavenly Host with the Shepherds watching their flocks by night, and the darkness about God dissipated by the Incarnation,—these inaugurations of the first Christian Religion,—with the awful beginning of the Jewish Religiosity.

XIX.—SOME THOUGHTS ABOUT CORRESPONDENCE.

In such difficult studies it is useful to lead the horse, or understanding of the Word, time after time, to principles in which thirst for truth may be satisfied, and the way refreshed. Let us delay here for a word about Correspondence ; since this fact, doctrine and knowledge, is so often referred to in these pages. Correspondence in the Word is between earthly and heavenly things. In the Ancient Church all the rituals were correspondences, and caused the presence of heaven to sincere worshippers. Placing things in a holy order, therefore, where the heart and mind were in the like state, had actual and active power from God to sanctify and potentize worship. There was Divine Spiritual Induction, as now by physical placements we have electrical induction : a proper plane from below to above and from above to below is the condition in both cases. This knowledge of spiritual correspondences came down from the earliest ages, when during the first celestial innocence it was in the mind from the heart of the Family of Man, and was as instinctive as the vitals of the body are now, and as the minds of animals and birds and insects are. There was, however, what there is nowhere but in man, a heavenly will to it, which was not instinctive, but free,—a free will. Nature so far as was good and useful, was transparent to this mind, flowed from it, and obeyed it by Correspondences. For man and nature were of one affection by act of God, and loved to correspond and converse, and so the world let man into her bridal rooms where she was continually married by new ends to her Creator, and where her teeming progeny of love was born. Therefore the science of correspondences was the science of sciences. In the Ancient Church the knowledge but not the instinct of it survived; a broken knowledge suited to the service of a more external Dispensation. Egypt possessed the scientific profession of it, and cultivated the "scientifics of the Church." It taught by the lore of most ancient symbols how worship could commune with heaven, and how those in heaven could flow into worship. It was an organized body of religion; a might and a power. The arrangement of Correspondences under the guidance of a pervading Revelation was like the build of the organization in a man, which while it answers to life and corresponds with it, brings life down into the body, and begs the question of life by being alive. So this organic science of the Church brought a fulness of life to faithful religious worshippers, and made them a body under an upper body in the spiritual heavens. This power when attained was subject to the state of the worshippers, and of the Church. The conscience formed to protect its integrity was corrupted by the free will of the members; oblivion came between worship and God, and the vehicles of divine truth were alienated. This was gradual, and the power of the knowledge was slowly lost. The refuse of it was more and more man-made, not God-made. It ruled minds from priestly dominion, and attempted to control the nature of things by Magic. Magic was not a false pretence but a false performance. The Egyptian Magicians had its powers. We have attestation of the spiritual lore of the Egyptians in the saying that Moses was learned in all their wisdom ; and the tradition of this wisdom was preserved in the legend that Greek philosophers resorted to Egypt as to a fountain of the truths of old. Herodotus also says that the gods once ruled there. It had been and was a real power as we see from Genesis, and continued to be such until the Ancient Church was consummated and judged, and the coincidence of its vastation in Egypt enacted in the overwhelming of Pharaoh and his host. The refuse of the religion, the survival of the dregs, which are always what can bear the degradation of surviving, dwindled into the perversions signalized in the temples and tombs, into the hieroglyphics concerning the glory of dynasties, but with remains of Ancient Truth, Justice and Judgment, in the book of the dead and their long-drawn destinies. Effective Magic, such as the Magicians opposed to the miracles of Jehovah through Moses, ceased, but still has left traces in all the centuries ; and witchcraft was dealt with in penal statutes till a late age in England and the United States. We also recal Lapland and Africa. A form of it consists in the arrangement of some mechanism meant to coincide with a future event, and thus to bring that event, whether death, or health, good or ill fortune, to pass, and so to control the stars. Rebellion is witchcraft, said Samuel to Saul. Superseding the Word of the Lord, and attempting to command the cosmos by your own invention, is spiritual rebellion.

When the Ancient Church was consummated and judged, and ceased to be a Church, a severe and limited system of correspondences was ordained, and magic and its symbols were forbidden. It is this iron discipline that we now meet with, and which we may reverently call Divine Magic in the stern walk of the Jewish Dispensation. There is continuity of the Revelations from Adam to Christ, and the might of Correspondences bares its arm in each, but with a different determination, because each several Church is two-fold, a Church in heaven and a Church on earth, and a Word written in correspondences is the uniting medium in every case between the upper and lower Churches.

XX.—JEWISH FREEDOM AND BONDAGE.

It does not appear that the Jews were condignly judged for cruelties other than those which were forbidden by the Lord in commandments, or through priests and prophets in the events of the history. The terrible processes of David were included in the general Israelitish mission of the extermination of the nations. The details belonged to the individuals, and to their several characters, and would be judged individually after death, and also committed to the bulk and record of the Jewish nature in the great Assize of the Consummation. So the Jews too had a comparatively free hand in a higher sense than Judaism permitted. They were not machines. But in regard to particular laws as symbols in the Divine Drama obedience was stringent, and life and death were at stake. This was exemplified when David numbered the people. We read the following:—
" Now these be the last words of David, David the Son of Jesse saith, and the man who was raised on high saith, the anointed of the God of Jacob, and pleasant in the Psalms of Israel: The spirit of the Lord spake by me, and His Word was upon my tongue. The God of Israel said, the Rock of Israel spake to me, he that rules over men must be just, ruling in the fear of God. As the light of the morning when the sun riseth, a morning without clouds; the tender grass out of the earth through clear shining after rain. Although my house be not so with God, yet He hath made with me an everlasting covenant, ordered in all things, and sure, for it is all my salvation and all my desire, although He maketh it not

AND THE OLD JERUSALEM. 49

to grow" (2 Samuel xxiii. 1–5). Then follow the names of David's thirty captains, and the exploits of his chiefs, the chiefs of the threes who were eminent over the thirty, making thirty and seven in all. Uriah the Hittite is the last enumerated. "And again the anger of the Lord was kindled against Israel, and He moved David against them, saying, Go, number Israel and Judah." Why was this anger kindled? The inventory of David's mighty men, and their exploits, and the *summum bonum* in Uriah the Hittite, is noteworthy. The only mention of the Lord in the chapter is where David would not drink of the water of the well of Bethlehem because it had value as the blood of the men that went for it in jeopardy of their lives. These were not actions commanded by Jehovah, or representative correspondences in the Dispensation. But David exulted in his own treasury of valour as its pieces were enumerated, and this led on to an infraction of a Divine command. The anger of Jehovah,—in the spiritual sense,—is David's manifested self-love. The avarice and lust were continued onwards now in numbering the people from Dan to Beersheba, that he might know the sum of the people. He first counts his guineas and then his farthings that he may be quite sure of his resources. He was warned by Joab and the captains of the host against counting the people, but his word prevailed against theirs. In consequence of David's disobedience, the destroying angel— spiritually, the crime of David—in voiding his representative veracity sent a pestilence upon Israel, and there died of the people from Dan even to Beersheba seventy thousand men. Jehovah sends no pestilences, but EPIDEMIC MAN falls from his own evil spirit upon his body, and kills himself.

"'To number signifies to arrange and dispose; and as it belongs to the Lord alone to arrange in order and dispose the truths and goods of faith and of love with everyone in the Church and in Heaven; therefore when this is done by man, as it was done by David through Joab, it signifies the ordering and disposition of such things by man and not

D

by the Lord; which is not to order and dispose, but to destroy."—*Arcana Cœlestia*, n. 10217.

If this be well considered, it explains why counting his armies, taking a military census, which all chiefs do to-day, was forbidden to David, because the Lord was his army, and seventy thousand deaths by pestilence were the spiritual measure of the offence whereby David denied that they were Jehovah's men and counted them as his own. Remembering all the previous deeds of the children of Israel in their battles, and believing the same literally, and that the power and terror of God was on these men against their enemies so that handfuls of them routed hosts; we may then know that the conditions of Israel's warfare were miraculous; and that whatever rebellion against command broke the obedience upon which the perpetual miracle of the Dispensation depended, in the act destroyed the foundations, and left Israel an easy prey to nations naturally mightier than themselves.

The avarice of personal glory, the deepest Miser and Hoarder of all, was dramatically or representatively stricken here in bodily deaths. For everything in the Jewish Economy was bodily and carnal, an outbirth of the Jews. The same things outborn from Christians are, mentally as well as bodily, propagated in modern states. The devastation of countries and waste of armies takes place under destroying angels, which are godless lusts of power; attributes of glory to nations themselves. Cupidities prowling after other lands, brooding revenges centuries long, schemes for universal dominion, mutual national hatreds and friendships of hatred all round; these and the parliaments of Atheistic Man make Christianity worse than Judaism.

It is noteworthy that the Jews of these late ages are not in the front in the conduct of wars, and that the worst part of their nature as it was displayed when Jehovah was their Ruler is dormant. Avarice is their hereditary passion, and financial ability the use of honest Jews to the community.

This latter is their best conversion towards Christianity ; and it is a sufficient and considerable fact. While they wail for their temple and their lost place in the Divine Drama, they may thank God that they are emancipated from its Letter, and that they sit politically and socially in so many countries under their own vines and fig-trees. We have succeeded to their Cross, but think to escape from the responsibilities which weighed upon the chosen people.

XXI.—SAUL AND SAMUEL.

An instance illustrative of the Jewish Dispensation occurs in the Word where Samuel presented Saul, the son of Kish, of the tribe of Benjamin, to all the people as king, and said, See ye him whom the Lord hath chosen, and all the people shouted and said, [God save the king] Let the king live. And Samuel said, Come, and let us go to Gilgal, and renew the kingdom there. Then recounting the Lord's doings from the days of Moses and Aaron to his own Priesthood, he thus rebuked the children of Israel for their wickedness: "When ye saw that Nahash the king of the children of Ammon came against you, ye said unto me, Nay, but a king shall reign over us ; *when the Lord your God was your King.* If ye will fear the Lord, and serve Him, and hearken unto His voice, and not rebel against the commandment of the Lord, then shall both ye and also the king that reigneth over you be followers of the Lord your God. But if ye will not hearken unto the voice of the Lord, but rebel against the commandment of the Lord, then shall the hand of the Lord be against you as it was against your fathers." —1 Samuel x. 25, xi. 15, xii. 12–16. "Then Saul, finding that the people were scattered from him, though he had been made king, and being afraid of the Philistines who were assembled to fight against Israel, did not wait for Samuel, who had appointed to meet him in Gilgal, there to renew the kingdom, but commanded the burnt-offering and the peace-offerings to be brought to him. And he offered the burnt-offering. And it came to pass as soon as he had made an end of offering the burnt-offering, behold, Samuel came. And Samuel said, What hast thou done? And Saul said, Because I saw that the people were scattered from me, and thou camest not within the days appointed, and that the Philistines assembled themselves together at Micmash, therefore said I, Now will the Philistines come down upon me to Gilgal, and I have not entreated the favour of the Lord. I forced myself therefore, and offered the burnt-offering. And Samuel said to Saul, Thou hast done foolishly. Thou hast not kept the commandment of the Lord thy God which he commanded thee, for now would the Lord have established thy kingdom upon Israel for ever. But now thy kingdom shall not continue. The Lord hath sought Him a man after His own heart, and the Lord hath appointed him to be prince over His people, because thou hast not kept that which the Lord commanded thee."—*Ibid.* xiii. 8-14.

Saul set the State above the Church, or rather became high priest by usurpation as well as king by divine right. But the matter for our perception here is still the revelation of the nature of the Jewish Dispensation. The king's anxiety and impatience, and in his fear of delay his wish to entreat the favour of the Lord, are obvious motives for his conduct, and if we put out of sight that he was under Jehovah, his offence might have been condoned If the reader is not careful to hold the conditions in mind, he may fall into the thought that it was hard that the first king of Israel should lose his kingdom on such grounds. But if you accept the letter of the Word, and the purpose of Jehovah in founding a representation of a Church on mere obedience to the spoken words of God Almighty,—to the bond of the Letter,—then Saul's misapprehension of his kingship becomes almost as marvellous from below as Jehovah's action before seemed from above. May we without irreverence liken the Jewish Church to a game at chess, only to declare that in such a combat, as between good and evil, the moves are fixed, and no exigence allows them to be departed from. The perception of this, we again repeat, depends upon our belief in the letter, and also in our acceptance of the new Revelation about the previous Churches, and the Christian Church which was to come. Natural mechanics came after celestial and spiritual dynamics.

We cannot but see that Saul had no knowledge of, or belief in, the conditions under which he was living, and that an impenetrable stupidity was manifested by the Jews generally in the same regard. Living under miracle and on miracle, they forgot this fact in the near presence of the greatest signs and wonders. The manifestation of Jehovah on Sinai, the casting of the golden calf, and the exultant cry, These be thy Gods, O Israel, which brought thee out of the land of Egypt, are almost synchronous events. Everything here signifies that a last remainder of man was being dealt with. This must be carefully taken into account in the theory of a case which has no parallel in other history. May we use a mythological trope in illustration. It shall be of Atlas, who was condemned to support heaven on his shoulders. His strength to do this depends upon an exact care of his mind and body: a wrong meal, a debauch in wine, a waste in his life, any disobedience to the needs of his singular service, a grain of unwillingness, make his state register a tottering foundation, and the weight of the sky sways to destruction.

In the Divine Word another event is declared. When Samuel tells Saul that his kingdom shall not continue, he says, The Lord hath sought him a man after His own heart, and the Lord hath appointed him to be prince over His people, because thou hast not kept that which the Lord commanded thee. David is here declared to be a man after God's own heart. The Lord knew what David was, and foresaw every deed that David would freely do in his lifetime. This characterization of David by the Lord as a man after His own heart requires neither more nor less than a *firm* knowledge of the essence of the Jewish Dispensation. Obedience to command in that dramatic Church militant was the essence. It seems to involve two elements. (1) The Jewish capacity for assuming an external religion under fear of punishment and hope of reward; and (2) the previous Jewish nature which was altogether intractable, and must be allowed to have its way where it did not infringe the borders of the strait commandments, laws, regulations, and directions of Jehovah. The man after God's own heart was one whose obediences to this regime so far exceeded his punishable disobediences, that the representation of an external Theocracy, however imperfectly acted, did not perish. All the war and the slaughter was in David's nature and in human nature, and Jehovah in commanding it made it representative of holy war between good and evil and between truth and falsity. How the case would have been with the Land of Canaan if the Jews had not been led against its nations by Moses and Joshua is a question which suggests itself, but it cannot be entertained in any case of theocratic history. Jehovah was the alone Agent, and apart from his Leadership the armies of the Jews were shadows.

It might be said that David in his long reign committed more infractions of *orders* than Saul, and yet he preserved the realm. But Saul clinging to his kingdom after he knew that the Lord had forsaken him, his demoniac possession and madness, his resort to necromancy, and above all his abominable hatred of young and wonderful David, and his attempts to murder him and to have him murdered, are strong notes of character. Yet none of these things is so much of the essence of his deposition and destruction as his two acts of disobedience, in himself offering the burnt-

AND THE OLD JERUSALEM. 55

offering and not awaiting Samuel, and in preserving Agag and the spoil of the Amalekites which Samuel by the Lord commanded him utterly to destroy. After this his prayers were of no offect; although he worshipped the Lord, the Lord was averted from him, and answered him neither by dreams, by urim, nor by prophets.

XXII.—IMPOSSIBILITIES WERE NOT ASKED OF THE JEWS.

With regard to the intractable Jewish nature which could not be reached by temporary fears or hopes, no impossible conditions were demanded of it. In the Psalms and Prophets it was tenderly addressed, and mercy and justice and brotherly love were enjoined as they were afterwards commanded by Christ. But they were interpreted as towards friends and brethren, and love your enemies was not expressed. These things were recommendations, not commands, and disobedience to mental injunctions did not infringe the Old Testament Code. Adultery was severely forbidden and punished, but taking to wife was interpreted according to the Jewish nature : it included polygamy according to regulation. The Patriarchs were polygamists, and the kings : David had as many wives as he listed; and it was not imputed to him for wrong. Solomon loved many strange women together with the daughter of Pharaoh. . . . women of the nations concerning which the Lord said unto the children of Israel, Ye shall not go among them. And he had seven hundred wives, princesses, and three hundred concubines, and his wives turned away his heart. For when Solomon was old, his wives turned away his heart unto other gods; and his heart was not perfect with the Lord his God, as was the heart of David his father. He went after Ashtoreth, the goddess of the Zidonians, and after Milcom, the abomination of the

Ammonites. And Solomon did that which was evil in the sight of the Lord, and went not fully after the Lord as did David his father. He built an high place for Chemosh, the abomination of Moab, in the mount that is before Jerusalem; and for Moloch, the abomination of the children of Ammon. And so did he for all his strange wives. For these deeds the Lord who had appeared to him twice, now said to him : I will surely rend thy kingdom from thee, and will give it to thy servant. Notwithstanding, in thy day I will not do it for David thy Father's sake, but I will rend it out of the hand of thy son. Howbeit I will not rend away all the kingdom, but I will give one tribe to thy son, for David my servant's sake, and for Jerusalem's sake which I have chosen.—1 Kings xi. 1-13. It is clear from this that the representation of a Church was perishing among the Jews, and that their adulterous lust was insatiable. Moses for the hardness of their hearts allowed them to put away their wives, but from the beginning it hath not been so.—Matthew xix. 8. Male and female made he them. For this cause shall a man leave his father and mother and shall cleave unto his wife, and *the twain* shall be one flesh.—Mark x. 5. The Lord did not answer the Pharisees respecting the polygamy recorded in the Old Testament. But the narrative of the letter shows that it was not adultery in that dispensation, and that the practice of it by David did not violate the scheme of Judaism; neither did the handmaids of the Patriarchs given by Sarah, Rebekah, and Rachel to their husbands to bear children to them. This was because the Jew then could not be kept to one wife ; his nature made it impossible, and therefore monogamy was not a life and death condition of the Dispensation, and polygamy did not preclude the miraculous communication of that religiosity with heaven. Conjugial love, which reigns in heaven, where Marriage is universal and perpetual, was not in those Jews, and the polygamy of that nation, with the other lusts of the internal man, was set on one side, or disregarded, when the daily performed representatives were translated inwards, and perceived above. The process of this transmutation has been already described (see pages 26-28).

XXIII.—INERADICABLE POLYGAMY, JEWISH AND MAHOMETAN.

Mahomet, whose supplementary religion wrought such effective good for a multitude of nations, destroying their idolatries, did not attempt to eradicate polygamy, which was hereditary over the whole world, and his Allah, like the Jehovah of the Jews, wrought with what was possible in the fallen and corrupt nature of man, in the interest of leading all, whether Jews, Mahometans, Africans, or Hindoos, by the gradual stages of possible change, towards the New Dispensation, in which again as at first one man will have one wife here and hereafter, and naturally and then spiritually, in heaven as on earth, they twain shall be one flesh.

We put in parenthesis here that missionary effort in instructing the heathen will have to follow Mahomet as he himself followed the Old Testament, and will not succeed in propagating the truths of the Old and New Testaments, if it is attempted to extinguish Polygamy and Idol-mediumship. The reception of the Divine letter of the Word unaccompanied by the dogmas of the Church will in God's good time do its work with Polygamy, and the White man, himself charged with the Bible, will take no steps towards inducing any chief to turn a crowd of faithful hard-working women who are indispensable to his industries, out of doors into unmerited want and degradation, because, not to his or their discredit, they are his wives. Let the Africans be under Jehovah for His time, until they have those new eyes which see Jehovah as Christ. We have used the phrase Idol-mediumship. It is different from idol worship, and the more the form is human to the worshipper, the more easily it may be the first step on which he kneels to the true God.

The form of God is divinely human. God is a Man. This truth, which was visible as Jehovah, and tangible as Christ, and audible in Genesis when "God said,"—for only Man says—is innate in every man, and embedded in every fetish, and can be brought out to acknowledged humanity according to Christian instruction and a life according to its simple teachings.

About marriage the Lord's words to the Sadducees are not followed out. Jesus said, Ye—the Sadducees—do err, not knowing the Scriptures, nor the power of God. For in the resurrection they neither marry nor are given in marriage, but are as the angels of God in heaven. But as touching the Resurrection of the dead, have ye not read that which was spoken unto you by God, saying, I am the God of Abraham, and the God of Isaac, and the God of Jacob? God is not the God of the dead, but of the living. The Lord lays down the Canon for understanding this revelation: it lies in knowing the Scriptures and the power of God. They, the Scriptures, are spirit and they are life. The Resurrection is the regenerate man and woman; here, by the question, in the heavens. Neither marrying nor being given in marriage is the Sadduceeism in them. What is being as the Angels of God in heaven? The next verse "which was spoken to you by God," answers this question. The God of Abraham, is the Divine truth proclaiming the celestial marriage, the God of Isaac is the Divine truth certifying the spiritual marriage, the God of Jacob is the Divine truth proclaiming the natural marriage. The three heavens attest immortal marriage with all their songs, psalms, and acclamations. And for whom? Not for the Sadduceeans. By the letter, and by the spirit, the parties in this ecclesiastical suit were seven dead men and one dead woman. Note the initial difference between the resurrection in which they are as the angels of God in heaven, and the resurrection of the dead, and that God is not the God of the dead. But God is the God of the living. Love is the life of man, and conjugial love the holy life in which two are one. And man and woman are man and woman for ever, married and conjoined either in the Abraham-heaven which signifies the celestial, in the Isaac-heaven which signifies the spiritual, or in the Jacob-heaven which is the natural, according to their place in Maximus Homo which is determined by the ardour and quality of their virginity and chastity here on earth. See Swedenborg's Revelation of the whole subject in his Book on CONJUGIAL LOVE, which will be the Canon for all races in the New Religion and its Churches, and will leave the Mahometan and the African to his own new and regenerating conscience confronted by the Word of both the Old and the New Testaments.

XXIV.—THE JEWISH DRAMA BECAME MORE AND MORE INEFFECTIVE.

It would appear that the sternness of Judaism was relaxed in the later stages of it, and that evil inheritance accumulated in the Jewish race age by age, as is always the case, in a falling mankind, though in no instance is there extant such a record of it as we possess in the Bible. While it took place, sins were overlooked legally, and condign punishment was postponed, and this was written of in the Word as the mercy of Jehovah, and as accorded for the sake of David. Polygamy grew monstrous, and Polytheism was the mind of it, and lust, the offspring of the two, multitudinous, peopled Jerusalem. From one source, David and Bathsheba, it is instructive to note what the Seed of a man means. In Solomon, the wisest of men, the builder of the Temple of Jehovah, murder and adultery were married as in his father David. Another subject to be opened is, that polygamy appears to have been restricted after the Babylonish Captivity. "In the post-Babylonian period monogamy appears to have become more prevalent than at any previous time; indeed we have no instance of polygamy during this period on record in the Bible, all the marriages noticed being with single wives. During the same period the theory of monogamy is set forth in Eccles. xxvi. 1–27. The practice of polygamy nevertheless still existed; Herod the Great had nine wives at one time. The abuse of divorce continued unabated."—*Smith's Concise Dictionary of the Bible*, Art. Marriage. Thus during the period alluded to some reformation took place, whether from example of Babylon, or from compulsion there, or from new thoughts instilled into the rulers. At the same time some glimmering light about a future state was inseminated into them. Such Reformations or Revivals are known in our countries as accompanying and to a certain extent mitigating the last days of dying States and Churches. They do not give life, but for a time they recall better ages, and keep hope and Remains alive, and thus prolong mortal days against the chronic and inveterate diseases which cause THE END OF THE CHURCH or of the Empire. It was in this way that the Reformation brought the Bible out of its sepulchre in the Churchyard. It was thus that the decline and fall of the Roman Empire was a death-bed for a thousand years.

But, moreover, as the Jewish Dispensation was drawing to a close, and Jehovah was leaving them to their own devices, the sense of a new freedom could not but be felt, and a new Atheism, what we call Agnosticism, concerning their guided supernatural past, must come as a paralysis upon all even external beliefs, and leave the Jewish mind open to both ethnic superstitions and philosophies. This, which modern writers generally regard as a distinct progress for Judaism, paved the way to the Romano-Judaic legality which ended in the Crucifixion of Christ.

XXV.—NEW REVELATIONS.

But spiritual reasons essential to the Jewish Dispensation governed in all these cases; reasons or causes which could not be discovered without a new Revelation. Things which are monstrous were permitted by the Lord. Hear then what Swedenborg says: "There are not any laws of permission by themselves, or separate from the laws of the Divine Providence; the laws of each are the same. Therefore it is said that God permits, by which is not meant that He wills, but that He is not able to prevent, in view of the end, which is salvation."—*Angelic Wisdom concerning the Divine Providence*, n. 234. "Solomon was permitted to inaugurate idolatrous worship of many kinds. This was in order that he might represent the Lord's Kingdom or Church, together with all the religious systems of the whole globe. For the Church established with the Israelitish and Jewish nation was a representative church; and therefore all the judgments and statutes of that Church represented the spiritual things of the Church which are its internals. The people itself represented the Church; the King, the Lord; David, the Lord about to come into the world; and Solomon, the Lord after his coming. And since the Lord after the glorification of His humanity had power over heaven and earth, therefore Solomon His representative appeared in glory and magnificence, was in wisdom above all the kings of the earth, and also built the temple. Moreover, he permitted and instituted the rites of many nations, through which the various creeds and practices in the world were represented. The like is signified by his seven hundred wives and three hundred concubines; for wife in the Word signifies a Church, and Concubine a Religion aside. . . . . Many kings after Solomon were permitted to profane the Temple and the holy things of the Church, because the people represented the Church, and their king, the head of them. And as the

Israelitish and Jewish nation could not long represent the Church, for they were idolaters at heart, so they receded in time from representative worship; perverting all things of the Church, nor resting until they had devastated it. This was represented [dramatized] by profanations of the Temple by their kings, and by their idolatries: the final devastation of the Church by the destruction of the Temple, by the carrying away of the Israelitish people, and the captivity of the Jewish people in Babylon. This was the cause; and whatever is done from any cause, is done of Divine Providence according to some law of its own."—*Ibid.* n. 245, 246. Granting that there must be a church on earth for man to continue to subsist here and hereafter, and that a representation or drama of a Church was the only Atlas left on earth to support the heaven, and that the Lord in His Divine Providence must make use of this support,—granting this, Swedenborg's Rational Revelation is as incontestable as the surest truths of mechanical or mathematical science. Yet beyond human finding unless God show it, which He has done.

XXVI.—THE MEDIUMSHIP OF DAVID AND THE PROPHETS.

When Christ was risen, and joined the two apostles who were going to the village of Emmaus, they had not truly believed what He announced before His Crucifixion. And now He said unto them, "O foolish men, and slow of heart to believe all that the Prophets have spoken. Ought not the Christ to suffer these things, and to enter into His Glory? And beginning from Moses and from all the Prophets, He interpreted to them in all the Scriptures the things concerning Himself." And when He stood in the midst of the eleven at Jerusalem, and showed them His hands and His feet, and said, " Handle Me and see that it is I Myself, for a spirit hath not flesh and bones as ye see

Me have," He then also said to them "that all things must needs be fulfilled which are written in the law of Moses and the Prophets, and the Psalms concerning me. Then opened He their mind that they might understand the Scriptures. And He said unto them, Thus it is written, that the Christ should suffer, and rise again from the dead the third day, and that repentance and remission of sins should be preached in His name unto all the nations beginning from Jerusalem" (Luke xxv. 28, 39, 40, 44–48).

Here the Lord claims the Scriptures as Himself the Word of God. To those to whom the Psalms are a daily Gospel, it is impossible to conceive that they refer to David and the Jews excepting in a temporal sense. They express the attributes and struggles of a Divine Man, a God, with His feet in the world, and struggling against the fetters of its flesh, to bring his Godhead into its Power, Kingdom and Glory. To David, on the contrary, his Psalms signify indeed his relation to Jehovah, his states and struggles of mind, but all temporal and personal, though taking in his posterity; his consciousness of the disobedience of his nation, and fear for the consequences of it to himself, his reliance on the promises to his Royal Line which he regards as binding on the Almighty: his adjuration of Jehovah to take his side against his enemies, to carry out his curses, and extend his cruelties. Within these lines David was a devout man, and sufficiently faithful to his dispensation to keep his throne in it, and die a king, and bequeath a kingdom.

Swedenborg throughout his works has to reveal about David, both as a person, and as a merely representative character. As a person he partook of the Jewish nature, especially in his capacity for an external worship of Jehovah, while such worship had no internal response in his nature and character. On this account, as a *dramatis persona*, he could receive from an angel of Jehovah, that is, from Jehovah Himself, *a verbal dictation* of the Psalms, having always some obvious reference to the man David, but also containing and hardly veiling a glory of Divine Truth and a fire of Divine Love which were irrelevant to David. He never proclaimed his own divinity; but it was impossible that he should not attribute to himself many of the expressions which are obviously divine attributes. This kept him to the representative worship of Jehovah; and was therefore an essential element in the Jewish Religiosity. Had he seen the coming Messiah in the Word verbally communicated, but inspired by Jehovah, he would not have been the Jew David. His love of himself and his descendants was in union here with the necessities of God's permission and providence, and he adored an external institution which suited his nature, and a word of the Lord which identified his name with a Royal Office, and did not make impossible demands upon him of self-sacrifice.

Few of my readers will object to be relieved from the "higher criticism" which tells us that David wrote but few of the Psalms, that his "last words" are partly his, and partly by some one else, etc., etc. To the main purpose here it is sufficient that these are divine Jewish writings with an inspired letter, and an internal sense.

These conditions must be kept up. As we have seen, nothing in David's mere selfhood prevented him from representing the Lord spiritually. This he did both in his lifetime, and by the Prophets after his death. "It is written of David that he shall be king over them; and they all shall have one Shepherd: they shall dwell in the land, they and their children, and their children's children, for ever." —Ezekiel xxxiv. 24, 25. And again, "The children of Israel shall return, and seek Jehovah their God, and David their King."—Hosea iii. 5. These words were written by the prophets after the time of David; and yet it is plainly declared that he shall be their king and prince; whence it may be evident that David means the Lord."—*Arcana Cœlestia*, n. 1888. Moreover every name in the Word, whether of kingdoms, countries, cities, or men, is a receptacle, and thus a repository, of the celestial and spiritual things of the Lord.—*Ibid*. The throne of David is not the kingdom David had, but the kingdom of Heaven; wherefore David does not signify David, but the Lord's divine Royalty; and throne signifies the Divine Truth which proceeds, and which constitutes the Lord's kingdom.—*Ibid*. 5313. I am the root and the offspring of David,—*Apocalypse*, xxii. 16,—signifies that He is that Lord who was born in the world, and therefore the Lord in His Divine Humanity. From this He is also called the Branch of David."—*Apocalypse Revealed*, n. 954. " He that hath the key of David, and openeth, and no one shutteth, and shutteth and no one openeth,—*Apocalypse*, iii. 7,—signifies, Who alone has omnipotence to save. David signifies the Lord as to Divine Truth. The key of David has a similar signification to the keys of Peter.—*Ibid*. n. 174. Enough has here been given to show that David in the internal sense, which is communicated for the new religion, denotes the Lord. And that His own conversation to the two disciples going to Emmaus was a declaration and prophecy by the Word made flesh, and who dwelt among us, of a Revelation which brings His omnipresence in the Old Testament from His own Divine Rationality into our most human certainty. His medium fulfilling this prophecy is Emanuel Swedenborg.

XXVII.—THE IMMANENCE OF JEHOVAH IN THE MOSAIC DISPENSATION.

Jehovah was near to the Jews in their Church Representation. It was a regimen of personal and national fear accompanied by signs and wonders; of threats and punishments; and of victories and worldly prosperity for legal and technical obedience. Jehovah spoke to Abraham and called him. He was an idolater at the time, and did not know

Jehovah, and therefore was more susceptible of the call to a new state than others in Syria among whom there lingered perverted knowledges of the destroyed Noahtic Church. He was indeed almost in the same religious state as the peoples around him; but, because he was emptied of the old religion, he could be spoken to by Jehovah for the new, and receive his Call. These characteristics were the beginning and seed of the Jewish Church. The Fathers of that Church were no better than the surrounding tribes, but they had a new word of Jehovah with them, which the others had not, and besides this, special fitnesses of dramatic emotional nature which have been dwelt upon frequently in these pages.

The Old Testament declares throughout, the visible and audible presence of Jehovah God. He said to Abram, Get thee out of thy country and from thy kindred, and from thy Father's House, into a land that I will show thee, and I will make of thee a great nation. He appeared to him at the place of Sichem, where Abram built an altar unto the Lord who appeared to him. The Word of the Lord came to him in a vision, and promised him a son and heir, and bringing him forth abroad, said, Look now towards heaven and tell the stars, if thou be able to number them; and He said unto him, So shall thy seed be. The Angel of the Lord also counselled Hagar, whom Sarai had given to Abram to be his wife, and prophesied to her of her seed, that it should not be numbered for multitude; and the Angel said, Thou shalt call his name Ishmael. When Abram was ninety years old and nine, the Lord appeared to him and said, I, the Almighty God! walk before me, and be thou perfect. . . . Thy name shall be called Abraham; for a father of many nations have I made thee. Of this we read in Swedenborg: "The letter H. was taken from the name Jehovah, being the only letter in that name which involves the divine, and signifies I AM and TO BE; and was inserted in the name Abram. In like manner with Sarai, who became Sarah."—*Arcana Cœlestia*, 2010. Jehovah was thus immanent in the names Abraham and Sarah. Again the Lord appeared to him in the plains of Mamre ; where three men stood beside him ; and he said, My Lord, If now I have found favour in thy sight, pass not away, I pray thee, from thy servant. . . . The three men turned their faces towards Sodom, . . . but Abraham stood yet before the Lord. . . . The Lord conversed with Abraham, who entreated his mercy respecting Sodom. Lot received two angels in Sodom whom the Lord had sent to destroy it. The Angel of God called to Hagar out of heaven, and said unto her, What aileth thee? Fear not, . . . I will make thy son, a great nation. God tempted Abraham to sacrifice his son, Isaac. Abraham's desire of ancient sacrifice came upon him, and through the substituted Ram, burnt-offerings, to prevent human sacrifices, were inevitable for the coming Dispensation. The Angel of Jehovah, not the Tempter, but the Divine Truth in an angelic personality, cried to him out of heaven, and forbade him to lay his hand upon the lad. He was literally obedient in heart to the God who tempted him, and to the angel of the Lord who forbade him to obey the temptation ; and the Angel of Jehovah called out of heaven the second time, and blest all his obedience in both sorts. For obedience was of the essence of his service.

This manifest Divine Government and Help, extended to the Father of the Faithful and head and heart of the Patriarchs, like the seed of a tree grows and ramifies through the Jewish and Israelitish history. The nations so long as they were under the theocracy, were led by Jehovah in all their wanderings, fed by Him in the desert, their thirst quenched by Him out of the flint which became a fountain of waters. Their ways were mere hourly open providences. Their victories were not their own, but the Lord's : number did not count in their battles, but a panic from immediate God overtook their enemies, and while the men of Israel obeyed, they had an influx with them which made them as the armies of Jehovah. Nature and human cunning yielded before them. The Red Sea and Jordan were streets with walls of water for their hosts. The walls of Jericho fell down before their trumpets. The miracles in Egypt dealt with man and nature as the ways of right and wrong deal ultimately with the mind and body of a man. Egyptian humanity and its world while Israel was kept servile, evilly treated, and held captive, were a hell of punishment and torment: and, in the end, of weeping, wailing, and gnashing of teeth for Pharaoh and his people. If the children of Israel had kept the commandments, and obeyed the laws and ordinances of Jehovah, they would have been even as natural children of the lowest heaven, walking rightly to each appointed end; time, space and person obedient to them, the forty years of wandering, a real dream soon over, and the promised land entered by the very men and women who had been led, with the pillar of fire by night and of cloud by day, from the bondage of Egypt to the land flowing with milk and honey. But miracle had two sides with them; for obedience, miracle of prosperity, of harvest, of increase of flocks and herds, and of propagation of their human race as the stars of heaven and as the sand of the sea; and for wickedness, miracle of destruction, as after the worship of the golden calf; of defeat, as of Saul's army by the Philistines; of pestilence, as when David numbered the people; of disaster from the wickedness of their kings; of captivity to Babylon, and of ultimate national extinction when from the temple at Jerusalem a voice was heard, God has departed. In the case of the Jews these events were miraculous on both sides, the good and the evil; for the Dispensation was a miracle; and not a man, woman or child of the chosen race from Abraham was beyond its sphere. We take the Word literally as it stands; and eliminate atheism and theism, denial, doubt, and criticism. This then is what may be called the Immanence of Jehovah.

The dispensation of Miracle which held the Jewish mind and nature in order to compel an external presence of God on earth, which for miracle was a necessity, was so indifferent a thing to the Jews, that they easily were seduced by the superstitions of the nations which promised gratification of their propensities. Miracle of Jehovah was indeed providential, but it was also providential that they should understand nothing of its spiritual import; in which case it ranks only with the desire which it promises to fulfil, or with the terror which it creates; and it is not separable, except by mere obedience, and the strong direction which this brings, from miraculous manifestations magically produced from the hells.

In this age we see an analogous coincidence. The spiritual world is now made known by open communication, and its wonders revealed, and to those who do not receive the true information, a way opens for their own inventions of many kinds, and spirits are invoked, and not the Lord, and have deceived many.

While often discussing difficult questions which arise in reading the Old Testament; such, for instance, as the destruction of the Priests of Baal by Elijah,—from the humanitarian point of view, a ruthless slaughter,—I have found that the correspondence of idolaters to infernal evils, the obedience to a command to extirpate the men which were the personifications of them; the miraculous power given to the Jews in the transaction, and the equally miraculous weakness with which these Priests, for instance, were smitten, are all, or in part, judged from the point of view of ordinary history. In this case the Jewish Theocracy is not consistently held as a fact; but the reader is a critic, happily without intending it, of the ways of God to man; which, however, are now justified as in no former age. This Theocracy, as it is our object to show, was a fatal divine necessity,* and as such was in the very atmosphere of Jewish Life.

The Divine institution and conduct of Judaism seems to be the most plainly revealed evidence of God in nature which we possess in Holy Scripture. The influx into a

* See especially Swedenborg's *Divine Providence* and *Arcana Cælestia*.

whole external mind ; into nature and sky and atmosphere ; into the ground; the physical plagues of Egypt ; the Lord on Sinai ; the supernatural harvests; the flocks and herds according to obedience ; the panics in hosts of enemies ; all these divine-natural circumstances are indeed immanence of Jehovah very close above and within the material sphere. The Lord bowed His heavens and came down. Heaven was under Him with all its angels ministering. He altered the atoms of His previous creation by adding fresh providences and powers to them. The Incarnation seems nearer to accomplishment by this immediacy of God in the mental, natural and physical world, when He was about to descend in Virgin Mary not as a thought or idea, but as the most substantial of beings, the Divine Truth in Heaven.

XXVIII.—THE MESSIANIC PROMISES.

For what reasons were the Jewish and Israelitish nation allowed to delude themselves into the persuasion that Jehovah had chosen them, and that He would come and personally lead them to supremacy? There were, as we read, several causes. " *One* was that by having to name and remember Him, they might be held together in His Worship in a brotherhood ; without which Jehovah would have no entry to any of them, and none of them would have had any access to Jehovah. It was then as it is to-day, no one has seen the Father at any time. The only-begotten Son who is in the bosom of the Father, He has declared Him. John i. 18 ; v. 37. No one comes to the Father but by Me. The *second* Cause why so frequent a prediction of the Lord's Coming was made, was, that the representative types of their Church, all of which had regard to our Lord, and the Church to be inaugurated by Him after the Advent, might serve them as so many pointings and symbols of their worship ; so that when He came, they should acknowledge

Him; and permit themselves to be introduced into the internal things of His Worship; and together with the nations which were around them, become Christians. The *third* Cause was, that by the recollection of His Advent, some glimmering notion or idea concerning the resurrection and eternal life might enter their thoughts. Otherwise, in their hearts they would say, What interest have we in the Messiah when we are dead, unless we are to return, and see His glory, and reign with Him? From this their religious invention (*religiosum*) poured forth a belief that at the time of His Advent they were to rise again, each from his sepulchre, and to return into the land of Canaan. The *fourth* Cause was, that in their states of vastation and oppression, when they were in trials and afflictions, they should be supported and healed, as their fathers and brethren were in the desert; for without such support and healing they would have loaded Jehovah with reproaches, and would have gone astray in multitudes from the representative worship of Him into idolatrous worship. For these causes the Advent of the Lord is so often predicted in the old Prophetic Word. For the same causes in the New Evangelical and Apostolic Word, the Lord is preached, and His Second Coming is predicted."—*Coronis*, n. 59.

We repeat here the reasons before alleged for the capacity of the Jews to become the subjects of an ultimate theocracy or material dispensation. They were above all the nations then extant capable of assuming and keeping up a holy external at the same time with a profane internal. Internal truth was thus precluded to them, and they could not profane it and make the holy external impossible, which latter would have taken place if the mind had recognized the higher divine light in an adequate conscience, and had abused it. Lack of interest in such truth, as irrelevant to their business and bosoms,—deadness to it,—prevented this. The theatric holiness thus had its field in the external nature.

The internal was thus closed against the internal things of the Word and the truths which the rituals represented, and the Jewish life with its passions went on unchanged in its motives, while the external life and daily conduct was forced to represent the order and mandates of heaven, but these also as modified into possible likenesses to the Jewish type. The Divinity communicated not through but to the Jew with heaven. So a representative or theatric Church as the last resort before the Incarnation was instituted. Forms and Ceremonies were its foothold; heaven recognized on the stage of the world: all the men and women merely players. It was a religious drama, in which the laws of heaven were acted in corresponding rituals and obediences and parts and characters under the command of Jehovah God; and no more was asked of the actors themselves than unswerving obedience to these externals. Yet the externals were not spiritually fruitless, for in living according to them the Jew led a life which is the way to his heaven after death. As we see in Blessed Mary, there was a remnant in the Jewish and Israelitish nations, and a considerable remnant; this is attested by John the Baptist, by the disciples, by the Seventy, by the Apostles who were sent forth to evangelize all nations, by the common people who heard Jesus gladly, by the great multitudes who resorted to Him and were healed by Him; by the thousands whom He fed with His miraculous loaves and fishes; by the fear of the Chief Priests, Pharisees and Rulers who crucified Him; by the first Christians who were chiefly Jews, and the first martyrs.

This latter requires to be said in addition to the sentence that the Jewish race was then the worst on earth; a sentence given them by their own leaders, judges, lawgivers, psalmists and prophets. It applies to the race collectively, and in its dominion, and in its being obnoxious to the show of a Church which came upon it from God. But it does not apply to the infants and little children whom Jesus loved, and whose angels always behold the face of the Father who s in the heavens ; it does not apply to the Magdalen ; or to the humble and simple men and women who were, so to speak, out of the priestly, governmental, Pharisaic, Sadducean and mammon-worshipping community. All these had the strain of Jewish depravity in them, as the Virgin Mother of Jesus also had, as we have the strain, deceitful above all things, and desperately wicked, of English depravity, but they had not added their own lives fatally to it ; and choirs of their hearts seconded the new promise, recognized their Lord's Advent, and entered the first Christian Church.

The Jewish Church, though merely external, and having the contrarious Jew for its exponent, as a religious drama incarnated in a peculiar people, was not, by virtue of the inconsistency between the congregation and the Church, a hypocrisy, as some might imagine from the mutual relation of the two factors, holy external, and profane internal. Jehovah is the God of all truth, of truth of the heart, truth of the mind, and truth of the outward man. His institute here was of the outward man ; the only man then left on earth ; for the Greeks with their "foolishness" were no exception. The Jews were incapable of perceiving more than their own privileges, of obeying more than literal commands, of fearing more than pain, adversity and poverty, of loving more than themselves and their descendants. The Lord knew every man of them, and "that they know not what they do." So when they obeyed the commandments including all the rule of their religion, they did it with a sincere external, and their conscience was not able from any spiritual instruction to rebuke them, and produce the battle of temptation between the inner and the outer man. A hypocritical religion is impossible : hypocrites may exist under any creed, and use it for their own purposes. A hypocrite mixes good and evil. He himself is evil good and good evil. The Jew is a natural substance ; the hypocrite is an unstable compound ; and after death the two elements in him are torn apart, and he alone almost loses personality, and so far as yet revealed is a sexless flitting phantom.

There were two churches before the Jewish Representation, the Adamic, and the Noahtic; and these died of their own accumulated corruptions, as all Churches and States have a tendency to die. Now the men in the decline of the Adamic or celestial or Heart-Church were the worst of all. Of them it is said in the letter of the Ancient Word, that on their account it repented Jehovah that He had created man, for the spiritual sense of which see the *Arcana Cœlestia*. A flood of lusts and persuasions against heaven, called in the letter rain from heaven, symbolized the consummation of the Adamic Church. The waters of the Red Sea were a second flood in the consummation of the Noahtic Church. A most evil nature was inherited from parents to children in the Adamic Church; and caused its extinction;* a lesser evil was in the generations of the Noahtic Church, by which it ceased to be a Church; and a more crass and material evil was innate in the Jews, and was dealt with by dispersion in the end of their drama.

The Jew was the worst race extant when the Lord was born of Virgin Mary, and His birth itself was an attestation of this, in consequence of the divine office which the human He assumed had to fulfil. Swedenborg, however, affirms that the Jew is not the worst race now. There were two worst races before him; worst for their times; and the worst varies with each Æon. The Christian world with its Consummated Church is in bad pre-eminence now, and embraces the area of civilization. The Lord as in a new sense is still the born King of the Jews. Hearken to this

* The serpent correspondentially was the incitement to the disobedience of Eve: the serpent, the perverted sensual degree of the Celestial Church, insurgent against the higher degrees. In the consummation of that Church the bells formed of it, the subtlest and most lethal of all, are of human serpents in inextricable folds, which are the lusts and persuasions that God is merged in these Adamites, and no longer exists but in them; so that they are Gods.—*Coronis*, n. 38.

Scripture: "*Verily I say unto you, This generation shall not pass away till all these things be fulfilled.*" The things alluded to are the portents of the last Judgment. On which passage Swedenborg remarks: 'These words signify that the Jewish nation shall not be extirpated like other nations. For as the tribe of Judah, more even than the other tribes, could be kept in a state of external sanctity, and at this day as formerly account those rituals holy which can be observed out of Jerusalem; and also retain a holy veneration for their fathers; and a particular reverence for the Word of the Old Testament; and as it was foreseen that Christians would almost totally reject that Word, and would likewise defile its internals with profanities; therefore that nation has been hitherto preserved according to the Lord's Words in Matthew. It would have been otherwise if Christians, acquainted as they were with internal things, had also lived as internal men. In that case the Jewish nation, like other nations mentioned in the Word, would have been cut off many ages since. '*Heaven and Earth shall pass away, but My Words shall not pass away.*' This declaration was made immediately after what is said of the Jewish Nation, because that Nation is preserved for the sake of the Word."—*Arcana Cœlestia*, n. 3479.

The above interpretation is of the internal sense, and man's capacity could not discern it if that sense had not been divinely opened. In the letter "this generation" was interpreted in its day as meaning that the prophecy in Matthew xxiv. 34 would be fulfilled in the time of the Apostles. But generation spiritually, and indeed most literally, as connected not with time but with engendering, means the Jew nature and nation in the midst of which the Lord stood. The literal sense here is the complex, continent, and basis of the spiritual sense. The heaven and earth which shall pass away, are the first heaven and the first earth which passed away, Apocalypse, xxi. 1: to understand which read Swedenborg's *Apocalypse Revealed*.

Swedenborg says again: "That race has been kept, and scattered about over a large portion of the globe, for the sake of the Word *in its original language*, which the Jews hold in greater sanctity than the Christians do: and in the several words of the Word there is the Lord's Divinity; for the Word is the Divine Truth united to the Divine Good, which proceeds from the Lord; and, through this, the Word is the conjunction of the Lord with the Church, and the presence of heaven. And there is a presence of the Lord and of heaven wherever the Word is read holily. This is the end or purpose of the Divine Providence in the keeping of the Jews, and in their dispersion over a large part of the globe."—*Divine Providence*, n. 260.

Thus the Jew has the conservation of the Old Testament committed to him still; but no race now has the New Testament in its keeping. There is, however, a new Church in promise, which will be the guardian of the whole Word. But the first Christian Church has fallen as the Jewish Church could not do; it had internal truths committed to it, and an internal mind which the Jew had not; and its decline, defection, and consummation have taken place under these conditions. The Jew had traditions, but not doctrines in our sense. He made the Word of none effect by his traditions. We, by the dogmas of Councils and by heresies besides, have precluded the way to the truths of religion derivable from the letter of the Word; and have filled the World with Atheism on the one hand, and with a new Judaism in formalism on the other.

XXIX.—THE EXPULSION OF THE JEWS FROM CANAAN.

"The Jews were expelled from Canaan lest they should defile and profane internal things by denial in that land, where, from the most ancient times, all the places had been representative of the principles of heaven and the Church. They were cast out for the further reason that representatives should cease." They were broken as the mediums between the Church on earth and the Church in Heaven. Had they remained in the Holy Places, and their rites and ceremonies been perpetuated by themselves, heaven ceasing to fill them, the superior state produced universally after the Lord came into the world, and participated in by them as an increase of their evil natural capacity—and a great capacity it is—would have led them into a worse superstition about their privilege and power as the chosen people; and in all the places for them haunted by this spirit, they would have found a fresh plane and occasion for their derisive denial of Christ the Lord and Saviour. Their love of the Old Testament would not have had the harmless function it now has, had they remained as a nation in Jerusalem. The work of Rome under Titus, the Consummation of their Æon, and the end of their unity as a nation, is accounted for on these grounds; as human history will some day in new ages be all judged and accounted for by spiritual causes discerned.

As a nation they were expelled from Canaan also on the ground that representatives should cease. That is to say, that no sanction of heaven should any longer appertain to sacrifices, external rites, forms and ceremonies. In this sense the rituals of the Old Testament were deprived of the divine influx which gave them sanctity and power during the Dispensation. Jewish worship was not abolished, but subsists still, and has its blessing for good Jews, as the Protestant and Catholic services have for good Christians, but it now belongs to a freedom common to all religions in decent political states, and carries nothing specially divine, only honest piety where it exists. Its miracle is over;—the Æon in which Jehovah controlled Nature for the Jews, when the land was God's, and the Sabbatical year yielded miraculous crops in the year of rest, the year of the Lord, the Jubilee; and when Jewish poverty was unknown, because Jehovah fed the obedient people according to His laws of needful bread whether in the wilderness or in Canaan. Representatives were abolished when the Lord assumed humanity and made it *in Himself* divine. He fulfilled the Word and was the Word made flesh : the ultimate declaration that God is a Man. Then a godly and an honest life became the sole foundation of heaven and the Church, the Lord being acknowledged as the Dispensation of it. As in Apocalypse : *I saw no temple therein, for the Lord God Almighty and the Lamb is the Temple of it.* Worship in His Freedom is thus left for each, and the sacraments of baptism inaugurating our natural lives and sanctifying our new lives, and of the Lord's Supper, in perpetual remembrance of His incarnation, remain as Representatives enacted and undergone by Himself; and perpetuating the ancient and most ancient days of representation.

The Rulers of Thought to-day will have it that there are none of these diverse Divine Æons. It is our day's work in the New Church to accept the Word of God as infinite in truth, goodness, love and light; and to abide by the results of such faith and acceptance. And the more we persevere in this course of receiving *precarious* intellectual daily bread, the more the Divine Word opens, and a mind is created before which important things for the immortal man receive their importance, and light things are dissipated. It is delightful to have the children of Israel made into object-lessons of "the Divinity that shapes our ends rough hew them how we will." In the long run, though not in this century, the result will be struck between the policy of the kingdom of God, and the ventures of Naturalism, and the sum will be declared in wisdom and knowledge between these two, in the several fields of progress, and in the interests and insights of the earthly man and the heavenly.

XXX.—A CHURCH MUST EXIST ON EARTH.

Whatever we have said hitherto flows from the necessity of a Church on earth answering to the Church in heaven. The reason of this necessity is unknown to Christians, for owing to ignorance of the spiritual sense of the chapters of Genesis from Adam to Abraham, the Jewish Church is the first with which they are acquainted in the Bible. Hence it seems as if the globe for long ages had had no visible Church upon it. This has been corrected if the reader wishes to learn, and the Adamic Church with one special Divine gift, and the Noahtic Church with another, have been revealed to view. *The human mind* was not otherwise created than by and in planes of Churches. Do not here think of ministering clergy, but of entire humanities fed with enthusiasm and light of revelation by their loving God. And *the human body* in its organization corresponding to the mind, is the evolution of one Ecclesia, or call of man by his Maker, after another; each organic body having a different reason for difference of being; and accordingly being different. Following this greatest of descents into creations, and after the fall of man seeing its fatal necessity, we have come to the Jewish Church prepared to understand its place in the work of Providence. It was a miraculous prop of the heavens when they would otherwise have tottered to their Fall. For heaven is not self-subsisting or self-sustaining, but exists continually, and so subsists, from the Lord. If these points are understood, the Jewish Economy takes its place as a new Revelation to the rational mind.

Now hear Swedenborg: In explaining Genesis vi. 13, I will destroy them with the earth, "It may," he says, "be observed that if the Lord's Church were to become entirely extinct on earth, mankind could in no wise exist, but each and every man must perish. The Church is as the heart which while it lives gives life to the vitals and members;

but when it dies all dies with it. So the whole race of mankind, even those who are out of the Church, derive life from the Church of the Lord on earth. The reason of this is at the present day quite unknown. Now the human race represents the natural body with its parts. In it the Church acts as heart; and unless there were a Church with which as a heart the Lord might be united through heaven and the world of spirits, disjunction would ensue, and, in consequence of this separation from the Lord, man would instantly perish. Hence, since man was first created, a Church has always existed. Even when the Church was about to perish, it still remained with some. This was the cause of the Lord's Advent into the world. Unless of His divine mercy He had come, all men must have ceased to exist, for the Church was at its lowest ebb, and scarcely any good and truth remained. . . . Unless the Lord had compassion on man, and conjoined him to Himself by the ministry of angels, he could not live a single moment. Of this man is ignorant."—*Arcana Cœlestia*, n. 637.

"'The powers of the heavens shall be shaken' (Matthew xxiv. 29). The foundations of the Church are said to be shaken when they perish. The Church on earth is the foundation of heaven. The influx of good and truth through the heavens from the Lord is ultimately terminated in the goods and truths which are with the man of the Church. But when the man of the Church is so perverted in his state as no longer to admit the influx of good and truth, the powers of the heavens are said to be shaken. Therefore it is always provided by the Lord that somewhat of the Church remains, and that when an old Church perishes, a new Church is instituted."—*Ibid.* n. 4060.

" The communication of heaven with man is a necessity of the existence of the human race: a communication hrough the Church. Otherwise men would become as beasts."—*Ibid.* n. 4545.

" If charity were in the first place, and faith in the second, the Church would have a different face; for then none would be called Christians but those who lead a life according to the truths of faith; that is a life of charity. Men also would not then make many Churches by distinguishing them according to opinions concerning the truths of faith, but they would say that there was one Church, in which all who are in the good of life are found; not only those who are within the region where the Church is, but also those who are outside it. Then the Church would enjoy enlightenment about those things which belong to the Lord's kingdom; *for charity enlightens.*"—*Ibid.* n. 6269.

"The Societies which constitute this order are scattered all over the world, and are those who are in love to the Lord, and in charity towards the neighbour. These scattered Societies are gathered together by the Lord, and also represent one man, as do the societies of heaven. They are not only within the Church, but also outside it; and taken together, are called the Lord's Church scattered and gathered from the good of the whole world; and this also is called a Communion. This Communion, this Church, is the Lord's kingdom on earth conjoined with the Lord's kingdom in the heavens; and thus conjoined with the Lord Himself."—*Ibid.* n. 7396.

"There are most general principles of the Church which enter into all religions, and make this communion. These principles are the acknowledgment of God, and a good life" (*bonum vitæ*).—*Divine Providence*, n. 325.

"The Church cannot exist with man unless its internal be spiritual, and its external, natural; there is no such thing as a Church purely spiritual, or a Church merely natural. . . . Therefore heaven could not subsist without the Church with man, nor the Church without heaven. . . . Thence the angels bitterly lament when the Church on earth is desolated by falsities, and consummated through evils; and liken the state of *their* life then to sleepiness, . . . but when the Church on earth is restored, they liken the state of *their* life to wakefulness."—*Coronis*, n. 19.

In reading these extracts, bear in mind that there are no angels created such from the beginning, but that all in the heavens have been men and women and children on some planet-earth. The spiritual world in the complex is the gathered sum and census from all worlds and ages of these populations.

The necessity of a Church finds a parallel necessity in government and subordination in order that citizenship may exist. We have no examples of the existence of civil society under any other conditions than that of power and force organized and legalized from above downwards. The Church also is as visible as the State, and, when it is not perishing, more potent. While the man in civil society is organic through human agents of his own kind, under the Providence which cares for political states, the man in religious society is organic through ecclesiastical and angelic powers under God-Man, whose kingdom on earth is the Church.

XXXI.—THE WORD, THE CONJOINING MEDIUM.

The word which was spoken by the Lord through Moses and the Prophets and through the Evangelists, descends through the heavens, and in each heaven is clothed with a sense adequate to the Angels there. In the celestial degree or the highest heaven where love to the Lord begets wisdom and the faculties of this degree, the word is celestial; in the spiritual degree or the second heaven, the Word is spiritual. Below these senses the natural heaven has a pure natural sense adequate to the understanding of the third degree of heaven, the celestial-natural and spiritual-natural; in which the other degrees are represented in a lower and more external form.

With this coheres the Letter of the Word, which is the presence of the Lord in the true church and its worshippers on earth.

The Word is thus one as the Lord is one, but becomes various as the Divine Person addresses Himself to each Heaven, to every angel in each, and to every man in the Church. The variety flows out of the method of correspondences whereby all creation is effected. The spiritual Sun, the Sun of Righteousness, which warms and illuminates the Angelic Heavens, is the source of creation; Jehovah God resides in it, and through its righteous heat and light, the Word which is with God is spoken forth as the alone reality of love and power. It is spoken into forms, appearances of the Being who is ineffable, but who presents Himself to us as His Images, by an Image of Himself as the Son of Man in the Word. The forms are according to the heavens, more and more ineffable and inconceivable, and imperceptible to man in their ascent. But the highest plane corresponds to the second, the second to the lower, and the lowest. This lowest is our Written Word, the Old and the New Testaments.

It flows from this account that correspondences of outward things to inward states are transmutable in an upward series into meanings after meanings as they ascend. Our Word, Jewish, and Christian, is written in our realm of nature, in which *space and time and person* are present everywhere to our faculties. These three real natural omnipresences have no existence in the spiritual world. Everlasting appearances of them have existence there instead of the fixations themselves. In the spiritual world the objects may be called fluid fixations. So all the objects of nature are reproduced and represented there, and indefinitely more and more on the higher mountains of love and light. Objects are created in a moment according to signification; for they are all parts of the language of the Word. The Lord converses with His heavens from these His Divine Manuscripts, these floral and faunal scrolls of living lands and skies.

So He does talk with us in His Bible, the Word, and it is the trysting-place in which He is present to the Christian World. The Word contains all the prayers and praises that the contrite and troubled heart, or the joyful mind, can offer to His throne. And in reading it with sacred attention, a hierarchy is reading it with us. By induction of the Word itself, our wants of love and life are supplied in the reading. The natural images of the letter suggest their spiritual likenesses, and another letter is gradually given in us as a higher Bible. Next, the spiritual kingdom is in the same Word with us in the Church on Earth; but with a penetration before which the letter of the Church has again disappeared, and truth leading to good is made objective in resplendent mental narratives of form. Higher still the celestial heaven is in direct perception of good itself as central; the flaming light of which is the highest perpetual self-evidence of the Divinity of the Word.

All is effected by CORRESPONDENCES. Science, which as yet knows nothing of this term, may illustrate it by Sir William Grove's teaching of the "Conversion of Forces." According to this doctrine, energy is stored in nature, and by suitable mechanical contrivances, and the motion of these producing friction, and interior relations in substance, new kinds of force are developed. So that motion, heat, light, magnetism, electricity, and no doubt many other forces, are all modes of motion; each one being a new power, and given out to a new contrivance which can receive it, and reactively manifest it. All this is within nature, and so to speak in one plane; but the products in the series appear very different. Now before motion put Will as correspondent to energy; and will is humanly alive, and life uses all these powers and forces for definite ends; and distributes them according to Uses or Functions. And so the Divine Will by the Word in prepared minds makes the heat and light of men. The heat here is love, and the light is wisdom.

"The sense of the Letter of the Word," says Swedenborg,

"is that through which there is conjunction with the Lord, and Consociation with the Angels. The conjunction is not apparent to man; but it lies in the affection for truth, and in the perception of it; thus in the love of the Divine truth, and the belief in it, in the man himself. Consociation with the angels of heaven takes place through the sense of the letter, because there is a spiritual and a celestial sense in the literal sense; and the angels are in the above two senses. They are evolved from the natural sense of the Word, or the sense of the letter, while a true man is in that sense. The Evolution is instantaneous; consequently also the Consociation. By much experience it has been given me to perceive that when I read the word in the sense of the letter, a communication was made with the heavens; now with one of their societies, now with another; and that those things which I understood according to the natural sense, the spiritual angels understood according to the spiritual sense, and the celestial angels according to the celestial sense; and this in an instant. As this communication has been perceived so many thousands of times, not a particle of doubt remains to me about it. . . . The spiritual angel evokes the spiritual, and the celestial angel the celestial. They can do no other; for the things are homogeneous to them and consentaneous to their nature and essence."

"Let this be first illustrated by comparisons with the three kingdoms of nature. *In the Animal Kingdom.*—Out of the food when it is made into chyle the veins drink and evoke their blood; the nervous fibres their juice; and the substances which are the origins of the fibres, their animal spirit. *In the Vegetable Kingdom.*—A tree with trunk, branches, leaves and fruits stands upon its root, and out of the soil through the root extracts and evokes a more crass juice for the trunk, branches, and leaves, a purer juice for the flesh of the fruits, and the purest for the seeds inside or within the fruits. *In the Mineral Kingdom.*—In the bosom of the earth in certain places there are minerals impregnated with gold, silver and iron. Out of exhalations treasured away in the earth, the gold draws its own element, the silver its own, and in like manner the iron."

"Now by an example let it be illustrated how the spiritual angels extract their sense, and the celestial angels theirs, from the natural sense in which the Word dwells with man."

"Commandment, '*Honour thy Father and thy Mother.*' Man by father and mother understands the father and mother on earth, as well as all who are in the place of father and mother: and by honouring he understands holding them in honour and obeying them. A spiritual angel by father understands the Lord, and by mother, the Church; and by honouring he understands loving. But a celestial angel by father understands the Lord's Divine Love, and by mother, His Divine Wisdom; and by honouring, doing good from him."

"Commandment, '*Thou shalt not steal.*' Man by stealing, understands literal theft, defrauding, taking his neighbour's goods away from him on any pretence. A spiritual angel by stealing understands depriving others of the truths of their faith and of the good things of charity by falses and evils. But a celestial angel understands by stealing, attributing to himself the things which are the Lord's, and claiming to himself His Justice and Merit."—*Holy Scripture*, n. 62-67.

XXXII.—THE DIVINE VALUE OF THE LETTER.

The internal sense is established as a fact of divine language beyond all doubt for those who study it reverently and with competent open minds. Those who are not able to see it for themselves should take it on trust from others, as we accept astronomy, mathematics and dynamics from their professors. First let them consider that the Word of the Lord must have a divine life and soul in it. And then further, that a great part of the Word is only worthy of the divine utterance when something is meant that is not apparent to them in the letter. So let them know, if they do not see, that "Blessed are they who have not seen and yet have believed." True testimony is the first essential of evidence. This testimony is uncounted thousands of years old, being from the beginning; and is as new as heaven is new, being reasserted in this new age for every honest faculty in the mankind of to-day.

The letter is the basis of the internal sense, and in its interest requires to be gravely entered upon as a divine letter. The spiritual sense once seen testifies that the letter is a part of the LOGOS. The view thus attained is given first especially to the rational and intellectual mind. Therefore we counsel the gentle reader to brace his heart and its faith to a complete admission of the presence in God's Word, of first a divine letter, proved to be such by the spiritual sense. Let there be light is the first utterance of the Word; divine internal, intimate light. The letter of it has a divine sense in every iota. It has a natural sense besides as it appears to the natural man. With the faith that this is so, religion can be revealed religion, and be taken seriously; which Renan thought a mistake: but his church in his early days had foreclosed against him the divinity of the written Word, and the grave function of that divinity.

What is called the "higher criticism" is the *post-mortem* examination of the dead Word; that is to say, of the Letter denied to be divine. It has its uses. But it tends to no direct religious service for man. It is arrested by the letter, and would spend ages, during which generations wanting the Word are dying, in knowing who wrote half this Psalm, and who wrote the other half; whether John's Gospel can have John of the Apocalypse for its writer, since the narrative and the vision differ in style; whether the great earthquakes in the Apocalypse are not plagiarisms from natural earthquakes which took place near Patmos; whether the

Sermon on the Mount was ever spoken by Jesus Christ, as it is not signed by any reporter who took it down, and who would himself need to be countersigned in long succession; whether the Beatitudes are not invention, like Hannibal's speeches in Livy, like those of Galgacus and Agricola in Tacitus, and like those of Abraham and Moses in Josephus; whether the Gospels were ever heard of until they were forged in the second or third century; and whether unclassical Greek is not an unpardonable sin, and a capital shibboleth against scholarly inspiration. These queries, which cannot be answered to satisfy those who put them, keep the mind from looking at the revelation, now made in full light, of the existence of a Divine Letter, the basis of the Word, and written Correspondences which open one heaven after another for the men of the Church.

We stop then to say that without discouraging any honest study, or biblical learning which reverences spiritual religion, it is not of prime consequence to the New Church who wrote the Books of Moses, the Four Gospels, or the Apocalypse, the Psalms, or the Prophets; or at what date they were written, or in what place or language. By the internal or spiritual sense Jehovah God wrote them all; and through the celestial and spiritual senses under the Divine sense, dictated them at last, word by word, to the chosen men who penned Holy Scripture. The spiritual sense, divinely revealed, is therefore demonstration of the divinity of the letter. This view accepts the opened Word, and prepares the way for the New Church to lie upon its breast.

At the same time, if supernally gifted insight has need of unlocking any external problems suggested by the Scriptures, solutions can come to the believer which are not for the scientist, to whom the Word itself is a dead letter.

XXXIII.—THE LORD'S PRAYER.

The letter indeed wants attention from a higher scholarship than has yet touched it. This it will receive only when it is taken seriously as filled with a plenary inspiration of meaning, and as one identical natural and spiritual language from Genesis to Apocalypse. So it should be rendered from Hebrew and Greek with a prayerful obeisant exactitude. At present this is not the way, but the letter is the victim of style, and varies from the original to avoid repetition and please the ear. Liberties are taken against which conscience would rebel if the letter itself were known to be divine. Hence a new translation will arise from the pressure of this doctrinal faith. Look at the Lord's Prayer. Unaware that the Word is literal to a divinity within it, the translation abolishes distinctions plain in the Greek. Let us endeavour to translate it approximately; if not for use in families praying, yet for insight in reading.

"Father of us, Thou in the heavens, hallowed be the name of Thee; the kingdom of Thee come; the will of Thee be done, as in heaven, also upon the earth; give to us to-day the bread of us, the needful; and forgive us our debts as we also forgive our debtors; and lead us not into temptation, but deliver us from the evil one; for of Thee is the Kingdom and the Power and the Glory unto the Ages. So be it."

Let it read baldly at first unsmoothed by style. We can get used to this, or be instructed to amend it, if access of divine life flows into our hearts from more faithful words. Father of us puts the Father first, and makes us also thereby substances. The substantive pronoun *us*, which would be lost in the adjective "our," takes its sense from the Father of us. Us is a social word; here, with this Father, a spiritual family abiding in its life in the prayer, and a greater family as the consociate body moves forward in regeneration.

The fatherhood of God to us is prayed first, and our sonship is bespoken from the heavens. In my Father's house are many mansions; the prayer is to the Father, recognized in the manifoldness of His heavens. Our versions ignore this. Here in the natural sense all worlds are named, for the heavens representatively are the Starry Firmament corresponding to the spiritual heavens. Father of us who art in the heavens, Hallowed be the name of Thee. The Personality is preserved in the pronoun name of Thee, but merged in the adjective pronoun, Thy name. Name is all that by which the Father is known and worshipped: the name of everything recalls all that we know of it; so as Christ is all we know or can know of God, Christ is His name; and thus Christ is the Father of us, who is visible, and we do not pray to the Father *in* Christ who is invisible. Father of us, hallowed be the name of Thee. Come the kingdom of Thee. Be done the will of Thee, as in heaven, also upon the earth. Heaven here is single and singular: not the house of many mansions, but the one will of the Father of us, for heaven is the Lord's will. And heaven comes first as His will there, and the prayer prays for the will also here, that the earth may be the Lord's. Give us to-day the bread of us, the needful: take no thought for the morrow, the morrow shall take thought for the things of itself: here lies the prudence of being under the Providence of the Father of us. The bread of us, our vital support in our work and works, in our thoughts and hearts, is the Divine truth of the Word instructing, guiding, and obeyed; and when carried out in the duties of our calling, the Divine Truth in our business and bosoms is *made good*—is a word made flesh in us. It is the Bread *of us*, for it is broken differently for each of us, and the sacramental pieces are the soul's constant individual sustenance. And forgive us our debts as we also forgive our debtors. Here acknowledgment of the infirmity of us enters the prayer; we owe what we cannot directly pay, but the Father of us remits the love

due to God when we obey His New Commandment, in
loving man, the erring, the enemy, the neighbour ; in loving
our selfhood by reducing it to order. The higher debt is
forgiven when we become the images of the Father of us in
forgiving the lower. So, and not otherwise we love the
Father of us, and can receive His love. Into the love of
the brother whom we have seen flows the love of the Father
whom we have not seen. And lead us not into temptation.
It seems as if the Father of us does lead us into temptation.
He does try us, and form our minds even by appearances,
as by letting us see the sun go round the world, and then by
giving us a mind above sight He lets us know that the world
instead goes round the sun ; and that the appearance is *a*
fact but not *the* fact. This makes the sun both natural and
rational, an ascent from sun to sun. So the Father of us,
the One in the heavens, clothes Himself with Seeming, to
come to very sense where nothing is but all things seem ;
and then He calls forth will of mind to uncover the Divine
Truth by slow degrees ; for we tolerate it slowly, and by
Æons. Then we find that the Father of us never leads
into temptation, but that another father of us, namely, our
proprium, does so lead. All temptation is pleasant ; to
comply with it at the time is pleasure ; great or little it is
delight ; the delight of yourself, of your evil propensity, of
indulging your weakness. This delight of yourself, the
hereditary and acquired man, must be called forth to be
resisted and conquered. You yourself stumble into it inevitably sooner or later, here or in the spiritual world, but it
is all the world of the Father of us, and by its very nature it
finds out every evil and every weakness, and He permits the
finding out, and uses it for justice and judgment. This
world is a wilderness for trying the children of Israel by
forcing them to expose themselves, as in the days of the
golden calf ; and Canaan is the result for what is left of their
increase after forty years : 40 always signifies temptation ;
and extermination is the commanded though not perfected

result for the same selfhood represented in the lowest degree by Jew and Canaanite alike.*

But deliver us from the evil one. There is no abstract evil; there is always an evil somebody, an evil man, individual or collective. The first evil one is yourself; the heart or *me of you*. This heart or love associates with its similars in this world; and as it is reformed or regenerated in a good life, with better and better similars. It also consociates with it invisible similars in the spiritual world, calls them to it, and lives from them; from the hells if an evil life is being led on earth; from heaven if the days are good and the nights are true.

For of Thee is the Kingdom, and the Power, and the Glory unto the Ages. So be it. Of Thee gives a more obvious sense of the procession of the Kingdom, the Power, and the Glory than the adjective Thine in the Bible; and Christ here declares that these divine attributes procced by Ages or Æons: as when He also speaks of the consummation of the Age or Æon, which the Versions make into the end of the world. Amen, So be it, is the plenary hope and submission of our Christ's prayer to Him the Father of us.

"We" are placed before the "Father of us," and earth before heaven in our Versions; whereas the order of the prayer prescribed by Christ is from the Father of us in a descending series, from God in the heavens to God in heaven, and from heaven to earth, and from earth with its supports of truth to be made good, through active love of the Lord and the neighbour, against all temptations, until we can hope and pray for delivery from the evil one; and then the prayer quits ourselves, and ascends to the Father. As Charles Augustus Tulk used to say to me, the Lord Christ's prayer is a little Gospel following our Father Christ's

* The Jewish host represented the Lord Christ in putting off by death the entire humanity which left Egypt except Joshua, which is also a form of the name Jesus.

life from His birth on earth, and through His conquests, to His resurrection and ascension; to His dominion, His omnipotence, and His Glory.

Now hear Swedenborg:—" It was given me to perceive angelic ideas in the Lord's Prayer about the words, ' Lead us not into temptation, but deliver us from the evil.' By the good spirits who were near, the thought of temptation and evil was rejected by a certain idea perceptible in me; and this rejection went on, till nothing but a purely angelic conception, namely, of good, without any idea of temptation and evil remained; the literal sense thus altogether perishing. About this good in the first degree of rejection, innumerable ideas concerning it were formed; such as, how good comes out of man's affliction; and yet affliction comes from man, and from his evil, which has its punishment inherent in it. To this was adjoined a species of indignation that any one should suppose that temptation and the evil of it can have any other origin; and that evil should be connected in their thoughts with the Lord. These ideas were purified as they ascended higher; and the degrees of ascent were represented by the rejections, which were effected with a velocity and in a manner inexpressible, until they passed into the shade of my thought. They were then in heaven, where there are ineffable angelic ideas solely concerning the good of the Lord."—*Arcana Cœlestia*, n. 1875.

" Whilst reading the Lord's Prayer morning and evening, it was evident to me that there are things innumerable in the ideas of thought, and that those things which are contained in order are from the interiors. On these occasions the ideas of my thought were constantly open towards heaven, and innumerable things flowed in, so that I observed clearly that the ideas of thought conceived from the contents of the prayer were filled from heaven. And such things were also poured in as it is impossible to utter, and also impossible for me to comprehend; only I was sensible of a general affection resulting from them. And the things

which flowed in were varied every day. Hence it was given me to know that in the contents of this prayer there are more things than the universal heaven is capable of comprehending. And that with man more things are in it in proportion as his thought is open towards heaven; and that fewer are in it in proportion as his thought is closed."
—*Ibid.* n. 6619.

Those who regard the Letter of the Word as Divine, will, when sufficiently strong in natural and spiritual knowledge, and the good life of it, translate with a felicitous fidelity unknown at present, but inspired out of the connectedness of the internal sense. In the mines of the letter they will find veins of gold which hide themselves from the prospecting of old scholarship. The whole Word requires to be brought to us afresh as a living letter. This is particularly wanted in the Psalms. The translation of the Word, and the restoration of it where the letter has been corrupted or violated, will advance and grow in truth and light as the New Church itself advances in life; and the English language and literature will partake in the illumination. For the Word is the first source and the last giver of nobleness and dignity to every tongue; yea, the languages of so-called heathen races are no longer perishable when the Bible is brought as a coal from the altar, and touches their lips.

XXXIV.—GOODNESS AND TRUTH ARE THE TWO SIDES OF THE WORD.

One thing in conclusion may be announced here from Swedenborg as essential in the Word. It is a body of truth which, like the divine humanity which it is, has a right and a left side to it throughout. In this respect it is an exemplar of all life, and as God is a Man the Word is a Man. The right side corresponds to the Will, the left to the intellect. You see this most easily when you think organically. Whatever enters the mind by the senses and the understanding, moves the will in some degree, and what is a thought in the understanding, in stirring the will becomes an affection of it. In application to these two faculties the Word has usually two terms which betoken their union. The Word is itself the Divine Marriage of Good and Truth. So nations and peoples are used; nations having reference to good and peoples to truth. The same terms imply also evil and falsity according to the series in which they are used. This bilaterality depends upon the correspondence of the Word with humanity, and with our mental organization. The reader will notice it readily in the Psalms, where most verses exhibit it. Clauses also are married to each other, and personal names. See especially Psalm lxxviii.: Give ear, O my people, to my law; incline your ears, O my people, to the Words of my mouth. The verses in this Psalm are in almost uniform reduplication, as a bilateral mind and man; and a third clause is often added, a trine dimension, wherein the Word stands on its Divine Feet. So we have the heavens declare the glory of God, and the firmament showeth His handiwork. We have justice and judgment in many texts: Judah and Israel. In countless instances Goodness and Truth, Love and Wisdom, Affection and Thought, are represented; and the one term is the will-side, and the other the intellect-side. The movement of life in the mind or spirit cannot exist without this twofold compact, for mental existence is a process from the will to the intellect, and a conjunction of the two into one, preliminary to deed. The will is the motive, the understanding the means. Some delight of life always accompanies the continual momentaneous unition of the will and the intellect; or otherwise motive, and consummation, would die. Think then that here the Word comes organic from the Divinity who is a Divine Man as Divine Goodness and Divine Truth; and that the constant reduplication in the Word is no arbitrary form of language, but that our spiritual existence is in plenary correspondence to it, and that the oneness of our minds depends upon the marriage union of the two elements signified by the Lord when He says, If ye know these things, blessed are ye if ye do them. The will and the understanding are the twain who are to be one flesh here.

XXXV.—THE KEEPING OF THE JEWS FULFILS PROPHECY.

For deprived as they are of inheritance in the land of Canaan, and now after long ages native in many other lands, and all these nominally Christian, the Jews are in part voluntary exiles, we will not say, prisoners, in the dominions of the only Messiah who has come out of the prophetical Writings. Where will they find another Messiah whose dominions compare in extent or human pretension with His? They are under His religion, though, now like Christians themselves, not of it; and in this still blessed England they are in the enjoyment of their synagogues, and of all privileges which spring from a toleration which is not Jewish historically, nor Christian either, but in the spirit of the New Church and its New Age.

This conversion of the Jews into good subjects of Christian States must imprison the evil nature denounced to themselves by Jehovah dictating the Old Testament to its Historians, Psalmists and Prophets. Qualities repressed, 'cabined, cribbed, confined' for thousands of years, and now not by persecutions, but by even justice of laws common to Jew, Christian, Mahometan and Hindoo, must become more passive, more retiring into backwardness of organization, more patient of impossibilities, and more capable of giving in and of sometimes dying out. We know that radically the Jew is an exception to this rule; but externally he obeys it; and when the old persecution ceases, and politic brotherhood reigns for all good citizens; and when the astonished Jew hears of a religion brought forth from his own Old Word (which has among its tenets that the Jew is by no means wanted by the New Christianity, but that the Old Testament wants him to stand by it when the Old Christianity deserts it), he may lose, if Jehovah so ordains, somewhat of the toughness and obstinacy produced not by his nature but by oppression and persecution. If he has been a martyr in a bad cause, still he has been a martyr, and the blood of martyrs is the seed of the indomitable. Failing this, without ceasing to be a Jew, a wise ductility may solicit him. One thing we know, that his Jehovah, who is our Christ, affords him every betterment that his character admits of; although that character for divine purposes keeps him a Jew. This is the meaning in Matthew. "This people's heart is waxed gross, and their ears are dull of hearing, and their eyes have been closed, lest at any time they should see with eyes, and hear with ears, and should understand with heart, and should be converted, and I should heal them," xiii. 15. See also Isaiah vi. 10. So it is not his restoration to Canaan which will fulfil Prophecy, but his permanence as a Jew. He is prevented by Jehovah from entering into the internal things of the Jewish Dispensation, *which are Christianity*, because he would profane them: his avarice, and immersion in this world's interests exclusively, alienate all interest in spiritual things excepting under the divinely given stimulants of remote Messianic promises. These he interprets for himself into earthly dominion and privileged humanity and superiority. An emphatic person, he holds that he is chosen by Jehovah who is no respecter of persons. Yet he is chosen in the sense that his self-love, which cannot be crushed without annihilating him, is laid hold of to function as the property-possessor of a Word which is accommodated to his character, and every iota and tittle of the bare letter of which he regards with a superstitious reverence; even as thaumaturgic or magical.

The function of avarice is well discerned by Sir Thomas

Browne. "Trust not," says he, "to the omnipotency of gold, and say not unto it, Thou art my confidence. Kiss not thy hand to that terrestrial sun, nor bore thine ear unto its servitude. A slave unto mammon makes no servant unto God. Covetousness cracks the sinews of faith; numbs the apprehension of anything above sense; and, only affected with the certainty of things present, makes a peradventure of things to come; lives but unto one world, nor hopes but fears another."—*Christian Morals*, sect. viii.

Christians, not yet instructed in the internal sense of the Word, are busy with the conversion of the Jews. They may now know the reason why their efforts will be fruitless. The Jews are kept for use and service till the Second Coming of Christ, as is plainly revealed in the 24th chapter of Matthew. They are in a sense under the special protection of Christ Who is Jehovah; not indeed as any longer the representation of a Church, but as fulfilling a use essential to the offices of a New Church, which has to enter upon the whole Word, and restore the truths of the Ancients.

An attempt not pretending to benevolence is made by the Czar and his ministers to exterminate the Jews from Russia, or to compel them to embrace Christianity. We have seen that Judaism is not a hypocrisy, but a religiosity of racial and national self-interest, induced by Jehovah upon a unique external capacity of religious seeming; and which thus contains at the core a mightily strong nature of persuasion. This intervention of divinity still extant with the Jew makes it perilous to treat him as an ordinary puppet for the Greek Church to dandle. A contest with a divine Arbiter may break the bones of the greatest monarch. The consequences will not be discernible as such because the causes are not admitted. But political demolition of an ancient religion whose externals were divine, and whose Word is so still, by another religiosity whose externals are human and superstitious, is nothing less than the annihilation of religion itself in the government which enacts it. It is more dangerous now than the persecutions of the Papacy, and the *auto da fe* of the Inquisition. And looking upon it as a sign of the times, which signs the Lord enjoins us to notice, this contempt of men's souls by Czarism spiritually brings forth Nihilism, the special contribution of Russia towards the rejuvenescence of society. Providence shows correspondences* by perpetual coincidences. Each form of atheism brings its own monstrous births.

XXXVI.—THE FOOD OF THE JEWS DIVINELY ORDAINED AND LIMITED.

It was the character of the Jews as being the most external of all nations, or as carrying their holiness outside themselves,—being thus and then the worst of nations,—which forced the existence of the mere representation of a Church, when that form, and obedience to it, was the one resource left to the Lord for supporting the ancient heavens and saving the human race. The same character made the representatives grievous, and the carrying out of them atrocious. If Romans, Mexicans, or Peruvians had been chosen under the same necessity, their bad qualities must have largely entered into the representation. For the representation is made of the stuff of the actors themselves to such an extent as that they can act *in it*. We are obliged to reinforce this; for it is the one point likely to be forgotten, and the point which is cardinal to the understanding of this Essay.

The diet of the Jews was representative, and breach of its prescriptions was on pain of death. Clean and unclean animals were signalized, and foods with spiritual correspondences on which they were forbidden to enter. " The reason why it was so severely prohibited to eat blood and fat was, that by such eating was represented the profanation of

* See my work, *Epidemic Man and his Visitations.* Speirs, 1893.

Divine Truth and Divine Good. For the Israelitish and Jewish nation lived in externals separate from internals; therefore in no Divine Truth and in no Divine Good of faith and love, but in external worship alone. They were in the love of self and the love of the world above other nations; consequently in the evils thence arising,—in contempt of others, enmity, hatred, revenge, fierceness, and cruelty. Hence also it was that internal truths were not revealed to them; for if they had been revealed they could not but have profaned them. Therefore they would have represented profanation if they had eaten blood and fat."—*Arcana Cœlestia*, n. 10033. This prohibition with regard to blood "which is the life" is carried out to this day by the Hebrew people, being one of the rites which does not depend upon their presence in the Holy Land.

Some modern higher critics claim Moses as a cunning sanitarian and medicine man, who foresaw by genius the food that would build a strong race, and issued a dietary accordingly, adding a superstitious authority to give the prescript weight. Whatever wholesomeness might lie in obeying the Levitical prohibitions and permissions of foods, the existence of the most active nations upon a diet that makes no account of the Old Testament table, is evidence that sanitation is no master-key to the law we are considering. The key is theological and of Jehovah; and the prohibition of blood and fat is a cardinal instance commanding all the rest. Let not the phrase be misunderstood that the Jewish Dispensation in its greatest and least aspects was commanded by a Divine Magic throughout. Magic can bear this highest sense. In it the supernal wisdom makes use of the catenation of external means to induce the descent of divine and to us miraculous power. Evil Magic is an imitation of this, effected by some knowledge of correspondences, as it was in ancient Egypt.

Our constant assertion of the doctrine that Jehovah stood immediately over the Jews, and miraculously and in veiled personality commanded them, is not more repetitious than the same statement is in the Word, and than the denial of the fact is in the commentators. Those who do not deny it, neglect and forget it.

Speaking of the food forbidden to the Jews, Sir Thomas Browne remarks : " Withal in this distinction of animals the consideration was hieroglyphicall; in the bosome and inward sense implying an abstinence from certain vices symbolically intimated from the nature of those animals ; as may be well made out in the prohibited meat of Swine, Cony, Owl, and many more. At least the intention was not medical, or such as might oblige to conformity or imitation. . . . The Jews refrained from swine at first symbolically, as an emblem of impurity ; and not from fear of the leprosie, as Tacitus would put upon them."—*Enquiries into Vulgar and Common Errors*, chap. xxv. p. 142, 2nd ed., folio 1650. Thomas Browne, Doctor of Physick at Norwich, was a profound Bible commentator, and by his gracious interpretations and divinations seemed already to rejoice in his pregnant genius at the promise of Swedenborg's day.

It were to be desired that every thinker on the Jewish Dispensation would read the *Arcana Cœlestia*, vols. xi. and xii., where the Garments of Holiness, the Altar, the Tabernacle, the Institution of the Sabbath, and in general the Ceremonials and holy arcane structures belonging to the Mosaic Law, are explained in the spiritual sense. No earthly romance awakens such wonder ; no moral theology is so commanding; no science of principles is so central and far-reaching : no demonstration of the presence of Deity in the world and its design so absolute as the demonstration of the presence of the Lord in the Word, revealed by Him in withdrawing the Veil from the Letter. O that our Church of England, in place of wasting itself upon fruitless efforts to make inspiration scientific, would deign to look upon inspiration itself in glory here.

This spiritual or internal sense answers the question of

inspiration by showing us pieces or specimens of it from its mine which underlies the entire Word. The old Churches, Roman, Greek and Protestant, possess no such evidences of the existence of such a sense, nor consequently of the inspiration of the letter. The Word says, "the letter killeth," which is a declaration that there is a Spirit which redeems the letter, and filling it with life, enables it to give life and not to kill. While the letter alone is in evidence, and a verbally concurrent spiritual sense is unknown, what is the meaning of inspiration? It is interpreted to mean that God has inspired into certain men, chosen and fitting instruments, to write by their minds under Divine influence a holy scripture containing truths necessary for our guidance and salvation, as Cicero and Seneca were inspired to write good moral truths, and as the best writers of all times have been helped providentially to give light to their races. In this case, all these inspirations are embedded in the substance of the letter. You may write religious and moral treatises from them, but your dissertations are no specimens of inspiration. Failing to acquire any sensible knowledge of this, you subject the letter to criticism rather than to translation; and your discredited letter, half-demolished and then passed *through* a number of other minds, you postulate as inspired when you interpret it into ecclesiastical dogmas. Your opinions here are your own interpretation, not the inspiration of the Divine Word. The Divine Word was with God, and was God: how different that Word from the letter. The Divine Word is settled in heaven: how different that Word. The Word was made flesh, and dwelt with us, and we saw His Glory; the Glory of the only begotten of the Father. How different that Word from the letter. Shew us then the way of eliciting the breathing spiritual sense from the seemingly motionless and speechless literal sense, that the letter may be seen to be divine, to breathe, to speak, and to live. The way of the Lord was to descend as the Word through the three heavens, of Love, of Wisdom, and of Works, and to clothe that Word with the speech of each, and as the Son of man thus garmented with His own Divinity to come as an Angel Person to Lawgivers, Prophets, Psalmists, Evangelists, and to him, "I, John," of the Apocalypse, and to speak *to* them, not *through* them, a literal Word in the languages of certain chosen nations whose minds and events prepared their chosen men to be obedient penmen of the letter. The Jewish dispensation employed men exactly competent to this office for the Old Testament; the Jewish character in them fitting them to receive it for Jewish use. And now therefore we have the heaven of the internal sense, and the earth of the external sense; the one corresponding to the other; the literal supporting the spiritual, and the spiritual inspiring the literal. And demonstration is here to satisfy every faculty of every mind made free by the truth; for if any one asks you what inspiration is, you can give him an object-lesson, specimen-proof, and sample of it, by taking the literal sense of any psalm, or of any chapter of the Apocalypse, and opening it word by word into a coherent higher chapter; the attesting grammar and dictionary of your single interpretation being the answerableness and compliance of the entire Word.

The Letter was compulsory to the Jew in his day, and the spirit was precluded to him. The Spirit is preached to Christians by the entire Word, and the letter without it killeth. Is it not all-important to know now that the Spirit is a substantial book and volume for a higher brain with angels reading it in plane after plane above and within the lower brain for the letter. When we advert to Archæology we may speak of inspiration again later on.

XXXVII.—THE RESTORATION OF THE JEWS.

The Jews as the Nation and People of the Old Testament and the Mosaic Dispensation will not be reconstituted in the Holy Land. No crusade or anti-crusade will be undertaken for them. They will have no Messiah such as they have looked for. They are averse to the New Jerusalem. This Jerusalem in the spiritual sense is the City into which all who endure to the end, whether Jews or Gentiles, will be gathered. The Lord of that city is no respecter of persons or of races as such. All who are in the good of love and the truth of faith will be its Jews, its inhabitants, its Israelites in whom there is no guile. It descends from God out of heaven; and is again the Divine Truth now as the doctrine of the New Religion. City here, the concentrated grouping and habitation of the elect, the streets of their divine order, signifies Doctrine. Doctrines are the intellectual precepts corresponding to the mental affinities of a spiritual-celestial civilization, or a heavenly citizenship in the Church of the Lord. True doctrines, says Swedenborg, constitute the Church, and a life according to them constitutes Religion.

This function of true doctrines is plainly shown in the internal sense of the Apocalypse, now the most open Book of the Word *to open minds*. From ignorance of that sense the Christian world interprets the promises made to the Jews in the Old Testament as indicating that they will be restored to the Land of Canaan, and will re-inhabit the Old Jerusalem, making it the centre of the world. Christians, in this consummation of the age, and end of the Church, are like the Jews in their state, and believe that the choice and salvation of man are dependent upon Divine Mercy irrespective of life and character; and so they easily imagine that the Jews and Israelites were chosen in preference to every other nation, and therefore were more excellent than the rest; as the Jews and Israelites themselves believed. Hence most Christians fall into the further belief that that nation once chosen will be chosen again, and be brought back into the Land of Canaan, according to the sense of the letter.

In connexion with these subjects we repeat what Swedenborg says in another place: "The representative of the Celestial Kingdom began to perish when the Jews asked for a king; and therefore in order that this representative of the Lord's kingdom in the Heavens might still be continued, the Jews were separated from the Israelites; and the Jewish kingdom represented the Lord's celestial kingdom, and the Israelite kingdom, His spiritual kingdom."—*Arcana Cœlestia*, 8770.

And again: "The Jewish kingdom represented the celestial kingdom, or the Lord's Priesthood, and the Israelite kingdom the spiritual kingdom or the Lord's Royalty. But the latter was destroyed when nothing spiritual remained with them. Whereas the Jewish kingdom was maintained *for the sake of the Word, and because the Lord was to be born there.* But when they had completely adulterated the Word, and thus could not know the Lord, then their kingdom was destroyed."—*Apocalypse Revealed*, n. 350.

"By Judah is not meant the Jewish nation, for this was nothing so little as a celestial church. As respected love to the Lord, and charity towards the neighbour, and faith, it was the worst nation of all. And this, from its first fore-elders to the present time. When the Jews turned aside from their rituals to idolatries, they represented infernal and diabolical things."—*Arcana*, 3881.

XXXVIII.—THE FUTURE OF THE JEWS.

We have seen that the Jew is a providential antichrist, because it would be worse for him and for the Church in heaven and on earth if he had believed in Christ. His self-love is enlisted in his Old Testament which promises him so much, and he shows his faith in himself by feeding on the promises. He has tenderness for himself, as who should say often, Poor dear Jew! He has times and places of wailing. And he loves his own flesh and blood as when in Shylock he cries out, 'O my daughter, O my ducats, O my daughter'! He loves written bonds. Can we blame him? In a constitution formed and hardened for thousands of years, he is incapable of receiving spiritual truth, though now scarcely less capable than the Christians. His faculty is truncated by absence of interest in anything which is not of this world: the organs of the higher light, its eyes, are shut in him. In worldly things how great is his capacity! In the range of the sensual mind, mounting up as it does into the *simulacra* of all the higher faculties, he is intellectual, philosophical, artistic, musical. He makes a good unitarian, a good ritualist, and is addicted to the higher criticism; but the latter when without changing his Jewish foundation he parts unhappily with some of his reverence for the Old Testament. He can be a great lawyer, financier, and economist in Great Britain, and serve his father-in-law land in these capacities. He can be a great statesman on the lines of civilization, as we have seen in that free member of the English Church, that head of our proud nobility, that guardian of our empire and maker of its empress, him now regretted by our patriots, and once respected and feared by our enemies, Benjamin D'Israeli. A grand representative in our need of the severe quality of the tribe of Benjamin.

We come again to the question, What will be the future of the Jews? Like futurity in general, it is veiled. Of its events, of its days and hours, knoweth no man. For the most part it resolves itself into the question of the relation of the modern world to this conserved ancient nation. We may attract or repel their multitude in one nation or another, but we are powerless to exterminate them; or to melt them away by incorporation among our own people; or by any national or international action to overcome the Providence that forbids them as a nation in the Holy Land.

The Jew is a model of the selfhood of race-preserving nationality: dotted over all the countries of the world he is still a masonic magnetic nation from age to age. English, French, Germans lose themselves in foreign races after one or more generations; their faces alter to new social surroundings and influence of climates; but the Jew, however modified superficially, is true to his type. The most inflexible, he is also the most plastic, of natural men. He enters into every country and belongs to its laws; he adopts its language and becomes its citizen; but remains Judean. Whatever progress to a different goal than his own is made, is in seeming: he moves with the tide of the race in which he resides; but the movement is accommodation and not otherwise volition. He is related as a race to all races, and would fain in some sense be at their head, yet he has no interest in cosmopolitanism, or in the brotherhood of mankind; no interest in the breadth and height of theology, in the salvation of the Gentiles, in gathering all men into a Maximus Homo, and helping humanity to be one fold under one Shepherd. And where he enjoys political privileges, he is not, unless he is a fleshless Anarch, under the demagogue flag of liberty, equality, and fraternity.

It need hardly be said for the United Kingdom that no social problem can be solved by meddling with our Jews. It is a fair question whether any paupers or weaklings, Jews, or others, should be admitted into a country to share its always limited needs of work and supplies of food; and it is the right of a community to stop an immigration that is injurious to its own citizens. It is also right to supervise immigrants who import unwholesome circumstances, or abominable habits, or who live by sweating the poor, or competing injuriously with honest hire. Nations should keep the children they have bred, whether Jews or Gentiles, and not ship them angrily and impudently upon their neighbours. Each people is a body corporate, and should maintain its own personality as represented at a given time. Law should compel in these cases; but we are too busy feeding bad ambitions which pay us with diabetic sweetness of promises that run destruction, to attend to the integrity of our national state. We suffer from a bad disease of heart and reins; from debauchery by the poisonous honey of false hopes which waste our lives.

We have no rights against Jew or Gentile otherwise. Suppose that Abraham, Isaac and Jacob were all imprisoned, or banished, or Jerusalemized. Nominal Christianity inherits Judaism profoundly in its greeds, its worldliness, and its Babylonian love of rule. The Jew has remorseless Christian confederates and successors. The great capitalists of America in sheer wealth, and capacity of money-making without doing useful work, overtop the Jews; as did the Roman proconsuls and procurators who sucked the blood of provinces and nations in their day. France and England abound in floaters of huge loans to be wiled from small men's certainties and widows' mites. And as long as standing armies and rival navies last, and war expenses are periodical and growing, money will be made by capitalists and paper-promise men, by honey-sweet politically diabetic men, whether Jews or Gentiles. From Cæsar downwards, nay from Cæsar upwards, the Jews have helped fighting; and when Divus Julius died, they howled and wailed for him as for a very patriarch and brother. But now we have learnt our lesson about banks and loans; and if all Jews were to become Christians, finance would undergo little change. The heart of man, wild with false hopes, is at the bottom of Pandora's box.

The conclusion seems to be, both from revelation, history, and broad prudence, though not from French Antisemitism or Russian jealousy, or English proselytism, that it is easiest and best to leave the Jews alone, and under just laws like other citizens. They are of use wherever they are as law-abiding and as honest as their neighbours. Many of them are excellent. Who could have known Sir Francis Goldsmidt, and not say this? or Sir Moses Montefiori, or

Peregrine Fernandez, or John Elliotson ? The good Jews are humane to their own people and self-respecting. They have their poor always with them in a good sense. Their lack of spiritual faculties is inherited ; and is now providentially kept up through their active genius in worldly cares. Moreover, from the proselytizing side, nothing definitely better is offered them than their own religion ; and nothing doctrinal is offered them at all. Christ comes before them as one of three Gods, three God-persons, and they have been warned by Moses and the Prophets that their own proclivity is polytheism ; and they have been punished in the past, and lost Canaan, for falling into it. Chiefly because Christ fulfilled none of their ideas of Messiahship, and now for pretext because they are monotheists, they refuse the three Gods of the three mutually hostile Christian Churches. As to civilized laws, so far as they are an improvement upon former morals, the Jews are disciplined in the best way by enforced attrition with western communities who do not admit metaphor, parable and correspondence as veracity; their Orientalism is usefully tempered by a dead-letter of truth-speaking as a rule of life and business. So though the Jews will not change, they are outwardly modified ; and images of mercy and tolerance of a gentler kind than their own are held up before them. And no Providence denies to any individual of them to enter the New Religion. The doctrine that Jesus Christ is the Lord, One God in One Person, may be accepted as a continuation of their Jehovah, Who appeared to their prophets as the Ancient of Days in a human form. And when these new disciples read the Gospels, they will learn that Christ on the cross prayed the Father to forgive them because they knew not what they did ; and also told us that His death was of His own consent ; that no man took His life from Him, but He Himself laid it down. May we call this, for our brethren's sakes, divine confession and human absolution ?

Let us be then thankful for Good Use which is the desirable administration of all things; and let us pray for our brother, the Jew, that he may indeed be the trusty keeper and treasurer of the Old Testament, and clasp it in its everlasting Hebrew; and that our own Churches may sympathize with him in the trust; and still learn of the divine letter at his hands. For we know by a new revelation that he, the Jew, now in his best estate, is an ark and casket of the Psalms, and of Moses and the Prophets, and that he is enlisted in his very nature and its frailties on the side of this divine fortune.

XXXIX.—INSTANCES OF CORRESPONDENCES.

GOD AND JEHOVAH.—It is expedient to give some instances of the internal sense which characterises the Word, and shows its verbal inspiration; and which no writer, whether Archæologist or "Higher Critic," supposes to exist in the polytheistic writings of the nations. This shall be done as briefly as possible, and in simple language.

Goodness and Truth in their essence are One God. Where the Word treats of Truth, God is mentioned; where of Good, Jehovah. In the first chapter of Genesis, God is the Creator: the *six* days of Creation, from man's "earth without form and void," through his various stages of regeneration, up to the sixth day when he is an "Image of God," are his receptions of Divine Truths into his life. ELOHIM, gods, truths in the plural, are the Divine agent here. This is no recognition of many gods; but of the nature of Truth; for "divine truth is various, but divine Goodness is one."

In chapter two, Jehovah, the Lord, is the agent. The six days of labour are over: the image of God, the spiritual man, is created. He is not the end; truth never is, but life according to it; making it *good* in the spiritual man in charity. But there is a higher good to come, in love to the Lord. Until this is effected, man is still the dust of the ground. Man is now taken on the seventh day, no longer by God, but by Jehovah, and formed into a "likeness of God"; or a celestial man; an end of creation; where before there was no man to till the ground. "The celestial man is the seventh day on which the Lord rested." In him, the celestial degree of life, love has gained the dominion; and what was still the dust of the ground correspondentially, is Adam, the Lord's primeval man.

So there are not two creations, an Elohist and a Jehovist creation, but one with no break in the narrative; and there are not two documents put together, but there is one divine organ of continuous correspondences, introducing us for all ages into a knowledge and acknowledgment of the primeval or Adamic Church.

There is no more need for two creations here than for several creations in one human life; a boy is born; a man appears in the course of him, where there was no man; but the one life accounts for both without insisting that the boy was one being and the man another; or that two makers were demanded for the two. A rude analogy, but it may help.

Without Correspondences, such things could not be written, without a knowledge of them the writings cannot be understood. This is the true most ancient and ancient learning by which we can commune with the mode of being, thinking, and speaking, which belonged to the first regenerate men. It is the lore of the Garden Eastward in Eden. When Jehovah's love and Adam's love were in harmony, man in conjunction with heaven talked creations as Jehovah acted them. The Word was written in him. These men lived in the East, which signified love, and so were Orientals; but Oriental speech to-day, if more figurative than English, is averse to the words which named all the creatures and Jehovah sanctioned the nomenclature. Archæology is locked up in modern Orientalism; and has the privileges of it; but they are not celestial or spiritual; and apply to only one tier of mankind—"a single instance"—the natural man, the lowest man.

THE NEPHILIM.—Now regard another Correspondence. "When men began to multiply on the face of the ground, and daughters were born unto them, the sons of God saw the daughters of men that they were fair, and they took them wives of all that they chose. And the Lord said, My spirit shall not strive with man for ever, for that he also is flesh. . . . The Nephilim were in the earth in those days; and also after that, when the sons of God came in unto the daughters of men, and they bare children to them; the same were the mighty men which were of old, the men of renown" (Gen. vi. 1–5). "The giants, Nephilim, are those who, from a persuasion of their own rank and pre-eminence, regarded what was holy and true as nothing."—*Arcana Cœlestia*, n. 580. What are the sons of God here? In the spiritual sense there are no persons. The sons of God are the Divine truths which were given especially to that Adamic Church; its doctrinals of faith. They are also the truths of the Word for all ages. Christ is the Son of God as the Divine Truth in heaven. The text above narrates perversion. Therefore the daughters of men are corrupt desires; lusts; for the man here is "flesh." The union of these two, of the fleshly mind with religious truth, for carrying out infernal ends, produces mighty men of old, men of renown. 'Of old, signifies from the first, or, *as usual.*' It is intelligible to us from the events of every age. Our own worst states are so produced. When our desires pervert our consciences, and overthrow their monitory truths, we become mighty in selfhood, for we make truth itself into a lie and a flattery. On a large scale in the world, the monster evils of mankind, hard and enduring, are the births of the union of our ambitions with our *Te Deums;* of our meanness and shame with our glory. So infallibility marries antichrist, and tyranny is at the altar with liberty, equality, and fraternity. The Nephilim of this age are here.

Have we not an abyssal instance of the sons of God, which are truths in their origin, going in to the daughters of men, which are desires permeating human nature, in the state of modern rivalry and warfare, personal, social, and national. The very Son of God Himself, the Lord Christ, in the theology of Christendom, absolves mankind from this earthly hell by atoning for it to the Father; and all that the sinners, private, public, and national, need do is, to lay hold on Him as their Justifier: they continuing in their sins, and never dreaming to get rid of them. Individual and universal selfishness and Bellona are here the daughters of men; and the Son of God of the Churches is wedded to them; and Giant Evils incurable, and that no brain can think beyond, Nephilim and Anakim, are born. Our Church wonders, and completes its duty by preaching penitence on Ash Wednesday.

THE FLOOD.—It is a spiritual event easily read after the correspondence of it is disclosed. "God breathed into man's nostrils the breath of lives, and man became a living soul." God's breath in man is man's life: it is his spirit. In Adam it was a pure life, for before the Fall Adam had not sinned, and was in no contrariety to Him whose breath was his life: man's breath and God's, man's spirit and God's, coincided. By Adam understand the first or Adamic Church. When that Church had corrupted itself, and was consummated, when man determined to be his own God, the life that God had given could no longer be breathed into him; but the effort he made to breathe from himself was what remained to him: the wrath of the tradition of the first respiration. This was more and more obstructed by the lusts and persuasions into which God no longer breathed, for their spirit was against His spirit, and man therefore ceased to be a living soul. As the Adam was thus, and as all will, thought, speech, and writing run in the streams of correspondences, this extinction of the respiration is called by the Divine Author of Genesis, the Flood. The world to-day lacks the elements of understanding this; because it does not study the science of correspondences; and also because it makes no account of the *doctrine of respiration*, which is the basement of the knowledge of the natural and spiritual life; and of the dwelling or intercourse of the soul with the body. See Swedenborg's *Animal Kingdom*, the Chapter on the Lungs. The Flood has constant analogies in this time. Truths of the past, which once possessed the people, become weakened by not being obeyed, and so ceasing to teach; and then they are suffocated by the onrush of flattering falses. This is known as the changing Spirit of the Age: *i.e.*, Breath of the Age. It is overflowed from time to time by a fresh wave of perversions from selfish ends which bribe consciences. In the earliest time, the falses were direful persuasions that man was God: now the falses of the *Zeitgeist* are antitheological: man is man, godless, and the kingdom of man is to come; the name of God is to cease. Little children in fair France are to forget it.

EGYPT.—The names of nations in the Word do not mean geographical places and their inhabitants, but great organic humanities at work: thus faculties of man; the vital things of Churches. And Churches are not ecclesiasticisms although they may contain them, but divine dispensations coinciding with the above humanities; and meant for guidance and salvation in their Æons.

Egypt illustrates this. In the Ancient Church it signified the culture of the Sciences of that Church. Let us try to understand this. The lower base of every Church, as indeed of all life, must be its sciences: the known things in its natural mind: its natural theology born of Revelation. What were the Sciences of the Church? They were divinely-authorized rituals and reverences which brought heaven near to the Egyptian man, so that when he, faithful to God, was in them, the corresponding plane of worship and precept was filled in his mind with the influx of God. They are called Sciences of the Church; but the word science rather means what we should call applied science than anything apart and abstract. They were the truths of the real presence arranged to ensure that Presence. Truth for its own sake which we sometimes hear of, has no place here : all the truths of the Word are divinely *interested*, and are only true to the glory of God, and the good of man's estate ; according to the formula of that Egyptian mind, Francis Bacon of Verulam.

Well, Egypt signified this *Cultus*, this kind of worship before it fell : it was endowed with the remains of the science of correspondences ; of which hieroglyphics as they now stand are the last " remainder-biscuit." Some man who has two spades, both ace of spades and king of spades, both spiritual spade and natural spade, will one day uncover things which are hieroglyphic of the Ancient Church, and no longer of Menes, Rameses, or Meneptah. It is impossible that the most ancient of the nations of the Noahtic Church can have spent its symbolic and lingual mind on the names of dynasties and their glory, or its religious mind on polytheism, and on an animal worship which was signalized as idolatrous even in the time of Moses.

A great people which corresponded in its mental organization to the science of worship, its divinely given natural forms and comeliness, must have undergone long ages of decline before its hieroglyphic genius became a Cadmean Letter, or its Jehovah was lost in a pantheon. Materialism, Churchyardism, must have destroyed the simple belief in immortality before a nation could look upon its mummies as its future state, and its funerals as its fee simple in immortality. Scientifics, however, when they fall, believe in death and change, and not in life and regeneration. We in our day are Egyptian in our belief in a future life : according to orthodoxy all our dead are slumbering in their graves awaiting a final judgment in this little planet which would not hold the gathered nations if they rose.

With regard to the first state of Egypt, when it was

a leading faculty and organ of the Ancient Church, Swedenborg says:—"From ancient times the Egyptians knew Jehovah. They had among them the representatives and significatives of that Church. The Egyptian hieroglyphics are nothing else. By them spiritual things were signified. They also knew that they actually corresponded" (*Arcana*, 7097). Also, "By Egypt was meant a church which in the beginning was pre-eminent; so Egypt, before its Church was devastated, is compared to the Garden of Eden, and to the Garden of Jehovah (Gen. xiii. 10; Ezek. xxxi. 8); and is also called "the corner-stone of the tribes, the son of the wise, and of the kings of antiquity" (Isaiah xix. 11, 13).

After this digression, the reader is requested to hold fast the doctrinal revelation that Egypt and its Nile, and all things in it, have reference in the Word to the scientific plane and degree of man and the Church. Egypt signifies the merely natural man, mere knowledge, facts, scientifics. Its mummies are facts to-day: you know the very face of Rameses in Cairo still as it protrudes into the nineteenth century.

Being scientifics, as we have no representative scientifics of the Church of to-day except Baptism and the Lord's Supper, Egypt for us descends to mean the scientific principle in all of us, and in all our nations. It means all the facts of knowledge which we most value, and which are the scientifics and thought-resources of our lives. To them we continually go down as to Egypt.

With respect to this phrase we read thus: "Everywhere in the Word it is said, 'to go down from the Land of Canaan to Egypt,' and to 'go up from Egypt to the land of Canaan.' The land of Canaan signifies the heavenly, and Egypt the natural. Canaan, the heavenly kingdom; and Egypt, the goods and truths of the external church, which for the most part are scientifics" (*Arcana*, 5406). "In a good sense Egypt signifies the scientifics which are of service *for the form of the Church* " (n. 5580).

Egypt had remarkable relations to the Jews personally and nationally; and these are only explicable by the revelation the New Religion now possesses that Egypt corresponds to the scientific mind. Abram journeyed south, and went down into Egypt to sojourn there; for the famine was grievous in the land where he was. When he returned from Egypt with his wife, Sarai, he was very rich in cattle, in silver, and in gold. An Egyptian handmaid Hagar, as it were substitutionally married to Abram, bears him his firstborn, Ishmael, and prepares the way for the birth of Isaac. But of Isaac when there was famine in the land, beside the first famine in the days of Abraham, it is said that the Lord appeared to him, and said, Go not down into Egypt; dwell in the land which I shall tell thee of, the land of Gerar. The reason why Isaac was not to go down into Egypt is given in the *Arcana Cœlestia*, n. 3368, where it is treated of at . length. Abraham sojourning in Egypt represented the Lord's instruction in scientifics when He was a child. Isaac represents the Lord's entry into the rational; and now that He would not look to scientifics but to rationals. The subject is too abstruse for these pages; but can be approached by the reverent reader who desires to be instructed in the different functions of rationals and scientifics in man's regeneration; and of how rationals receive light from the Divine, and then enlighten scientifics.

Joseph also is sold into Egypt, and Jacob sends his sons there, and goes thither himself. The children of Israel become a people in Egypt, and are prepared for the possession of Canaan, and the representation of a Church there. These events signify the indispensable character of Egypt in constituting the Ancient Church, which was the foothold of God's human creatures in the World from Noah to Abraham, and to Moses.

Yet another event occurs in the Word. After the Lord was born, and the Wise Men, the Magi, had fallen down and worshipped Him, and opened their gifts; and were departed, "behold the angel of the Lord appeared to Joseph in a dream, saying, Arise, and take the young child and his mother, and flee into Egypt, and be thou there until I bring thee word: for Herod will seek the young child to destroy him. When he arose, he took the young child and his mother by night, and departed into Egypt: and was there until the death of Herod: that it might be fulfilled which was spoken of the Lord by the Prophet saying, 'Out of Egypt have I called my Son.' .... But when Herod was dead, behold an angel of the Lord appeareth in a dream to Joseph in Egypt, saying, Arise, and take the young child and his mother, and go into the land of Israel: for they are dead which sought the young child's life. And he arose, and took the young child and his mother, and came into the land of Israel" (Matthew ii. 11). This event is connected in the word with two causes, the escape of the young child from the murder of the Innocents by Herod, and the pressure of Divine order in the Lord's entry into a natural human mind, and its glorification by His life in it. Respecting this we read as follows. "In the Ancient Church there were doctrinals, and there were scientifics. The Doctrinals treated of love to God, and of charity towards the neighbour. The Scientifics treated of the Correspondences of the natural world with the spiritual world, and of representatives of spiritual and celestial things in natural and terrestrial. Joseph was made to go down into Egypt. The Lord is represented by Joseph. Hereby then is signified, that when the Lord glorified His internal man, that is, made it divine, He first imbued the scientifics of the Church, and from and by them made progress to things more and more interior, and at length to things divine. It pleased Him to glorify Himself, or to make divine, according to the order in which He regenerates man, or makes him spiritual: namely, from external things, which are scientifics and truths of faith, successively to internal things, which are of charity towards the neighbour, and of love to Himself. Hence what is signified in Hosea xi. 1, 'When Israel was a child then I loved him; *and out of Egypt* have I called my Son.' These words were spoken of the Lord. See Matthew ii. 15."

This revelation from the Word begins to clear our eyes and conceptions about the nature, process, and end and object of the INCARNATION, and what the divine man did for man in reconstituting the human mind, first in Himself, and then for our whole natural humanity. He overthrew the Hells by resisting them. He made them level with man's power of resistance, and so gave man back his lost freedom. He atoned for no sin, past, present, or to come. But he made us all capable of working out our own salvation, and also then of being strong in faith and love to acknowledge that He fights when we fight; and that He alone, veiled Lord God Almighty, is our Victory and our Heaven.

We adduce one more mention of Egypt commenting on the same text. "Scientifics are things which they who are regenerating must first learn, since they are a plane for the things of the understanding; and the understanding is the recipient of the truth of faith; and the truth of faith is the recipient of the good of charity. That the scientific principle was the first plane to the Lord when He made His human, divine truth, or the divine law, is signified by the Lord when an infant being brought into Egypt. By scientifics are not meant philosophical scientifics, but scientifics of the Church " (*Ibid.* n. 6750).

There are many passages in the Word which signify the perversions of the natural mind and scientific principle denoted by Egypt. " Isaiah xxvi. describes the state of those who wish to be wise from themselves in things of heaven and the church. Of them it is said, 'Woe to them that go down to Egypt for help, and do not look to the Holy One of Israel, and do not seek Jehovah.' The imaginary things which come from the fallacies of the senses are 'the horses of Egypt on which they stay.' That the natural man does not understand divine things from himself is signified by 'Egypt is a man, and not God.' That such intelligence is from the *proprium* in which there is no life, is signified by 'his horses are flesh and not spirit.'"—*Apocalypse Explained*, n. 654.

" In seven chapters in the Revelation the consummation of the present Church is described in like manner as the devastation of Egypt. Both are described by the like plagues, each one of which signifies some falsity which furthered its devastation even to destruction. Thus this Church which is at this day destroyed is also called Egypt."—*True Christian Religion*, n. 635. "'The city which is called Sodom and Egypt, where also our Lord was crucified.' The two infernal loves which are the love of dominion from the love of self, and the love of reigning from the pride of one's own intelligence, are here signified. Sodom means all evil from the love of self, and Egypt instead of Gomorrha all the falsity thence derived." May we not say that Sodom involves all atheist right to do whatever we lust and like with our own souls and bodies, with ourselves, and with others, and with all living creatures; that it means, infernal godhood; and that Egypt here is the skilful genius and working hypothesis of Atheism universally applied by Sodom in the killing of conscience. Christ is crucified in all the abominations, cruelties and vivisections of these two. They are a hell of the present mind. The modern Church condones them.

SWEDENBORG.—The Commissioner of the New Dispensation, Emanuel Swedenborg, guarded and guided by the Lord from his birth onwards, was also sent down into an Egypt where no theologian had preceded him. He was committed to natural science. In its pursuit he saw that the highest natural sciences, namely, of anatomy and physiology, were then in honest plenty, like the seven kine, fat-fleshed and well-favoured of Pharaoh's dream, and which fed in a meadow: and like the seven ears of corn on one stalk, full and good. So with such a harvest before him he also foresaw that the grain must be stored in good doctrinal barns, since dearth might follow; "for unless," says he, "I mistake the signs of the times, the world's destinies are tending thitherwards." His insight and onsight were borne out; for the Egypt which has since followed is of the lean kine of materialism which but for him would have eaten up the fat kine; and of the thin ears which would have devoured the seven good ears. In his time under this Joseph the scientific earth brought forth by handfuls. "And he gathered up all the food of the seven years which were in the land of Egypt, and laid up the food in the cities. The food of the field which was round about every city laid he up in the same." Cities in the Word are doctrines. Thus he stored and garnered in these the abundance of the true corn of natural knowledge. The cities or doctrines for the wealth of storage were many; and many were wanted, for the corn of life when seven years means holy truth of state in the mind, or truth tending to good, is "as the sand of the sea," exceeding number. We know the names of these cities. They are common senses about nature divinely illustrated, digests and inductions, intuitions into ends and purposes, divinations of natural wisdom poured into vessels of faith. The field is the human body in which all the organs and spheres become doctrines. Individually they are the "Doctrine of Forms, of Order and Degrees, of Series and Society, of Influx, of Correspondence and Representation, and of Modification."

Perceptions of what the life of the body is; of how it is alive simply because it answers by perpetual service to the living soul which has to dwell in it: of how the body is the image and face and literal sense of the soul; and the soul, the model, the idea, the first form, the substance, the force, and principle of the body, entered the mind of this non-medical physiologist, who stood on a mountain of no professional partiality. He has left universal truths yet to be recognized in the Animal Kingdom, meaning thereby the Soul's Kingdom, the human form, not the republic of

Zoology. Of these uncoverings we may chronicle the doctrine of the heart, how that it, like the will to which it corresponds, makes and modifies for its own purposes in its walled house, what it contains; in the case of the heart, the blood, which it next circulates. This doctrine, of the heart as the supreme voter and ordainer of excellence and ranks in the blood, dimly held by many, was fixed into verity by Swedenborg. He also divined and showed that the brain is faculty in every spherule, and is distinctly various in all its globes of animations as the mind is various; representing also a partible genius corresponding to the moving sciences and skills of the universe of creation: how from the soul which is an inner brain, it builds the body according to all natural light and knowledge and all physical departments made alive. The doctrine of Uses is always the beginning and the end: the Circulation of Uses. This is the Circle of Life. The use of the body to the soul is intended in all the organism. Signal to the writer among these scientifics and rationals and spirituals is the uncovering of the spirit which human breath is: the use of the lungs in breathing. "For the lungs not only respire themselves but make the whole organic body to respire along with them." Swedenborg has established in spirit, in reason, and in science under it, the end, use and purpose which is served for man and his life in that his body from head to foot heaves and falls, and makes space in every atom of it by the motion wherewith the lungs set it walking into mental and bodily function. And this motion has nothing to do directly with the breathing in and out of the air in the chest through the mouth. It is the freewill of the body itself.

First a SEER through the medium of organic doctrines, this instrument in realizing the Lord's Second Advent was sent down into the Egypt of the eighteenth century; into scientifics far outlying the Church scientifically; into mines and smelting works, into mechanical inventions, into theories of chemical forms, into cosmic speculations, into the schools of old and new philosophy, into the workshop and the dissecting room ; into whatever would contribute by education to the betterment of his native land, especially in this regard into Algebra and Mathematics. Nor did he disdain to help his king in war, and his country in great mining and engineering works. But as we said above, all was preparatory : a means to uncover to himself, and discover for mankind, the doctrines and disciplines lying in the science of the organization of the human form : for this is the form of forms : the divine form, the form of heaven, and the form of humanity under heaven.

I revert to say again that up to this time the spiritual cognition of the human body began and ended with Swedenborg. Since then cognizance has been manifold but unspiritual : life unrecognizable, and soul not admitted. One reason, apart from the End of the Church and the proud sensuality of the age, has been that the experimental insight into the corporeal frame of man has been more and more under medicine and surgery, and motived towards professional renown and remuneration. Trade-medicine is the death of spiritual insight into the bodily image of God which a man is. When vivisection is added to the horrors of unlimited surgery, the last connexion between medical insight, and the soul, mind and body of mankind is ruptured. So physiology through professionalism has nothing to do with men's souls, but everything with their miserable bodies and pockets. And through the annexation of physiology to medicine, the whole of the organic world from protoplasm to humanity has been treated as an outlying empire of the Physicians, and Darwin and evolution are the tyranny of it : the survival of the fittest, the strong confounding the weak. Like Solomon's seven hundred wives and three hundred concubines, natural history, penetrated by the push of all constituents from below, lies wealthy before us. This has supplied motive to live in a hopeless and death-bearing age ; and all that is won will be claimed in time to a greater than Solomon. Meanwhile present hope lies in the entry of a true Christian Religion, and in its theology becoming the proprietor of the natural body of the soul; and in its Professors annexing this great present black Africa of physiology, to their sphere of influence, to reconnect it with its proper life.

Emanuel Swedenborg was installed in this work; so that when you read his *Animal Kingdom, considered anatomically, physically, and philosophically*, you are reading of soul, mind or spirit, and body, when you are reading of the forms and functions of your organism. To be competent to this showing, he underwent representatively the discipline of Israel, the spiritual man, in Egypt from Joseph to Moses. He thought to pursue the same path on the plain of nature, and did not know for what mission the knowledges and sciences had been used to train him. But " he went out to seek his father's asses, and found a kingdom." Asses again are scientifics, where horses are understandings. And the kingdom was an open intercourse with the Lord, an opening of the spiritual sight, an opening of the spiritual sense of the Word, and of the doctrine of the Divine Human, the revelation of which is the Second Advent.

Register here then that the natural and scientific is the basis to mankind of the New Church, and that the great developments of this age in applied sciences and uses, in themselves neutral, can be preparations for an intellect descending from God out of heaven, which will lay hold of them and make them into means of influx, purging them of the Atheism which comes from below. The temptations of Egypt, the trials of materialism and its infidelities, can be the means of first riddance for the men of thought and speculation, from the Red Sea. The simple in faith will follow them not knowing that they follow, and be safe.

ASSYRIA, ASHUR.—The largest instances making history in the Jewish Dispensation lie in the transport of its nations into other lands. And now, since we have the spiritual power which commanded these movements revealed to us, and the spiritual sense of it accounting for each event, we know in the first place that the sons of Jacob and children of Israel were sent to school in Egypt before the spirit of the Ancient Church died there, that they might be imbued with the scientific principle, in order to begin to be the representation of a church. Strange, Reader, is it not, that a nation should be moved about bodily to represent a divine principle? But representation and correspondence is the veiled Cosmos, and principles not seen are the thick darkness about God. First school, and then punishment in manhood. Egypt = science ; but Assyria = reasoning. Israel = the spiritual man represented or dramatized. When this man fell before falses and into evils, he fell by reasonings against true and good principles. So ten tribes of him, Israel, were carried away bodily into Assyria, and until this was done, representation was not satisfied. The inner and outer Cosmos, Israel and Assyria, became what they really were—one ; and Israel left its simple good folks at home in Samaria, and herself never came back. She was not lost, but was eaten up by Assyria, and became of her body. Then Judah = the celestial church or man represented or dramatized. The evil into which this churchman fell was the love of dominion over souls. When this love gains the mind, it stands papally between the Lord and man, and persuades man that the church is between the Creator and the creature, and that an intermediate person as head of the Church is as God on earth. This perversion and infernal dominion against the real presence, the holiest gift to man, is Babylon. So when Judah sank representatively under this sin, and consummated it in her wicked kings, she was representatively, that is, really, carried away to Babylon, and the Divine Order enacted the correspondence, and the unity of evil and punishment was the unity of Judah and Babylon in the Babylonish Captivity. For reasons already given Judah was brought back, though Israel was not. The Scripture does not record the next event, excepting in the Lord's words as prophecy of the Last Judgment in Matthew. It was the end of Judah ; not this time by the Babylon of the Euphrates; but by the historical Babylon, Rome, which as a principle of dominion, and where the Church is treated of, as dominion over souls, is signalized throughout the Apocalypse. This was the last dispersion, and this was the final levelling of Jewish pretension and religiosity in the impartial Divine Cosmos; in which the use of the Jewish nature was reserved; as is the case with all natures while they last; that is, while the Divine Providence can make use of them in conducting humanity to a goal.

The seemingly abstract principles of good and evil are here made into broad concrete history. The supernatural is for ever the brain and nerve of the mundane story. In the Word it is the whole flesh and blood of man, and by divine appointment alone he lives and moves and has his being in it there.

Now hear Swedenborg on the spiritual signification of Assyria: "That Assyria denotes reasoning is evident from the Word. It is constantly taken for those things which are of reason in both senses; namely, for rational things, and for reasonings. By reason and rational things are properly meant those things which are true, but by reasoning and reasonings, those things which are false. Because Assyria signifies thus it is for the most part joined with Egypt, because reason and reasoning are from scientifics."—*Arcana*, n. 1186.

"Assyria signifies reasoning in Isaiah x. 5, 7, 13. 'Woe to Assyria, the rod of mine anger, he thinks not what is right and his heart meditates not what is right. He hath said, In the strength of mine hand have I done it, and in my wisdom, because I am intelligent.'"

"Nineveh signifies the falsities of doctrinals. There are three falsities of this kind from three origins. The first is the fallacies of the senses, the darkness of an understanding which is not enlightened, and ignorance. Hence the false called 'Nineveh.' The second origin is from the same

cause, but with a predominating desire either of innovating, or of being pre-eminent. The falsities thence derived are 'Rehoboth.' The third origin is of the will, thus of cupidities : the not being willing to acknowledge as truth anything but what favours cupidities. The falses thence derived are called 'Calah.' All these three kinds arise by means of 'Asshur,' or reasoning about the truths and goods of faith."
—*Ibid.* 1188.

"Assyria signifies the rational mind, as in Ezekiel xxxi. 3, 4 : 'Behold Assyria is a cedar in Lebanon, beautiful in branch, and a shady grove, and lofty in height ; and her shoot was among the thick fronds. The waters made her grow, the depth of waters exalted her, the river drawing round about the plant.' The rational is called a cedar in Lebanon."—*Ibid.* 119.

"When a man is natural he is in Egypt ; when he becomes rational he is in Assyria ; and when he becomes spiritual he is in the land of Canaan, or in the Church."— *Apoc. Expl.* n. 654.

"'In that day there shall be a path from Egypt into Assyria, so that the Assyrian may come into Egypt, and Egypt into Assyria,' signifies that then the rational will be opened for them by means of scientific truths, in order that man may view the scientific things which are of the natural man rationally, and thus intelligently. In that day Israel shall be the third with Egypt and Assyria, a blessing in the midst of the land.' This signifies influx into them both from spiritual light. Israel is the spiritual man who has light from heaven ; Egypt, the natural man who has light from the world ; and Assyria, the rational man who is midway. He receives light from the spiritual, transmits it into the natural, and enlightens it. 'Assyria, the work of my hands,' is the rational man not from himself but from the Lord."— *Ibid.* n. 654. Since the spiritual is that from which what is rational and scientific is applied to genuine truths, Israel is called the inheritance, and Assyria, the work of my hands ;

and Egypt, the blessed people, because all things are together in their ultimate, the scientific."—*Ibid.* n. 340.

This passage from the Authorized Version is as follows: "And the Lord shall smite Egypt, He shall smite and heal; and they shall return to the Lord, and He shall be entreated of them, and shall heal them. In that day shall there be a highway out of Egypt to Assyria, and the Assyrian shall come into Egypt, and the Egyptians into Assyria, and the Egyptians shall serve with the Assyrians. In that day shall Israel be the third with Egypt and with Assyria, a blessing in the midst of the land: whom the Lord of Hosts shall bless, saying, Blessed Egypt my people, and Assyria the work of my hands, and Israel mine inheritance" (Isaiah xix. 22–25).

Assyria, which we are specially considering here, is used, as shown by these extracts, in a good, and in a bad sense. The Ancient Church was established there, and the Ancient Word, and that Church underwent decline for ages, and was consummated, and then helped in the consummation of the Israelitish Church. In its later history and as we also know it from the monuments, Assyria was cruel, and 'Woe to the bloody city' is written of Nineveh in Nahum. To the modern reader, especially if he be a politician to-day, this sanguinary character may seem to militate against the signification of Assyria as in its perversion denoting or corresponding to reasoning, for reasoning is Parliament in strict definition, and how reasonable Parliament is! But looking into history, what has been more bloody on both sides than reasoning? Religious controversy and its battles, the wars of Iconoclasts with Image-Worshippers from Byzantium to Rome, from east to west in Christendom, the burning of heretics in all lands, the mutual hatreds of the three great Churches, Greek, Catholic and Protestants, and the malices of Non-conformity, are indeed an Assyria, to which, as all springing from personal power and national reasonings, we may well fear the prophet's denunciation of Nineveh, Woe to the bloody city. *Odium theologicum* is the name of this Assyria.

As an outcome of the furnace of hot reasoning, the goddess of reason was enthroned in Paris in the days of its bloody Revolution. Here was another Assyria, typically cruel, a political Assyria, after all religion was dead.

In regard to the spiritual signification of these nations, as well as to the other alleged correspondences, if his heart is not averse to the existence of such things, we counsel the reader to try them while reading the Word, to prove to himself whether they yield the sense claimed for them. Try thus Egypt, Assyria, Israel, Babylon, in their contexts, on both sides, good and evil. It was by trials that the hieroglyphic and cuneiform were confirmed as languages. Go down into Egypt here by patient experimentation. Prove and hold fast that which is good.

XL.—THE DIVINE NATURAL.

It is said in Matthew that as the women went to tell the disciples of the resurrection, "Jesus met them, saying, All hail! And they came and held Him by the feet, and worshipped Him" (xxviii. 9); and in Luke, "Jesus Himself stood in the midst of them, and saith unto them, Peace unto you. But they were terrified and affrighted, and supposed that they had seen a spirit. And He said unto them, Why are ye troubled? And why do thoughts arise in your hearts? Behold my hands, and my feet, that it is I myself: handle me, and see; for a spirit hath not flesh and bones, as ye see me have. And when He had thus spoken He showed them hands and feet. And while they yet believed not for joy, He said unto them, Have ye here any meat? And they gave Him a piece of a broiled fish, and of an honeycomb. And He took, and did eat before them" (xxiv. 36–42). The Lord proved His identity to their doubting hearts by showing

His hands and His feet as the parts where the crucifixion had left its marks. In John the Lord again showed the disciples His hands and His feet; and again specially to Thomas, who would not believe until he saw in His hands the print of the nails, and thrust his hand into His side. "Then came Jesus, the doors being shut, and stood in the midst, and said, Peace unto you. Then saith He to Thomas, Reach hither thy finger, and behold my hands; and reach hither thy hand, and thrust it into my side, and be not faithless but believing. And Thomas answered and said unto Him, My Lord and my God" (xx. 25-28).

After this Jesus again showed Himself to the disciples at the Sea of Tiberias, and caused them to take on the right side of the ship a great draught of fishes; and when they came to land, they saw a fire of coals there, and fish laid thereon, and bread, and Jesus said to them, Bring of the fish which we have now caught; which Peter obeyed; and Jesus saith unto them, Come, dine. Jesus then cometh, and taketh bread, and giveth them, and fish likewise. This is now the third time that Jesus showed Himself to His disciples after that He was risen from the dead" (John xxi. 1-15).

In these events, which happened in nature, the Lord not only proved to the doubting minds of the disciples His identity, but also that He remained a Natural Man. We nowhere read that He was seen of the Jews; the narrative is as it were in another nature, but in nature still. He "showed Himself" to whom He would. They could not themselves say, Lo here, and, Lo there, to Him; the women and the disciples did not look for Him; in the instances of being seen, He "showed Himself," that is, revealed Himself. He came in when the doors were shut, and stood in the midst; not through material obstacles; for there were none such. Yet He was a Natural Man. He rose from the tomb as such. We men are raised from our graves as spirits, leaving the body to decay, and quitting our natural materiated frame for ever. To angelic and human sight He left nothing in the sepulchre except the linen-clothes, and the folded napkin of the head. And He thought it good to preach "that a spirit hath not flesh and bones as ye see Me have:" and to confirm this as a divine announcement, proving it to two senses, sight and touch.

Herein we see the consummated end of the Incarnation; the Lord having made the Word flesh, that is, natural flesh; that is, in Him, Divine Flesh: having glorified His humanity; having put on the Divine Natural and the Divine Sensual. So He is the Divine and Infinite Man in fulness and power, in sentient infinitude and omnipotent natural will. So in Him dwelleth all the fulness of the Godhead *bodily*.

The only thing rejected was what Swedenborg denominates *the Corporeal*, that which makes our bodies and minds limited and extant: the dead matter which fixes us men to a spot of ground, and imprisons us in a covering which enters into all our thoughts and feelings, and tells us that we are finite; the mind being imbued with the consciousness of this dead experience; and the memory sealed up to it. If we lost this here or hereafter we should have no basis, but should be instantly annihilated. In our spiritual world it is made *latent*, as an invisible and unrecognized stratum under us; and being latent, the mind after death, in the heavens, partakes of the spiritual realm, and the Lord's mercy and gift there makes the love and wisdom adopted into the character into a moving image and likeness of the Infinite and the Eternal. But the fixity of the corporeal man must be stable at the lower end, or the Lord's gift would have no permanent matrix to inhere in. Immortality is only possible by having its everlasting ground in a first and past mortality.

The whole of this narrative is adapted, by plain declarations, and by speaking correspondences, to teach us women and men,—the women were first with Him when He rose; and first of all Mary Magdalene,—that the Lord after Death, and in His resurrection-body, was in nature, was a natural man. He demonstrated this by another sign than mere sight and hearing; He took dinner with the fishermen, His disciples. It is recorded in three gospels that He ate before them, or with them. He supped with two disciples going to Emmaus; having joined them on the way; their eyes being holden that they should not know Him. "And it came to pass as He sat at meat with them, He took bread, and blessed it, and break, and gave to them, and their eyes were opened, and they knew Him, and He vanished out of their sight" (Luke xxiv. 30, 31). The spiritual sense of breaking bread, and giving to them, is "instruction in the good and truth of faith, through which the Lord appears" (*Arcana*, 9412).

Note.—The Author possesses an engraving from Rubens (date 1643) representing the Supper at Emmaus, with an inscription much in keeping with the doctrine of the Divine Natural inculcated here:—

> Mihi quantus ignis torret? inæstuas
> Amore quanto? Substituit Deum.
> Deum reponit. Mira rerum
> Vox opifex, taciturna vulgo:
> Audita cœlo: manibus impiis
> Horrenda: nobis gratior: se obtulit
> Interminatus: quo locorum
> Insideat, fugo suspicari.

Translation.

How great a fire burns within me!
How great a tide of love swells in Thee!—
He has made Himself as God!
He brings God back!
Voice wonderful, Creator of all things!
Not spoken to the world;
Heard in heaven;
Terrible to the impious crew.
Too gracious to us-ward.
He shows no bounds to His dominion.
I forbear to look up to the seat where His throne may be.

Now let us further hear Swedenborg where he opens the passages in the Word concerning what the Lord ate, as recorded in Matthew and in John. First as to fishes generally. "The reason why the 'creatures of the sea,' or fishes, signify scientifics, is that the sea signifies the natural man. So the fishes in the sea are the scientifics themselves which are in the natural man. . . . Spirits who are not in spiritual truths, but only in natural ones, which are scientifics, appear in seas, and when looked at by those who are above, as fishes : it is their thoughts which proceed from the scientifics which they hold, which so appear. . . . The ideas of those who are natural and think from scientifics only are turned into the forms of fishes" (*Apoc. Expl.* n. 513).

"The honeycomb and the broiled fish which the Lord ate after His resurrection, signify the external sense of the Word; the honeycomb its pleasantness" (*Ibid.* n. 619). "The broiled fish signify the natural as to truth from good." In the correspondence they representatively absorbed the truth that He was a natural man; they had dined with Him as such, and His resurrection was not to disprove it for the disciples representing the Christian Church.

He was the same Divine Natural Man in heaven and above the heavens, as then on earth.

Again we read : "The like things are signified by the catching of fishes by the disciples after the Lord's Resurrection. The reason why the Lord manifested Himself while they were fishing, was, that to fish signifies to teach the knowledges of truth and good, and thus to reform. By the little fish upon the hearth was signified the knowledge of truth from good; by the little fish, the knowledge of truth ; and by the hearth or fire, good. At that time there were no spiritual men, because the Church was completely vastated, but all were natural; and the reformation of these latter was represented by that fishing (*piscatura*), and also by the fish upon the hearth" (*Apoc. Expl.* n. 513). "The first animate things in the [human] creation of the fifth day in Genesis are called the fishes of the sea and the birds of the heavens" (*Arcana*, n. 11).

"He who knows that such people and things are signified by fishes can see why the Lord chose fishermen for His disciples, and said, 'I will make you fishers of men.' Also why the disciples by the Lord's blessing caught a vast multitude of fishes. Why the Lord caused the tribute to be paid from the fish. And why, after His resurrection, He gave the disciples fish and bread to eat, and commanded them to preach the gospel to *every creature ;* for the nations they converted were in general truths only, and in natural truth more than in spiritual" (*Apocalypse Revealed*, n. 405).

"Peter's taking a fish out of the sea, and finding in its mouth a piece of money, which he gave for the tribute, represented that the lowest natural, as a thing that serves, would do this ; for fishes signify this natural" (*Arcana*, n. 6394).

Swedenborg, speaking of himself, says : "I was once asked, 'How I, at first a philosopher, became a theologian?' I replied, 'In the same manner that fishermen became the disciples and apostles of the Lord.' I added that I also from early youth had been a spiritual fisherman. My inquirer then asked what I meant by a spiritual fisherman? To which I answered, 'A fisherman in the spiritual sense of the Word is a man who investigates and teaches natural truths, and afterwards spiritual truths in a rational manner.' He enquired how this is demonstrated. I said, From these passages, ' The waters shall fail from the sea, and the rivers shall be wasted and dried up. Therefore the fishers shall mourn, and all that cast a hook into the sea shall lament ' (Isaiah xix. 5, 8). And respecting the sea whose waters are healed, 'The fishers shall stand from Engedi even unto Eneglaim ; they shall be a place to spread forth nets ; their fish shall be according to their kinds, as the fish of the great sea, exceeding many' (Ezekiel xlvii. 10). Also this, 'Behold

I will send for many fishers, saith Jehovah, and they shall fish them' (Jeremiah xvi. 16). Hence it is evident why the Lord chose fishermen for His disciples, and said, 'Follow Me, and I will make you fishers of men' (Matthew iv. 18, 19; Mark i. 16, 17). And why He said to Peter, after he had caught a great multitude of fishes, 'From henceforth thou shalt catch men' (Luke v. 6, 10). I then demonstrated the origin of this signification of fishermen from the *Apocalypse Revealed*, thus :—As water signifies natural truths, as also does a river, so a fish signifies those who are in possession of natural truths; whence fishermen are those who investigate and teach the truth. On hearing this, my questioner raised his voice and said, 'Now I can understand why the Lord called and chose fishermen to be His disciples; and therefore I do not wonder that He has also called and chosen you; since, as you observed, you were from early youth a fisherman in a spiritual sense, that is, an investigator of natural truths. You are now become an investigator of spiritual truths, because these latter are founded upon the former.' To this he added, being a man of reason, 'The Lord alone knows who is the proper person to apprehend and teach or communicate the truths which should be revealed for His New Church; and whether such person is to be found among the dignitaries of the Church, or among their domestic servants.' . . . He concluded by saying, 'Since you are become a divine, explain what is your system of Divinity.' I answered, These are its two principles, 'THAT GOD IS ONE, and THAT THERE IS CONJUNCTION OF CHARITY AND FAITH.' 'Who denies these principles?' said he. I rejoined, 'The Divinity of the present day when interiorly examined'" (*The Intercourse between the Soul and the Body*, n. 20).

These texts from the Word, and explications of the spiritual sense by Swedenborg, furnish a cumulative evidence that fish, fishing, and fishermen have a subjective spiritual meaning in both the Old and the New Testaments, and that

that meaning gathers itself up in the great draught of fishes taken by the disciples, and again by Peter, the truth of faith, when the Lord commanded it after His resurrection. All the circumstances of the narrative in Luke xxiv. not only cohere but conjoin as it were in a living mathematical teaching or doctrine. The Christian Church takes little notice of such evidences of the Divinity of the Word. All we have found in Kitto's *Cyclopædia of Biblical Literature*, under the article *Fish*, is, " That on the walls of the oldest Catacombs of Rome the representation of the $IX\Theta Y\Sigma$ (Ichthus) is frequently discernible, and always interpreted as an emblem of the Saviour." In my work, *Oannes according to Berosus*, I dealt at some length with this subject, and show that the signification of fishes from the records of the Ancient Church, was what Swedenborg declares to-day; and that Oannes, the fish man, came from the Erythrean sea to teach the Babylonians in their first and better days the truths of the Word and of life.

Rational men must be caught, at first netted, by natural truths, for they are fishes in the sea, and at sea, immersed in the strong naturalism of the age. Even the scientisms with no fish in them are a flood needful to drown the falses of the vastated Church. We are living in the end of the Church: its dead body so afflicts many ardent scientific minds as to force them into denial of the Word. To them we appeal with the spiritual sense. To them the knowledge of the Divine Natural is especially necessary. It will enable them to see God in Christ, and Christ now through a revealed rationality, and as not only the Divine Infinite of Theology, but as the Divine-Human Infinite of Sacred History.

The Lord in the process of His glorification, and before He had put off the corporeal, appears as a Man in History, and thereby has given, and still gives, a fixed object of love and worship, which is confirmed, and cannot be abolished, in the natural mind. He is our God, and we are invited to be His mother and His brethren. And our love must be translated also into intellectual faith. For His divine is illimitable. He is One above the heavens, divine in heaven, divine celestial, divine spiritual; and in heaven and on earth, divine natural. There is no duality or trinity of persons here, but He is one Man. He is Creator, Redeemer, and Saviour. Of His Creatorship we read in Swedenborg: "Commit your thought to the angelic idea of God as a Man, and remove as much as you are able the idea of space, and you will approximate in thought to the truth. . . . God, who appears far above the spiritual world as a Sun, to whom there can be no appearance of space, is not to be thought of from space. On this condition it can be comprehended that He created the universe not out of nothing, but out of Himself. Also that His Human Body cannot be thought of as great or small, or of any stature, because this also attributes space; and hence it is that He is the same in the first things and in the last, and in the greatest things and the least, and moreover that the human is the inmost in every created thing, but apart from space. . . . In God there is Love and Wisdom, there is Mercy and Clemency, absolute Goodness and Truth, because these things are from Him. . . . No one of these things is possible apart from man; man is their subject; and to separate them from their subject is to say that they are not" (*Divine Love and Wisdom*, n. 285, 286).

So now we understand that the Lord in Jesus Christ gives us a fixed object of Divine Worship before, and hence after, His Resurrection and Ascension; and when He had put off the spatial corporeal, that He revealed Himself as the infinite natural, not as a spirit but as a man, "For a Spirit has not flesh and bones as ye see *Me* have." He came into their midst when the doors were shut. He showed Himself to them as He would. He held back their eyes from knowing Him when present with them. He was known to them in the breaking of bread, and vanished out of their sight. He talked with them face to face, and yet "He said unto them, 'These the words which I spake unto you *while I was yet with you*, that all things must be fulfilled which were written in the Law of Moses, and in the Prophets, and in the Psalms concerning Me' (Luke xxiv. 44). And He declared His immediate Presence and Omnipresence to them as to His Church to come, in saying, And Behold, 'I am with you all the days up to the Consummation of the Æon. So be it'" (Matthew xxviii. 20). He had every quality we conceive of spirit, and yet was a Divine Natural Man.

As in His appearances, so in His disappearance. Of this last event there is no record in Matthew, but that "after the Chief Priests had given the soldiers money to say that His disciples came by night and stole Him away while we slept,— that then the disciples went away into Galilee, into a mountain where Jesus had appointed them; and when they saw Him, they worshipped Him, but some doubted. And Jesus came and spake unto them saying, All power is given unto *Me* in heaven and in earth." In Mark it is said, "So then after the Lord had spoken to them, He was received up into heaven, and sat on the right hand of God." In Luke, "And He led them out as far as to Bethany, and He lifted up His hands and blessed them. And it came to pass while He blessed them, He was parted from them, and carried up into heaven."

So after His Resurrection the Divine Natural Man did not appear as an object of vision except when He *made Himself visible*, and at the last disappeared when He was parted from them and received up into heaven. His pictorial ascension making beautiful our Cathedrals, helps many natural minds, and is of good use; but the Word has a spiritual view, and the Lord is parted from us, and no longer visible, when His light and love transcend all our faculties. It is even so with all revelations, nay with all subjects; when they exceed our capacity, they are "in the shade of our thoughts," and they vanish from our lost attention. The Lord in All

Power sits on the right hand of God; spiritually again, the Omnipotence of divine truth is signalized. The Divine Man as one of ourselves before His death, in memory and thought intercedes between our unbelief and the divinity which He is after His resurrection and ascension. But in both characters He abolishes fear, which accompanies the manifestation of a spirit, by His Real Presence as a Divine Natural Man.

What further was done by these representatives : by the Lord eating with the disciples ; by His causing the great draught of fishes ; by His showing Himself to them, and vanishing from their midst ? By creating a new natural faith in the minds of the women and the disciples, He founded the infancy of a Church which became a support in the world to the Ancient Heavens. He also fulfilled the Word, dictating to the Evangelists and again to John in the Apocalypse, a plain natural Logos, nowhere written without a parable, and therefore with a spiritual meaning and universal correspondence in it for the heavens, and a doctrine and natural message for men. So He fulfilled the Word, not only by obeying it, but by completing it in Himself and in His contract and legacy, the New Testament.

The Lord put aside by His own right hand and His holy arm the Jewish nature which He took upon Him by being born of Blessed Mary ; and therein He glorified His humanity, and made it divine. Was this consummated when He said as in Matthew, " My God, my God, why hast Thou forsaken Me ?"? Was this the last struggle with the maternal humanity, and the last state of humiliation ? In Mark He spoke the same words, and "cried again with a loud voice, and yielded up the ghost." In Luke it is further written : " When He had cried with a loud voice, He said, Father, into Thy hands I commend my spirit, and having said thus, He gave up the ghost. And knowing that all things were now accomplished, that the Scripture might be fulfilled, He saith, I thirst. Now there was set a vessel full of vinegar; and they filled a sponge with vinegar, and put it upon hyssop, and put it to His mouth. When Jesus therefore had received the vinegar, He said, It is finished: and He bowed His head, and gave up the ghost." Note also His declaration in John x. 17, 18, "Therefore doth my Father love Me, because I lay down My life, that I might take it again. No man taketh it from Me, but I lay it down of myself. I have power to lay it down, and I have power to take it again. This commandment have I received of my Father."

Was the Divine Natural accomplished in the Lord in putting aside the Jewish nature? This He put off in His life in Judea. In His death and resurrection He rejected the elemental man which is necessary to our existence and subsistence in this world; the case of matter which fixes us here, and by which we mean the limitaneous substances and laws of nature. He rose with His own divine body, His virtue, and with nothing else. *We* have need to be clothed with matters and substances derived from the dead fire of the sun of this world. It gives us fixed memory and personal ego and identity. Our two memories, the outward memory of the deeds done in the body, the inward, of the account and balances of conscience, are our book of Life, according to which we are judged; and become permanent characters for good or for evil. The Lord had no such Book of Life, but the Word which He fulfilled. So the substances and matters which once formed a part of the body derived from the mother were rejected because they had no function and no Use. So the Lord first put off Jewish Nature, and conquered heaven and hell and the world thereby, and then by His own Merit, He put off by death· whatever was dead in fixed nature, and added the natural degree to His Divine Life, becoming a Divine Natural Man.

AND THE OLD JERUSALEM. 141

XLI.—THE CANON OF THE WORD.

We have seen throughout that the Word is characterized by the possession of a spiritual sense, which has been revealed, and demonstrates its divinity. It is also important where our belief in Holy Scripture comes in question, to find corroboration from another point of view, which however leads up to fundamentally the same demonstration. We have again to travel over the sacred ground of Luke, and to listen to the Lord on the walk to Emmaus, and at the supper there. In a *Review of the World's Religious Congresses*, by the Rev. L. P. Mercer of Chicago, which that enlightened New Churchman has sent me, I find a valuable paper by the Rev. Frank Sewall of Washington. In the course of this lucid document, he says : " The Christian Scripture, the Holy Bible, is written in two parts, the Old and the New Testament. In the interval of time between the writing of these two parts, the divine truth and essential Word, which in the beginning was with God, and was God, became incarnate on our earth in the person of our Lord Jesus Christ, He, . . . 'the true light that lighteth every man that cometh into the world,' placed the seal of divine authority upon certain of the then existing sacred scriptures. He thus forever fixed the divine canon of that portion of the written Word."

"The Divine Canon is declared by Him where He says : '*All things* must be fulfilled which were written in the law of Moses, and in the Prophets, and in the Psalms concerning me.' And further: 'O fools, and slow of heart to believe all that the Prophets have spoken ; and beginning at Moses and all the Prophets, He expounded unto them in all the Scriptures *things concerning Himself.*' The Scriptures of the Old Testament thus enumerated as testifying of Him and as being fulfilled in Him embrace two of the three divisions into which the Jews at that time divided their sacred books. These two are the Law (Torah), or the five books of Moses, so called; and the Prophets (Nebiim). Of the books contained in the third division of the Jewish Canon, known as the Kethubim or other writings, our Lord recognizes but two: He names by title the Psalms; and in Matthew xxiv. 15, when predicting the consummation of the age, and His own Second Coming, he cites the Prophecy of Daniel. . . In the words of Jesus Christ the Canon of the Word is established in a twofold manner. First, intrinsically . . Second, specifically, by naming the books under the three divisions, the Law, the Prophets and the Psalms. The Canon in this sense comprises the five books of Moses or the Law; the books of Joshua, the Judges, First and Second Samuel, First and Second Kings, or the so-called earlier Prophets; the later including the four great and the twelve minor prophets; and finally the Book of Psalms. The other books of the Old Testament are Apocrypha."

"These divine books, besides being thus set apart by Christ, declare themselves to be the Word of the Lord in the sense of being actually spoken by the Lord, and so constituting a divine language."

The writer proceeds to give scriptural and rational evidence to show that the Gospels and the Apocalypse are part of the Word. "Only to these books could one presume to apply the words written at the close of the Apocalypse, and applying immediately to it: 'If any man shall take away from the words of the prophecy of this book, God shall take away his part out of the book of life, and out of the Holy City, and from the things which are written in this book!'"

Good bread this of yours, dear brother Sewall, in the great Hall of the "RELIGIOUS SYMPOSIUM."

XLII.—THE FOUR GOSPELS.

Believing these canonical books of the New Testament to be literally divine, and knowing that they vary in their accounts of the same occurrences, we may fairly ask How far are they historical? We need not cite the apparent dissimilarities in the four narratives. Learned Christians have sought to reconcile the divergent statements, and so to establish a "Harmony of the Gospels."

May the truth be that the Gospels embrace what is called history, but are not limited by it, or included in it, and that hence they are not in any ordinary sense critically historical? If we look closely at it, there is no such thing as fixed history; every event of the day, even every photograph, though definite as nature, depends on its point of view, and every variation of this gives a new portrait, as it were another event, another face, a different place. History lives upon research and discrimination, upon a many-motived love of old facts about nations and peoples, with a delight in filling up each *hiatus*, as *maxime deflendus!* It craves accumulations, and its greatest works and authors differ, even clash, concerning actual events, but more entirely about the interpretation, consequences, and the good or evil, of men and things in the past. For History is made of the voices and verdicts of the Historians. To Suetonius, the Emperor Tiberius is a monster of iniquity; to Velleius Paterculus, a true man at first; and to a class of learned historians to-day, a great ruler consistent throughout to his early fame. To Cicero, Julius Cæsar is a destroyer of virtue and liberty; to Froude, he is a supreme man, a Cæsar indeed, an author and perpetuator of Roman greatness. To Sallust, Catiline is a cruel, remorseless rebel; to a liberal professor to-day, he is a noble and injured gentleman, led into revolt by faction, injustice, and contumely. The secular historian, looking for flesh wherewith to cover the bones of the past, never has enough of new and curious traits; for history would fain accomplish the impossible in giving itself a fixed reality alien to the temporalities of this world.

Shall we be wrong in agreeing with Carlyle that Shakespeare was the greatest of our historical geniuses, because he was a poet of poets. If this be allowed, the recording scribe stands aside, and a higher and more liberal faculty presents another ideal of scripture suggested by imagination, and by *art and its perspective.*

That new ideal may help us to come nearer to the method of the Word. Here we mean the Gospels especially, because, treating of one Life and one Person, they give us different accounts of the same event and apparently contradictory particulars. We select an instance which occurs in all the four Gospels. It concerns the crucifixion and the two robbers who suffered with Jesus.

It is written in Matthew: " Then are there two robbers crucified with Him, one on the right hand, and one on the left. And they that passed by railed on Him, wagging their heads. Likewise also the chief priests mocking, with the scribes and elders said, He saved others, Himself he cannot save. He trusted in God; let Him deliver him now, if He will have him; for he said, I am the Son of God. And the robbers also that were crucified with him, cast upon him the same reproach " (xxvii. 38, 39, 41–44).

In Mark: "And with him they crucify two robbers; the one on his right hand, and the other on his left, and the Scripture was fulfilled which saith, And he was numbered with the transgressors. . . . And they that were crucified with him reviled him " (xv. 27, 28, 32).

In the first place, consider these narratives as independent texts, as written from the internal sense downwards, and as containing internal history as well as external. The crucifixion itself took place, and was written of among other important ends to fulfil prophecy. As witness these declarations: "After this Jesus knowing that all things were now accomplished, that the scripture might be fulfilled, saith, I thirst." "The scripture was fulfilled which saith, He was numbered with the transgressors." " These things were done that the scripture should be fulfilled, A bone of Him shall not be broken. And again another scripture saith,

They shall look on him whom they pierced." These things declare the end and purpose of the narrative, that the True Christian portion of the Word might be written. We have dwelt on the office of the Word as ministering to those who read it worthily the conjunction of earth with heaven; the conjunction of the church above with the church below; the conjunction of men with angels. For this and in this the scripture is fulfilled. The ancient and the modern heavens are linked in the fulfilments. Thereby deep calleth unto deep.

Let us then regard these fourfold scriptures as each filled with its own internal sense, and as written to exhibit it. And let us endeavour to see something of that sense in each case.

"The passion of the Cross was the last of the Lord's temptations, through which He fully united the human to the divine, and the divine to the human. Through the passion of the cross He did not take away sins, but carried them." "The Lord in the midst" represented the crucifixion in Himself of the Jewish nature which died on the cross, and was put aside and rejected. The crucifixion of the malefactors represented the rejection of the Jewish Church: the end of Jehovah's contract and covenant with Judah, the end of the Æon. It terminated there and then. The narrative in Matthew is fulfilled with details, history within history. The two robbers come after the soldiers who set up over his head his accusation written, THIS IS JESUS THE KING OF THE JEWS. One robber on the right hand, and another on the left. These now are dominants in the spiritual sense. The robber on the right hand represents the evil of the Jewish Church, the robber on the left hand represents its falsity. It had robbed the Lord of all His attributes = the evil side; and triumphed in the accomplished end = the false.

They that passed by reviled Him, wagging their heads; and saying, Thou that destroyest the Temple, and buildest in three days, save Thyself. If Thou be the Son of

K

God, come down from the Cross. These are the external men of the Jewish Church; its evil side, of which unbelieving Thomas was the good side: the scientists of the Crucifixion. Wagging their heads = scepticism idiotic with cunning sensuality. To prove that the Divine Martyr was the Son of God, they asked Him to come down from the Cross, and save *Himself.* See Renan's *Vie de Jesus.* He who was voluntarily dying to save the world!

"Likewise also the chief priests mocking, with the scribes and elders, said, He saved others, Himself He cannot save." Here the chief priests, the heads of the Jewish Ecclesiasticism, the scribes, the custodians of the written Law, and the elders, the official rulers of the people, assailed Him with hypocrisies, evil goods, and lying truths. For the Jewish Church in representative conclave admitted His miraculous deeds of good, and also that being Salvation Himself He cannot be saved. They also asked Him to falsify Himself by making Himself the King of Israel, that by coming down from the cross they might believe in Him. He trusted in God; let Him deliver Him now, if He will have Him; for He said, I am the Son of God. They admitted His trust in God as His Father, and mocked at it, and prescribed the conditions under which He would be acknowledged as a divinity, the Son of God. And the robbers also that were crucified with Him cast upon Him the same reproach. The robbers were orthodox in the same Ecclesiasticism, and subscribed the articles of the passers-by, and of the chief priests, elders, and scribes. As the ultimate confirmation of this state, they represented the whole Jewish Church in defection and consummation. "Now from the sixth hour there was darkness over all the land until the ninth hour." The land here is the representative Jewish Church. The darkness is of the hells opened, and the Sun of Righteousness eclipsed. From the sixth hour to the ninth hour is the end of Christ's passion, and in that end the loud voice wherewith He yielded up the ghost.

AND THE OLD JERUSALEM. 147

Observe the completeness with which in few words the whole Jewish dispensation, under the Babylon of Rome, the king-maker, is brought into a final unity, and is all upon the cross, and its litany of blasphemy inaugurated; and then is summed up in the two robbers. After the soldiers' superscription of accusation, the whole sense evolves from the words, *Then* were there two robbers crucified with Him. These embracive robbers were also the passers-by, the chief priests, the scribes, and the elders, and most significative yet, and last and least, the condemned twain themselves. They were the clerks who said Amen to the chief priests, scribes, and elders. A synagogue of Satan.

Nearly the same words are used in the Gospel according to Mark; it is also said regarding His crucifixion with a robber on one side, and a robber on the other, that herein "the scripture was fulfilled which saith, And He was numbered with the transgressors." The occurrence of an almost identical text in the two first Gospels is a testimony of two witnesses to the weight of the letter here. The condemnation and rejection of the Jewish Church is the sum of it. These synoptical accounts seem to be the ultimate or lowest degree of the fourfold Evangel.

In Luke we have another elevation. Its letter is thus: " And there were also two others, malefactors, led with Him to be put to death; and when they came into the place which is called The Skull, there they crucified Him, and the malefactors, one on the right hand, and the other on the left. And Jesus said, Father, forgive them, for they know not what they do. And parting His garments among them, they cast lots. And the people stood beholding. And the rulers also scoffed at Him, saying, He saved others; let Him save Himself, if this is the Christ of God, His chosen. And the soldiers also mocked Him, coming to Him, offering Him vinegar, and saying, If thou art the King of the Jews, save Thyself. And there was also a superscription over Him, THIS IS THE KING OF THE JEWS. And one of the malefactors which were hanged, railed on Him, saying, Art not Thou the Christ? Save Thyself and us. But the other answered, and rebuking him, said, Dost thou not even fear God, seeing thou art in the same condemnation? And we indeed justly; for we receive the due reward of our deeds: but this man hath done nothing amiss. And he said, Jesus, remember me when Thou comest into Thy kingdom. And He said unto him, Verily I say unto thee, To-day shalt thou be with Me in Paradise" (xxiii. 32–43).

This account is a milder indictment against the Jews, and has in its midst the words, " Father, forgive them, for they know not what they do." The rulers also, as unbelieving Jews, had ordinary natural reason with them in saying, He saved others, that is, we admit so much; but now, as ourselves the greatest authorities here, let him give us crowning proof, let him save himself if this is the Christ of God, His chosen. We have been His chosen people; and God has done miracles for us: Why cannot this man if He is the Son of God? Here, if they had not first crucified Him, they were within Jewish rationality. The malefactor also behaved with great naturalness, and something like faith, when he said, Art not thou the Christ? Save Thyself and us. The Jews demanded proof positive, not knowing that there was a divine reason opposing their sensual reason. The malefactor on one side demanded to be saved from the consequences of his guilt, including the desire that his fellows crucified with him should also be miraculously released. The worst of him was that he knew he was guilty, and was not conscience-stricken; and perhaps echoed the chief priests with a purpose. The other malefactor owned to his ill-doing, and had the heart to rebuke his fellow, and to tell him to fear even God, seeing that death, and meeting with God, was before him. And instead of asking of the Lord to be saved from the cross, he besought to be remembered by Jesus when He comes into His Kingdom.

Each interpretation of the Word rises from the internal

historical sense where events are recorded, to a deeper internal sense in which the persons disappear, and the spiritual states which they signify remain. Perhaps a single compound state is portrayed where several persons are named, just as one individual man may have several differing and even warring elements in action within him at the same time. In the Word these may be represented by various persons. In Matthew and Mark the Jewish Church in all its hierarchy converged at last to the two robbers who were crucified with Jesus ; and these two are one mind, which represents the evil and falsity that robs the Lord of His rule in the soul, and crucifies Him.

In Luke, in the third crucifixion, another letter has other life in it. Light is divided from darkness as in the Book of Creation. The Lord is about to ordain a singular remnant of the Jewish Church. In the one perception of the Messiah-ship, and in its recognition of the awe of Messiah on the cross,—a faith rare and exemplary,—the malefactors, who are one in condemnation, represent repentance on the one hand, and evil rejected on the other, like the butler and the baker whose dreams were interpreted by Joseph. 'Lord, remember me when thou comest into Thy Kingdom,' is a plain recognition of Jesus on the cross as the Messiah, and that His kingdom is not of this present world, and yet, according to the natural mind of the Jew, it is to be a kingdom somewhere. The disciples showed the same mind when they disputed who should be greatest in His kingdom, when a little child was set in the midst. This illustrates the use of the Messianic promise to the Jews, and its working where their faith is real, to exact a belief in a future life ; not a myth of heathen immortality learnt in the Babylonish captivity ; but a hope beaming from their own scriptures when hard times press them and mortality is closing round.

The rejection of some conspicuous evil from the heredities of the Judaism which even here from the cross was to be inserted into the Life of the future, is represented by the penitent malefactor rebuking his fellow in crime, pointing him to God, confessing the sin of both, and the justice of their punishment, and telling him that He who is in their midst, on the cross, had done no wrong. The preservation of Judaism recognizing its Messiah is presently indicated here. And its self-love, believing that it is still the chosen people, malefactor as it is in one sense, keeps it to its own piety, and leads it to represent the custody of its Messianic Word. The promise by Jesus, " Verily I say, This day shalt thou be with Me in Paradise," signifies a state of the Christian Church, derived from the Jewish, in which the Messianic promises must be long held in a literal sense before anything spiritual can be received. Other things might perhaps be taught in this third Crucifixion to Christians, such as immediate resurrection after death ; but such resurrection is only bodily. 'This day' is *this your state*, and rather signifies that a repentance having the promise of remission of sins, is the way to heaven ;. that the beginning of it is accepted by the Lord ; and that persistence in it is the way onward. As long as the state lasts, the paradise-promise accompanies it. Under these conditions fulfilled "this day" involves for ever.

The railing or blaspheming of the recalcitrant malefactor expresses the evil which was rejected. He said to Jesus, "If Thou art the Christ, save Thyself and us." Another reading is, "Art Thou not the Christ ? Save Thyself and us." This infidelity of state follows the same demand made by the rulers, the people, and the soldiers. The malefactor repeats almost their words, but includes himself and his companion. The rulers said, " He saved others, let Him save Himself if He be the Christ, the chosen of God ! " The soldiers said, "If Thou be the King of the Jews, save Thyself." " And a superscription also was written over Him, in letters of Greek, and Latin, and Hebrew, THIS IS THE KING OF THE JEWS." The malefactor's appeal to the Christ to prove His Messiahship by saving those who were being crucified, is here in the text ; for Christ stands for the Messiah, the Anointed, the King. Again, as in Matthew and Mark, the Jewish Church represented on the cross converges to an ultimatum, but now towards the single malefactor who desires to be saved in his sins. Christ's silence to his petition represents rejection of this evil falsity scandalizing the cross. It rebukes all Churches which base religion on any other foundation than reform of personal character through regeneration of the heart.

Finally, the words exchanged between the malefactors represent the rending in twain of the Jewish Church from the top to the bottom. The passage between the contrite male factor and Jesus is the remnant represented by "this day" or state imported into the first Christian Church.

In John's Gospel we have a fourth Word about the crucifixion. By consent of many pious readers of the Bible, this Gospel is higher on the mountains of Revelation than Matthew, Mark, and Luke. Edmund Sears, in a delightful book, dares to name it THE HEART OF CHRIST.

"In the beginning was the Word, and the Word was with God, and the Word was God. The same was in the beginning with God. All things were made by Him, and without Him was not anything made that was made. In Him was Life, and the Life was the light of men. And the light shineth in darkness; and the darkness comprehended it not. And the Word was made flesh and dwelt among us, and we beheld His glory, the glory as of the only begotten of the Father, full of grace and truth" (chap i.).

This exordium is in complement and contrast to the genealogy of Christ in Matthew from Abraham to David and from David to Joseph the husband of Mary; and to the genealogy in Luke from Joseph, the "supposed" father of Christ, upwards to Adam the Son of God. In John there is no genealogy but "the divinity, humanity, and office" of the Lord. This is concrete theology, corresponding to the concrete creation of the spiritual heavens and the spiritual earth in Genesis; the Word—God said—being the agent there, and the Word with God and being God in John here.

These particulars prepare the mind for a different dictation and inspiration of the letter in the Fourth Gospel. In Matthew and Mark the natural side is more represented, in Luke the spiritual side, in John the celestial side.

Let us attend diligently to the Divine letter now in especial reference to the circumstances of the fourth crucifixion.

"And it was the preparation of the Passover, and about the sixth hour : and he (Pilate) saith unto the Jews, Behold your King! But they cried out, Away with Him, away with Him, crucify Him. Pilate saith unto them, Shall I crucify your King? The Chief Priests answered, We have no king but Cæsar. Then delivered he Him therefore unto them to be crucified. And they took Jesus and led away. And He bearing His cross went forth into a place called from a skull, which is in the Hebrew, Golgotha. Where they crucified Him, and two other with Him, on either side one, and Jesus in the midst. Then the soldiers, when they had crucified Jesus, took His garments, and made four parts, to every soldier a part ; and also His coat. Now the coat was without seam, woven from the top throughout. They said therefore among themselves, Let us not rend it, but cast lots for it, whose it shall be : that the Scripture might be fulfilled, which saith, They parted my raiment among them, and for my vesture they did cast lots. These things therefore the soldiers did. Now there stood by the Cross of Jesus, His mother, and His mother's sister, Mary the wife of Cleophas, and Mary Magdalene. When Jesus therefore saw His mother, and the disciple standing by whom He loved, He saith unto His mother, Woman, behold thy son. Then saith He to the disciple, Behold thy mother! And from that hour that disciple took her unto his own" (xix. 13-18, 23-27.)

In the natural sense the first malignity of the Jewish rulers and people gives place in this Gospel to charges of blasphemy in making Himself the Son of God, and of treason in not denying that He was their King. The rage of the Jews against Him is more represented here than in the other Evangelists; and Pilate's conscience, his expostulation with the Chief Priests, and his longing to save Jesus, are strongly written down.

The Jews crucified Him and two other with Him, on either side one.

All that Christ underwent was representative of the state of the Jewish Church. The crucifixion represented in bodily cruelty the hatred of the Jews to the Divine Truth, which their evils murdered in themselves. He, the Lord, suffered all things and the passion of the cross at their hands. Herein He resisted not evil. On the other hand His assertion of His own power and kingdom over His own people, and over the sick, the poor, the needy, the dying, and the dead, was absolute. The miracles which He did were of this omnipotence. Because He had come into the Jewish race, nation, and Church, He Himself took on Him both characters; of representing Jewish evil and wrong by suffering their inflictions and not resisting, and also of manifesting divine authority in the Judea and world which He had made, and which knew Him not. His own natural mind, which was as one of ours at first, underwent states of humiliation in which His Godhead was obscured to His humanity; and then states of glorification when some word of the Father in Him was made flesh by His virtue, and became a divine nature. These remembrances may help the reader to expect that the internal sense of the Word, especially where the tragedy and judgment of the human universe are spoken forth, contains unexpected revealings.

Observe therefore first that the robbers of Matthew and Mark, and the malefactors of Luke, are not extant in John's Gospel. If we were dealing with history written by man without being also inspired and dictated by God, we should justly say at once that of course what one Gospel has said is clearly implied in the series of the same events, whether it be stated or not, in the others. And therefore that the two crucified with the Lord are identical throughout. But the internal sense which lives only within the verbal and iotal literal sense forbids any historical treatment of the kind. John's Gospel has no malefactors here, such as those of the first Gospels, and this for spiritual reasons. The difference of the robbers of Matthew and Mark from the malefactors of Luke, proves that rules of circumstantial evidence from Gospel to Gospel are inadmissible in dealing with the Word.

As Jesus took up His cross that His divine natural humanity might be purged of all inherited Jewish nature, that He might die to it; and as we also are to submit to the same discipline in our finite degree, in order that our characters may be subdued into consonance with heavenly order, so this our crucifixion beside Him cannot fail to be represented in all the Gospels. Crosses are in the path of life : calamities for the wicked, afflictions helping regeneration for the good. The soul who knows Christ, and follows Him, must undergo His cross ; not only bear it in the sense of carrying it to the place of a skull and then going his way in the day's life ; but also in measuring His affections and thoughts, His works or hands, His ways or feet upon it ; and by binding or nailing these to its confines, make them conform to the two commands of love to God and the neighbour, until their old nature is remote and their apparent death gives new life to the soul. This process, easy to write about, is seldom carried out far into life : its word is not often made flesh. But at least we see where the Divine exaction lies.

In the case of the band of men and women who were the first followers and disciples, the natural agony of all they felt and saw gives them in the internal historical sense, which is one degree above the Letter, a full title to be regarded as those who chiefly were crucified with Jesus. Mary perhaps on the left hand : the iron entered into her soul ; and John on the right hand. The dawning Church represented by blessed Mary was here made part and partaker of the great sacrifice; and it became the sole property of John whom Jesus loved. John = Good Works, the Good of Life. Other leading affections of the Church underwent the same agony from the cross; and Mary Magdalene came last, as in her the gates of hell had been sealed when the seven devils of profanation were cast out of her by Christ.

"Jesus saw" signifies divine perception for ordination of the faculties that were below Him in the Jewish nature, and which could belong to His Religion: the four women represent the affections of good which constitute the Church, and Mary Magdalene their devout adoption.

In recapitulation, the robbers in Matthew and Mark, as the condemned ultimate of those who railed on the Lord, were the sum and conclusion of the Jewish Church. The whole hierarchy was represented by the robbers, and that the end of its crimes had come upon it.

In Luke, the lowest remains of the Jewish nature and Church are represented; meaning by the remains the same as "the remnant of all nations which shall be saved." On the cross itself, Christ is acknowledged as the inheritor of the Kingdom, as the Messiah, by the one malefactor; and faith in a future spoken of by him in the words, When thou comest into thy kingdom, is answered by Jesus, This day shalt thou be with Me in Paradise.

A Roman declaration of kingship, which in its sense of kingdom in this world Christ had refused, was put upon the cross by Pilate: *Jesus of Nazareth the King of the Jews.* Remembering Christ's refusal, succession to the Jewish Babylon was here crucified in the first disciples, and forbidden to the coming Church. A Roman governor in temporal power had the declaration and accusation written. Rome has not heeded this part of the furniture of the crucifixion. Nor the fact that John = good works. Good in act is the possessor and owner of the Church, which was given to John on the cross by Jesus. Peter had been the rock under the Church, the faith that "Thou art the Christ the Son of the living

God." John as Love is in the first succession : both representatively, but not as persons.

From Noah as the initiation of the first spiritual Church which succeeded the lost celestial Church called Adam, the human will and understanding underwent successive declensions, until at length in the children of Israel these faculties were extant only as depravities. They had ceased from spiritual capacity, and were used by Jehovah God for interested obedience to a superstitious and sensual religion; that is, for the representation of a Church. This will and understanding covering thousands of years, and extant over the East in nominal churches, was crucified and rejected on the cross by the Divine Man who had borne it, and subdued it in Himself. A new heart and a new mind was given to the race of man in all universes by an event seemingly local, but which yet had such extension within it.

Some further explanation of divine history seems requisite here. Swedenborg has been made to furnish it. "The Lord," says he, "came into the world to save the spiritual." Before the declension spoken of above, in the ages when man, by obeying his newly-given conscience was still so far uplifted from selfishness and sensuality as to be capable of heaven, the natural world, as its function is, fed the spiritual world, and then the heavens, with good and true men and women, children of the conscience, and fathers and mothers of dutiful daily lives, and so the divine purpose was carried on. That purpose is, in the creation of the worlds of nature, to form of their men and women, of which this world is the nursery, an everlasting heaven where love and wisdom and their happiness can have a home. This end is accomplished so long as the river of new-comers from the earth, the thoracic duct of the *Maximus Homo*, as Swedenborg, the spiritual Psychologist, names it, contains a preponderance of regenerated lives in its ever-flowing current.

Here, Reader, reject all fallacies about churchyards as containing your dead ; about expectant Mummies waiting for their KA, and about Paul's Last Trump, and the resurrection of the body. The folk you are thinking of have gone on before, and are every one in the spiritual world; also have been virtually judged already according to their characters; will go to home, or to finality: and whenever a great Æon is accomplished may be rearranged in new mercies, or exactions, of divine order, as God pleases. So the individual judgment and general judgment, both of them always in the spiritual world, and only casually represented in courts of law and diseases and calamities and catastrophes in the natural world, have truth with them both. Understanding this, and believing in God, and a life after death, and that spirits eschew churchyards, you easily see that the state of the spiritual world, in a given age, is a knowable problem for the willing mind: a problem of emigration, and as it were colonization. You know who have emigrated. In a tumbling epoch it is a death-rate and death-life-rate of teeming magnitudes of evil, sensual, dishonest men and women fabricating new states and places whereby and wherein to gratify and propagate their realms of lust and falsity and ceremony. Mere *Census* is alone sufficient to show what sort of nations and peoples are proximately above us and below us *now* under these conditions; what they will all vote for, what sort of Parliaments they will have, what governments will be sweet to them, and what atheist priests, what Word, what god will be found in their churches or charnel-houses. To comprehend anything of spiritual history, which now is widely opened for us, it is first necessary to know that every woman and man is a permanent creature; goes as a spirit three days after death into another world, being drawn out of the dead body by the Lord; and there awaits either the second death, which is the life alien to God, or enters by the first resurrection on the road and way that leads to the home in heaven, and to the unfailing marriage in the home.

We come back to the question, How did Christ save the Spiritual. First, by assuming the Divine Natural in Himself.

By this means, which did not exist until His incarnation, a natural basis of virtue was added to the Divine Spiritual which existed from eternity, and then the whole Creation became Christ's. Man's Freewill, which is the whole man himself, was the only thing that outlay the Redeemer. In His Life from His birth to His death on the Cross, He gathered round Him the Remains of the Church from Abraham downwards; the fishermen who could become disciples, the women who would be ministers, and the Magdalenes who would be humiliations. He built them up in His intercourse, penetrated them by His wonders of mercy, and instructed them by His Word. They were all natural men and women; He too was a natural man, Ιχθυς, and became the Divine Natural Man. They were new natural men and women, and as His Divine Natural communicated with and corresponded to His Divine Spiritual, so their natural could be regenerated or made spiritual; not at once, but throughout their lives, and in their descendants. Their innocent and honest naturalism is plain throughout the Gospels: they expected the day of judgment in their own lifetime: they were eager to sit on twelve thrones judging the twelve tribes of Israel: they took the Master's words in a literal sense with no spiritual reserve behind it. They did not heed what He said of His Resurrection. They were not only fishermen but fishes and fond of eating spiritual fish: they were natural men. And this, nothwithstanding that He taught them that He always spoke in Parables.

The restored capacity of regeneration, the power through their freewill of controlling the natural, and so bringing the spiritual into it, so that it became spiritual-natural, and leaving the natural basis, became spiritual after death,—made this world again into a Nursery of Heaven, fulfilled the divine law that heaven can never be full, but increases by fresh angelic populations, and the mundane divine law that regeneration of individuals fills the earth with inheritances of good men and women, who here are a basis to the Ancient

Edifices of God, and who now subsist in safety in the Divine Natural assumed by Christ.

The former natural capable of all this is represented in the Fourth Gospel by the two who were crucified with Christ ; these being the entire remains of the Natural Man which could serve as the "Tabernacle of the Son, which cometh forth as a bridegroom out of his chamber, and rejoiceth as a strong man to run a race. There is nothing hid from the heat thereof. In that heat the law of the Lord is perfect, converting the soul; the testimony of the Lord is sure, making wise the simple." This is an account of the capacity now first restored to the heavens and firmament of the Remains of the natural man consenting to share in the Crucifixion, and so to enter the path that leads to the spiritual man ; and that leads the spiritual man when adequate to contribute again to the fulness of the spiritual heaven.

These things become self-evident in the revealed doctrine of the Churches. The incapacity of the natural man to become unselfish and heavenly-minded during the Jewish Dispensation, and the restoration of man's freewill by the Lord's Incarnation, have been treated of throughout in this work.

We have now gone through the various Words of the Crucifixion in the Four Gospels, attempting to draw out from each a few crumbs of its own spiritual sense.

In Matthew and Mark the Jewish Church is crucified with and rejected by Christ on the cross, and perishes. In Luke a Messianic remnant is received, which if it will, can have an inheritance by and by. In John the Crucifixion is extended to the coming Church, its whole natural man is measured on the cross, which becomes the sign and banner of regeneration and salvation. The series is maintained.

The spiritual sense is the harmony of the Gospels for those who accept it: it proves that no finite man wrote these portions of the Word. They asseverate to subsequent mankind that the Lord controls His own records. The generation in the Lord's time attests Christ, and His life, death, resurrection, and ascension. The first Christian Church is the tree from the seed planted by Christ in the first disciples. The Second Christian Church as given to man fulfils the Scriptures completed in the First.

John, the evangelist, he whom Jesus loved, is the only disciple mentioned who witnessed the Crucifixion. The letter of his Word was dictated to him as Holy Scripture. The omission of detail as to those who were crucified with Christ is therefore not his omission. It has a divine purpose. And in this as the final and highest Gospel the signification covers the universal and general meaning in which the cross leads and will forever lead the generations on. The dictation to the four evangelists seems to culminate here.

There are some other things which are prerogatively brought forward in the Fourth Gospel.

"Then the soldiers, when they had crucified Jesus, took His garments, and made four parts, to every soldier a part; and also the coat: now the coat was without seam, woven from the top throughout. They said therefore among themselves, Let us not rend it, but cast lots for it, whose it shall be: that the Scripture might be fulfilled, which saith, They parted my raiment among them, and for my vesture they did cast lots. *These things therefore the soldiers did*" (xix. 23, 24).

To approach the spiritual sense of this scripture, remember that the person on the cross was the Lord God Almighty in the last act and hours of redeeming the human race. His garments and the coat cannot but ascend to a Logos commensurate with Himself. The Scripture sounding from Æon to Æon is fulfilled by what is done with these coverings belonging to the Lord's Body. The soldiers did what they did that the fulfilment should take place: *therefore* they did it.

The Lord's garments represented truth in the external form, and His vesture truth in the internal. The vesture is the spiritual sense of the Word; the garments are the literal sense, which is parted among the disputants. The spiritual sense, the coat is woven without seam from the top throughout. The top of the divine garment is the origin of that sense from Him who wears it, and from whom it descends through the heavens. Coming downwards it is Divine Truth Spiritual from the Divine Celestial. The coat being not divided signifies that such divine truth could not be dissipated because it is the internal truth of the Word. Casting lots for it signifies indifference of utter incapacity. It is not said that it had an owner among those who diced it away. The seamless coat is now with the New Church wherever the life represented by John, namely, good works, or good in act, is found. Observe that this "coat without seam woven from the top throughout" is a revelation only found in John's Gospel.

The reader, astonished that the Lord's coat without seam has such things in it, and such Scriptures heralding it a thousand years before the Crucifixion, will remember the exact clothing of Aaron that he might represent High Priesthood in the Church with the Jews : also that it is said in the Psalms, cii. 26, 27, "the heavens shall wax old like a garment ; as a vesture shalt thou change them and they shall be changed." We also read of garments of holiness, and that fine linen is the righteousness of the saints. In the Apocalypse it is written, "He was clothed in a vesture dipped in blood, and His name is called the Word of God," where the divine truth in the letter to which violence has been done is signified. A vesture there is truth investing good, and when predicated of the Word, the sense of the Letter. Again it is written, "And the armies in heaven followed Him upon white horses, clothed in fine linen, white and clean. . . . He hath on His vesture and on His thigh a name written, King of Kings and Lord of Lords." This signifies that the Lord teaches in the Word what He is, namely, the Divine Truth of the Divine Wisdom, and the Divine Good of the Divine Love ; therefore, the God of the Universe. The vestment signifies the Word as to Divine Truth, the thigh as to Divine Good.

L

The Word is full of instances of garments representing internal things. In the spiritual world every one is clothed according to his nature and character: the dress can come upon him without his consciousness. Also garments assumed cause the interiors to be for a time what the exteriors signify.

As a general form, truth is a garment which invests good, and natural things are sheaths, coverings, or garments which invest spiritual. The face is a representative garment to the interiors of the mind, and the body to the soul. Now apply the instances from Revelation to the vestments in the Fourth Gospel, and you will see what the things that have clothed the Lord must mean.

The Lord gave up the spirit before those who were crucified with Him had their legs broken by Pilate's compliance. The bodies were taken away, so as not to remain upon the cross on the Sabbath day,—the high Sabbath day. This was the end of the natural man and his Church ; on the part of the Jews, an end in profanation ; on the part of those who were crucified, an end in consummation of the Church, and in defection of the human race. Representatively Jesus was dead. The two who were crucified had their legs broken. The legs signify the lowest natural man, and his walk and way, his progress on his own basis from his own power. Of this the Psalm says, "The Lord delighteth not in the legs of a man." The legs thus broken = the suicide of human nature, dead in Church, in state, in will and understanding, in godlessness, and then in useless propagation. " But when they came to Jesus, and found that He was dead already, they brake not His legs. But one of the soldiers with a spear pierced His side, and forthwith came thereout blood and water." The infirm natural had deceased in Christ, the divine natural was in assumption. He, the first nature, was dead already ; the second nature advanced to completion. The bones which the soldiers did not break were the infinite basis and stability of it. We cannot think of Christ as dying on the cross as men die. The divine body which His life had implanted in the natural man suffered no extinction. It became in death His whole body, and did not die. " These things were done that the Scripture should be fulfilled ;—a bone of Him shall not be broken." The death was most real, because it laid aside the human natural. Its act was voluntary, and was imminent resurrection, because the Divine Natural Man was there. The bone here signifies the rock of the entire natural divinity.

When man dies a natural death, the spirit is still in the body, and remains there until the third day. Celestial angels sit beside the body, and await the fact of death, to awaken the new inhabitant, and to welcome him. The spirit is drawn out from the intricate flesh by the Lord's attraction, and by no power of its own. With the Divine Man the case is different. He gave up the spirit by His own deed, when He said, It is finished, = the Divine Use of His Passion is completed ; and He rose on the third day by His own proper Power of infinite Will and Wisdom. There was no interval but union between these acts of God. The third day signifies a full state, not a period of time. He was not in the grave as a man is, but the state of Glorification was going on. The days signify the order of preparation. When the Infinite Man comes, infinite operation and use are evidently in transaction. The three days signify omnipotent work for souls which no human thought can fathom.

But one of the soldiers with a spear pierced His side, and forthwith came thereout blood and water. This signifies the death of human nature in its relation to the Letter which killeth ; the blood, the death of the good that had been with it to the last ; the water, the death of the truth. The soldier's spear, the violation by man himself. The Divine Natural, the Divine Humanity, then remained alone to ascend to the Father, and with Him those whom He had prepared to institute the new race of men on earth, to repeople the spiritual heaven. For "the Lord came into the world to save the spiritual."

That a divine sense lies in the soldier piercing His side, is brought to our recognition by the words of John, who witnesses. " And he that saw, bare record, and his record is true, and he knoweth that he saith true, that ye might believe. For these things were done that the scripture should be fulfilled, A bone of him shall not be broken. And again another scripture saith, They shall look on Him whom they pierced." In the Apocalypse it is said, "'Behold He cometh with clouds, and every eye shall see Him, and they which pierced Him.' The clouds in which the Lord comes, are the sense of the letter, in which He will reveal Himself, and reveal the spiritual sense after the Last Judgment, at the end of the first Christian Church. And every eye will see Him, signifies that all those who from affection are in the understanding of divine truth, will acknowledge that sense. In the spiritual sense eye does not mean eye, but intellect. The others see, and also understand, but do not acknowledge. These are signified, because it follows that they also will see who pierced Him. These signify those who are in falses. By piercing Jesus Christ nothing else is meant than destroying His divine truth in the Word. Blood and Water are the Divine Truth Spiritual and Natural. Thus the Word in the spiritual and natural sense. And to pierce the side of the Lord is to destroy both by falses, which was done by the Jews. All things of the Lord's Passion represented the state of the Jewish Church with regard to the Word " (*Apoc. Rev.* n. 1).

The importance of these texts is attested by three memorable scriptures ranging over three dispensations, the Jewish, the first Christian Church and the New Church. The reader will find proof here that the Lord's garments and coat, His bone that shall not be broken, and His pierced side, are weighty with the Godhead of the spiritual Word; and that there is no rectitude or sound reason in taking the letter just as it is written, which is impossible, and being satisfied that religious justice has been done to Holy Writ :

that Christ's vesture means no more than yours or mine.

The Lord's words to Peter,—Simon of Jonas, thrice counselling him to feed His lambs and then His sheep, signify that all innocence of nature and of wisdom should be of primary concern in the life of a Church which makes three-fold profession of love to the Lord. But the prophecy, " When thou wast young thou girdedst thyself, and walkedst whither thou wouldest ; but when thou shalt be old thou shalt stretch forth thy hands, and another shall gird thee, and carry thee whither thou wouldest not ;—this spake He, signifying by what death He should glorify God. And when He had spoken this, He saith unto him, Follow me." The prophecy imports that faith represented by Peter would lose the mission wherein the truth had made it free, of commanding the union of faith with love as the life of faith and the means of Salvation ; and would in the end be enslaved and debauched by the growing depravity and falsehood of the Church, to teach justification by faith alone apart from works. Peter, faith, is thus carried whither he would not. The death by which he should glorify God implies this depraved faith dying, and good works, good life, honest Christian character in all daily callings, in a word, charity, which alone has true faith, taking its place. Peter's martyrdom is the meaning generally given to the prophecy. Every church, as Swedenborg says speaking of Babylon, begins as a virgin and ends as a harlot. When the latter dies, not as a martyr but as a malefactor, a new church is raised up, which glorifies God.

We will now adduce some words from Swedenborg. " John was the first of the apostles, because he represented the good of charity. That not Peter but John was the first is evident from the fact that John lay on the Lord's breast, and that he and not Peter followed the Lord." " The Lord said concerning John that 'he should remain until He came,' thus to the present day, which is the Advent of the Lord ; and therefore also, the good of life is now taught by the Lord for those who will be of His New Church, which is the New Jerusalem. As John represented the good of love, therefore the Revelation was made to him. Revelation from heaven which is really such, cannot be made to any others than those who are in the good of charity, or of love. Others can indeed hear the things which are from heaven, but they cannot *perceive* them." . . . John represented the church as to good works, and good works contain all things of love to the Lord and of charity towards the neighbour. . . . That the Lord's Church is with those who live in charity in act, or in good works : and not with those who are in faith separated from works, is signified by what is related in John xxi. As John signifies the goods of charity, or good works, and these constitute the Lord's Church, therefore not Peter but John followed the Lord, and the Lord said to Peter, If I will that he remain until I come, what is that to thee? Follow thou me. By which is meant that the good of charity will still remain with those who are the Lord's, even to the end of the Church, and when there is a new Church. And not with those who are in faith separated from this good. This is signified by these words to Peter, What is that to thee? . . . Peter said of John, What is this? that is, that it is not anything. Jesus said, If I will that he remain until I come, what is it to thee?" Observe that throughout the Lord's conversation he calls Peter, Simon of Jonas, which marks a change of representation in that disciple, whose decease as a false faith will glorify God.

These cumulative passages are adduced to reinforce the position of the Gospel of Love, the Heart of Christ, John's Gospel. The verbal inspiration of the Letter shines throughout it. And John as a representative speaks for himself, and yet not of himself, when he says at the conclusion, " This is the disciple which testifieth of these things, and wrote these things : and we know that his testimony is true." As the Word was dictated to John, so the Divine Natural Man, the Word, the Son of Man, the Son revealing the Father, here attests his Work complete in John. It is a direct voice from above.

"And there are also many other things which Jesus did, the which, if they should be written every one, I suppose that even the world itself could not contain the books that should be written. Amen." The Redemptive acts by which the Lord overcame the hells, and reduced the spiritual world to order, by which He glorified His Humanity and made it divine, and by which He became the Saviour of mankind, are in these four small books. The divine Author and Artist has written them from the ground of infinite Use which selects all truths as they are wanted. That use is indefinitely various, and the differences of its administration are not discrepancies which have to be reconciled by ingenious commentators, but wisdom to be seen and perceived from love of the spiritual and celestial senses which are intended. Each Gospel Word as a truth for application has infinite contents. Infinite things are compressed into the letter, that the world may have room for honest secular men. Take an example. "If thy right eye offend thee, pluck it out, and cast it from thee." Seen spiritually, the right eye which offends is the intellect charged by the corrupt will, and insinuating and dictating act. Here in the mind it is the organ of the vision of lusts. In these few words, human life is traversed from end to end, and books which would fill the world might be the history of the carrying out of it. All greed, evil mastery, and delight of self-love, are the lusts in the ban of this excommunication. The immensity of the work commended to us by our Saviour finds few echoes in our literature. And yet the work is imminent; for after death, when the tree lies, and the mind's habits in what little is left of the mind are immortal, the evil eye cannot be plucked out or cast away: it sees its love, and nothing else it sees, and drones on in its dead desires for ever.

In John there is no account of the Lord's Ascension. The Divine Natural Man proclaims His union with the

Father only in a special Gospel of Love. He disappears in witnessing to John.

So in endeavouring to elucidate the Four Gospels spiritually, we have first gone down into Egypt for the facts and knowledges of the Letter which has divine natural contents in it. We have then taken the pathway to Assyria, and found there the rational certainty that all things of the Lord, even His coat without seam, must be divine and infinite: Assyria, Reason, says *must be*. And then Israel is the third, the all in all, with Egypt and with Assyria; is the spiritual sense of the Gospels and of the entire Word; even a blessing in the midst of the land.

I conclude this section with the following extract from the PARABLE OF CREATION, by the late Rev. John Doughty: an exposition of the First Chapter of Genesis, which makes its spiritual sense self-evident, and prepares the reader to receive a similar sense in Holy Scripture throughout:

"The Word of God cannot be a book of natural history or science. It must contain, in its essence, only *spiritual* truth. As history, it must give only a history of the *spiritual* states of church or man. If, therefore, their surface appearances indicate that it is something else, those appearances must be false. The child might imagine that Æsop's Fables were given for the mere purpose of relating curious stories of the conversations of birds and beasts which took place in the long ago, but that does not prove the child to be correct. A belief in error never makes error true. But the well-instructed man knows better. He is fully aware that the real design of those fables is to teach a lofty moral by means of a written story.

"Much more is this true of the Word of God, of which the fables of Æsop are a faint imitation. History is here used not for the history's sake, but for the sake of the spiritual lesson which lies concealed within it. Geography is used, not to give any lessons concerning the relative situations of the seas, rivers or lakes, cities, countries or mountains of olden times, but because of their adaptability to expressing the relative spiritual situations or states of men. An account of creation is given, not with the idea of furnishing man with an epitome of geological science, but because it forms a fitting dress for the portrayal of the regeneration of man. As all Scripture is given in parables and for the sake of its *spiritual* teaching, a history of creation must be, in its essential meaning, a description of the creation and development of the *spiritual* nature within us. This is called by our Lord, the rebirth, or regeneration," pp. 34-36.

XLIII.—MARY MAGDALENE.

John's Gospel contains the following concerning Mary Magdalene which does not occur in the other Gospels :—

"She turned herself back, and saw Jesus standing, and knew not that it was Jesus. Jesus saith unto her, Woman, why weepest thou? Whom seekest thou? She, supposing him to be the gardener, saith unto him, Sir, if thou have borne Him hence, tell me where thou hast laid Him, and I will take Him away. Jesus saith unto her, Mary. She turned herself, and saith unto Him, Rabboni; which is to say, Master. Jesus saith unto her, Touch me not; for I am not yet ascended to my Father: but go to my brethren and say unto them, I ascend unto my Father and your Father, and to my God and your God. Mary Magdalene came and told the disciples that she had seen the Lord, and He had spoken these things unto her" (xx. 14-18).

This passage is full of Mary's kind affection: she craves Christ's dead body, and longs to take it away with her. She would not lose sight of it. She is a devout natural woman, through Christ in possession of herself. She is present at the crucifixion; first at the sepulchre on the morning of the resurrection; the first to see Jesus after He rose from the dead, and showed Himself unto her.

Jesus calls her Mary; she calls Him, Master. To which

he rejoins, Touch Me not. May we break this bread, and see a spiritual sense in it?

Mary Magdalene represents ardent natural affection for Jesus; natural devotion; a necessary accompaniment of the first Christian Church, founded as it was upon personal intercourse with the Saviour, and upon loving memory of brotherhood with Him, and of His wondrous words and works. Her history represents an uncontrolled spirit redeemed by Him : for out of her He had cast seven devils. All her behaviour when she supposed Christ to be the gardener, evidences her strong, unsuspecting natural affection. While this was dominant, He could be to her no more than a grand natural man. Touching Him then means loving Him from her *proprium*. He forbids her to touch Him as He has not yet ascended to His Father: her love has not yet apprehended Him as her God. She has her old familiar recognition of Him as He was before His death and resurrection in His infirm Humanity. Yet this ardent natural affection rebuked as it was, being a good love, is made the medium of a revelation from the Lord to the minds of His brethren, to whom Mary is told by Him to say, I ascend unto my Father and your Father, and to my God and your God. The abashed natural love becomes the means to instruction and revelation concerning the Lord's Divinity in His Divine Humanity. The Lord's brethren are those who hear the Word of God and do it : and He here spoke the Word to such. This is for the New Church, and belongs to the spiritual sense now revealed to it. Merely human affection for Christ, except with little children and simple minds, has detracted, and detracts, from the recognition of His Divinity; and has made it more obvious to think of Him in His Humiliation and infirm Jewish humanity than in His Godhead; to pity the Lord rather than to adore Him; to think of His flesh not as divine good, and of His blood not as divine truth, but as carnal and sanguinary real presence from His dead body on the cross; and so of the merits not of His life, but of His agony and death. The three great Churches have had their *Via Dolorosa*, and have dwelt minutely upon Christ's sufferings, having no knowledge of His victories over the Hells and over *spiritual* death. They have wailed over Him as a man of sorrows and acquainted with grief. Yet He said, just before His crucifixion, Daughters of Jerusalem, weep not for me, but weep for yourselves, and for your children. The natural affection for Him who took our flesh upon Him, and lived a divine life in it, making His humanity divine, can indeed never be abolished : it should live as a lamb in every little child : and wherever the Gospel is read or known, be it here on earth, or in the worlds of the spiritual firmament in the vast communion after death, this affection, from personal experience, or pious memory, should always rest as a reserve to our thoughts and feelings about our Saviour. But age by age as we know His Godhead by the process of our own regeneration, our love will be transmuted into a spiritual affection to which the Lord will appear in His Kingdom, Power and Glory. Rituals commemorating His suffering, fixed seasons of humiliation, relics authentic or not authentic, whenever the simple can be weaned from them, will disappear into relative unimportance. The New Church will be emancipated from the Crucifixion as a natural agony upon which the Lord after His resurrection ceased to dwell. It will live to ages of ages on account of the Spiritual sense which alone makes all Scripture divine : the Crucifixion now of our own evil and false proclivities will be the heaven and the blessing of it. For the sake of this we read in Luke, " Ought not Christ to have suffered these things, and to enter into His Glory ?"

XLIV.—RESIST NOT THE EVIL ONE.

Bear in mind that we speak from appearance when we say that the Lord rejected the Jewish Church. The converse is true. He did not resist evil. He came into the world into a Jewish humanity that could be tempted, and with a divinity in Him that could resist the most grievous temptations of earth, of heaven and of hell. This humanity could not fail to be assaulted by all these, for it was an opportunity for all ; and it admitted all; and when the assault took place, it admitted the evil to be evil, as it was ; and so held it as evil ; and then the divinity confronted it : in no wrath, in no anger : God is never angry with the wicked although He is angry with them every day, for His anger is Love, which when it looks upon them precipitates them downwards : being of opposite essence they cannot abide His truth which is the eye of His Love. It turns them inside out and upside down, and to regain their own state, they sink away below it.

Here we come upon that passage in the Sermon on the Mount, " Ye have heard that it hath been said, An eye for an eye, and a tooth for a tooth : but I say unto you that ye resist not the evil one : but whosoever shall smite thee on thy right cheek, turn to him the other also. And if any man sue thee at the law, and take away thy coat, let him have the cloak also. And whosoever shall compel thee to go a mile, go with him twain" (Matthew v. 38-41).

In a well-meaning book by Count Leo Tolstoi, *The Kingdom of God is within you*, 1894, this text has been made use of to set forth "a new Life-conception of Christianity," changing man's relation to the state, to social organizations, to his fellow-man, to the guardianship of property, and to the treatment of offenders against existing law and order. Especially recommending non-compliance with military service, and non-intercourse with legal tribunals. The scheme intends external reform from the ground of written Scripture, which is to be fulfilled by exemplary courageous men leading the way into a New Age of non-resistance, which is to bring in the Kingdom of God.

In using the WORD, our endeavour has been to hold to the very letter as the pillar on which its senses stand, and Count Tolstoi is an instance of how much danger of perversion and false dogma is incurred if this allegiance to verbal reality is disregarded. The Count has altered the letter into Resist not evil by violence, taking this transcript apparently from Adin Ballou. The text is *Resist not the evil one.* That the evil *one* is literally right is shown by the number of evil persons you are straightway commanded not to resist. *By violence* is an addition to the text. It abolishes the meaning of the command, and sets you forth on a career and propagandism of passive resistance: whereas resistance with no qualification is forbidden. The book itself proceeds on this mistake, and whatever political or social results it may have, they have no connection with Christ's doctrine of non-resistance. Tolstoi, though (p. 65) he once mentions Swedenborg disparagingly as among sectarian founders, is unaware of the spiritual sense which resides in the words, Resist not the evil one.

The command is evidently to an enduring or passive state. It was carried out by Christ in His active life from the beginning to the end. He, the innocent, the sinless, was the most tempting prey for all the hells; the Lamb to all their wolves. He was assaulted by temptation, and He conquered by seeing and owning it : He stood as Christ and the devil left Him. Each temptation made no mark on His inherited nature, but a white record of truth made good in His newly-planted flesh. That is not our case. We fall and fall, and the mind, the book of life, is a blurred record of good and evil. If we examine ourselves we admit continual failing; evil complexions to the neighbour, self-love and its greedy demands. Our present self-love is our ground of temptation; our past life, of rebuke. This rebuke is what we are not to resist. It comes from the same source with our temptations. It is the revenge of the Evil One for not being admitted as an associate on our way. If we went boldly on we should never be rebuked, but be received in the abyss under its triumphal arches into the skeleton arms of destruction.

This is to say, that by our evils we are in sympathetic alliance with the hells, and if they cannot make us worse, whenever low states of mind and body supervene, the devil, the accuser, turns over our book of life, and reads despair to us from its pages. Shall we dismiss him? Can we say to the Father of Lies who thus tells us his evil truths, Get thee behind me, Satan? Christ commands us in this case of accusation *not* to resist the Evil One. This means spiritually that we should not deny our evils however brought home to us. If one side of our internal man is smitten with just accusation, help comes from the Deliverer and Saviour in exploring the other side also: both are part of the peccant life. If the enemy will legally have our coat, and make the sins under it naked, we are to use our freedom to review the faults hidden till now under the cloak. If the Satan compel us to misery over the course and journey of our past lives, we are to double the mileage of our wanderings with him, and in this good way of repentance the evil one, not resisted, disappears. Swedenborg also tells us that such self-accusation, prompted by the hells, if it becomes too sore for man, is mitigated by instant angels, who take part with the penitent, and even excuse his errors and sins, as the devils and Satans aggravate them.

Distinction should be made between temptations and trials. Temptation involves attempted seduction by some pleasure agreeable to yourself, and which ought to be resisted because to indulge it is wrong. Discipline comes in here. Trial on the other hand is the pain of self-examination, and this, wherever it springs from originally, ought not to be resisted. Treatment for cure then follows it.

An eye for an eye and a tooth for a tooth means the opposite spirit to Resist not the Evil One. It discloses that man since the Noahtic Church and before Christ had no internal reward and punishment in him, but lived as an external natural man: his book of life was written out in this world, and no revelation was possible for him about another. He worshipped the evil spirits that he knew, and called them gods; and hatred and revenge were permitted in the legal eye for eye, and tooth for tooth. These things too are in the basis of our minds; and our difference from the old state is, that we are more capable of self-examination, and of literal acknowledgment of the Sermon on the Mount, and of the commands and precepts of Christ. The New Church which has come, and which is to come, now knows of the spiritual Word, and the Spiritual World, and of the Divine Natural Man, and will open the Æon in God's time, and lay bare every evil, public and private, with which the enemy of mankind helps the Friend of mankind in charging us. It is a truth that in our present condition, with our hearts and minds as they are, we need the Society of Evil Spirits to sustain our natures and characters, not in getting worse, but in mere existence, pending the slow process of our regeneration. If all our bad habits, which are equivalent to our evil familiar spirits, were suddenly removed, we should be remitted into a hopeless infancy on the road to annihilation, until we were revived by the corruption of evil communications. Self-love is the arm of the industry of the present world. Evil cannot be taken away except by regeneration, and most gradually. I rejoice to see that my old friend, Herbert Spencer, is aware of this troublous truth. Meanwhile the evil spirits who like strong drinks stimulate us to make our selfishness muscular and useful, whenever we determine to turn over a new leaf, and to refuse their comforts to our often infirmities, are in anger and fury, and the freshly sensitive conscience is their place of assault. Our past lives are made into frescoes on it. We are then to look on these steadily with acknowledgement of what the heart is, and in the prayer, Lord, be merciful to me a sinner, the devil will depart from us when he has performed his use. We submit to Count Tolstoi that this is a crumb of that bread which the Sermon on the Mount teaches in the Word, *Resist not the Evil One.*

XLV.—ESTIMATES OF THE BIBLE.

Swedenborg's dictum that it was foreseen that Christians would almost reject the Word of the Old Testament, finds confirmation on all hands in the Christian Church down to this day. Already Josephus, the Jewish Historian, and a Romanized Jew, was agnostic to the divine supernatural element in the Dispensation to which he had belonged. The first part of his standard book bears the appropriate title "The Antiquities of the Jews": whether this title was given by himself, or not. He regarded the earlier Bible narratives as a record of superstitions; and held that in his day God had forsaken the Jews, and gone over to the Romans. When he relates the miraculous passage of the Israelites through the Red Sea, he says that "he tells everything as it is written in the Holy Books, and doubts whether the sea went back of its own accord, or by God's special command. Every one might think of it as he pleased." Of God's coming down to Mount Sinai he says, "Let every one believe of it as he will: he relates what he finds in the Holy Books." With respect to the declaration that God was the Author of the Law of Moses, he expresses the same unconcern. So also of what is told of Jonah and Nebuchadnezzar. "In his second Book against Apion he says, that Moses from his justice and piety might very well judge that he had God for his guide; and when he had once persuaded himself of that, he did well to persuade the people to think so too; as the Greeks pretended to have their laws from Apollo, whether they really thought so, or thought it the best way to make them received of the people." Dr. Willes, the author of "Two Discourses upon Josephus" prefixed to the translation of that author by Sir Roger l'Estrange, adds to these statements, that "the disesteeming the rites and ceremonies of the Law of Moses, and setting so great a value upon the precepts of morality, are two considerable steps that Josephus made towards the doctrine of

Christianity." From which it might seem that Dr. Willes himself was an agnostic with regard to the supernatural character of the Jewish Dispensation, as well as of the Christian. For he says further that " when Josephus makes the Jewish religion to consist in piety, justice, concord, and observing God and His Providence, he comes very near the description of Christianity."

The Jews themselves during their miraculous time exhibited a wonderful capacity of forgetting Jehovah : under Sinai they lapsed into Egyptian idolatry. The causes of their oblivions were themselves supernatural in some sense. They were idolaters in heart, Jehovah was one of many gods, and their religiosity was superstition. So they were moveable from one manifestation to another, and had no central foundation in faith; no special love of their God: they easily worshipped the gods of the nations ; and when magical powers were exhibited, or professed, they went over to their Priests. Solomon did the same thing on the greatest scale. There is no such narrative of defections in the face of divine miracles as that presented in the Bible. Josephus inherited from the Jews, and disbelieving the authenticity of their dispensation, he was naturally disposed to see the Messiah in the Emperor Vespasian.

Throughout the Christian ages there has been no recognition of Judaism as a continuous miraculous dispensation in the sense in which we have been enabled to acknowledge it in these pages. It has not been looked upon as a body religious, held together by miracle and commandment, constituting a unique theocracy. Any rational account of it as such has never been attempted. To this time, it is for the Old Church and for those who outlie it, a hieroglyphic unread. We will not say that the Old Testament has not been accepted reverently and religiously, at least by Protestant Christendom ; but that nothing has been made of it to show its necessity from the past or importance for the future. Theology has not been able to justify the ways of God to man in this difficult field.

Acute scepticism about it has appeared in all countries and in every century; and Thomas Paine's *Age of Reason*, which I once read with admiration, gives a voice still to a large class impatient of their ignorance of the why and wherefore of the Hebrew story. Paine, as I recollect him sixty-six years ago, was not consciously impious, but if he had not been inflamed politically, could perhaps have received true Biblical information had it been forthcoming. His tract on *Theophilanthropy* is a declaration that religion is summed up in love to God and love to man. Although he was less mannerly than the moderns, who are in the full liberty of their opinions, and therefore under no excuse of irritation, he was a loud theist, and nothing worse.

Before this Thomas Hobbes was an acute commentator, and the student of his *Leviathan* will find sagacious observation and interpretation of the letter of the Bible. He was a Churchman, and also a theist, and addicted to historical criticism, and well worth reading for specimens of it. He sheds no light upon the supernatural side of religion, and does not find it in the Bible. Why is he regarded as an atheist? Perhaps because he denied freewill, and maintained that human actions are inevitable links in a pre-determined chain of causes and effects; and that good and evil men are fixed fates. Did not Calvin also hold the same.

Among the commentators Sir Thomas Browne is a signal exception to the understanding of the letter of the Old Testament. His strong faith often comes near to the spiritual sense, and discerns vistas of meaning that are hidden from those who regard the style of the Word as loose and indeterminate. His remarks on the foods forbidden to the Jews by the Levitical law have been already quoted. *The Pseudodoxia or Vulgar Errors* contains suggestive chapters on creation and Scripture history: and opens the Christian gospels as the heart of intellect alone can perceive them. Speaking of John on the text, *that John the Evangelist should not die*, he says: " He alone of the twelve beheld Christ's passion on the

Cross. Wherein the affliction that He suffered could not amount to less than Martyrdom : for if the naked relation, at least the intentive consideration of that passion, be able still, and at this disadvantage of time, to rend the hearts of pious contemplators, surely the near and sensible vision thereof must needs occasion agonies beyond the comprehension of flesh" (p. 305). And speaking of the Lord Christ he says, "In Holy Scripture it is recorded He sometimes wept, but never that He laughed. Which howsoever granted, it will be hard to conceive how He passed His younger years and childhood without a smile ; if, as Divinity affirmeth, for the assurance of His Humanity unto men, and the concealment of His Divinity from the devil, He passed this age like other children, and so proceeded until He evidenced the same. Nor need we be afraid to ascribe that unto the incarnate Sonne which sometimes is attributed unto the uncarnate Father, of Whom it is said, He that dwelleth in the heavens shall laugh the wicked to scorn." We proffer these extracts though somewhat apart from our remarks on the neglect of the Old Testament, to remind the reader of Sir T. Browne's claim to take high rank among those who have worked in the mines of Holy Scripture.

Theism with regard to the Old Testament is prevalent in the Church, especially among the learned. This must be so until the new revelations are received which allow them to accept the Letter just as it is, with no natural explanations ; and to be instructed and educated into the spiritual truths and reasons which infil and justify the Word throughout. The humble people in these late centuries have possessed their Bibles uninjured, and their faith has kept them out of the darkness which the learned have gathered round themselves as the Jews gathered for themselves the "thick darkness about God." The letter thus accepted by the simple has a pious modesty with it which is not superstition, but an earnest of enlightenment to come to these "souls under the Altar."

Dean Stanley's *Lectures on the Jewish Church* are a typical instance of learned and courteous dismissal of the supernatural element in the Old Testament. Throughout his attractive Guide-book the revelation of Jehovah is of God *in* man, and not of God *to* man. Whereas to the Jews there was no such revelation, for Jehovah was *with* them, but never *in* them. Supernaturalism was necessarily typical here; for the Jewish race was all mere human nature, and the Jewish dispensation had no nature to it, but supernal governance alone. Neither was the Jewish Race an instance of "the universality of prophetic inspiration. This," says the Dean, "extended to the whole nation. The history of Israel, from Moses downwards, is not the history of an inspired book, or of an inspired order, but of an inspired people." Moses contradicted this when he said to Joshua, "Would that all the Lord's people were prophets; and that the Lord would put His spirit upon them" (Num. xi. 30). So little were the Jews inspired in the Dean's sense, that their great Prophets themselves were not inspired excepting with obedience to verbal dictation; and neither they nor the people understood the prophecies, which never came through their own minds, but from without to their senses. As they were receptive of the dictation, so they were obedient to any open commands in it. The prophetical inspiration was confined to a few men; and consists in large part of the denunciation of the wickedness of the Jews and Israelites, and of the surrounding nations, Egypt and the others. Terrible immanence and pressure from Jehovah,—dictatorship from without, and stern commandment,—were on the one hand; and unquestioning obedience to rituals, and reasons which were beyond their understanding, were imperative on the other hand. The inspiration which the Dean is thinking of is that *virtus* and exaltation of human genius which all strong natures feel at times, and in which the Jews were not deficient. It led them in the end to attribute the work and Word of God to themselves. Josephus dared to conjecture this of Moses, and that he acknowledged Jehovah only to hold dominion over the people. Such hypocrisy is denounced against the children of Israel throughout in the Psalms. The two nations added to it century by century, until the consummation of their Æon, when the commingling of their supernatural leading with the pride of their hearts gave rise to loss of freewill, and then to demoniacal possession such as existed in the Lord's time.

It were easy to multiply instances of the Dean's agnosticism all through his pursuit of the Old Testament narrative. The account of Sinai has no objective reality left to it on the spiritual side; the natural scenery is florid, and Jehovah is a pallid oracle, not only invisible, but vague and unthinkable; whereas in the Bible His voice and His writing are the evidences of a God man. The objectiveness is so reduced that Moses acting on the host by hypnotism through "swarmery" might have been the juggler of it all. From the Dean's version, no remembrance of the events could be constructed. Bunyan's Pilgrim's Progress could be so treated, but not Holy Scripture. And the Dean is not candid like Josephus, who tells you to think what you like about the story. In treating of the destruction of Sodom, and the doom of the Cities of the Plain, the insinuation is that nature and not the Divine in judgment is the agent. "There is yet another occasion on which Abraham appears in connexion, not indeed with the revolutions of armies or of empires, but with the more awful convulsions which agitate the fabric of the world itself. What were the precise special means by which the fertile vale of Siddim was blasted with eternal barrenness— how and to what extent the five guilty cities of the plain were overthrown, is still a vexed question equally with theologians and geologists. We need here only consider the aspect of the catastrophe as it was presented to the Patriarch" (*Lectures on the History of the Jewish Church*, Part I., p. 46). The Scripture says, "The Lord rained upon Sodom and upon Gomorrah brimstone and fire from the Lord out of heaven, and He overthrew those cities, and all the plain, and all the inhabitants of the cities, and that which grew upon the ground" (Gen. xix. 24, 25). The Dean sees no precise special means of destruction in the Lord raining fire and brimstone, but theologians and geologists find a vexed question in it and join the patriarch and the Dean in gazing on the results; as if Abraham and they are scientist tourists unacquainted with their Bible.

One more indication of the fact that the Old Testament might die out as a portion of God's Word if it were left in the hands of the learned, who pervert it into fables as the Greeks perverted the religion of the ancient Church. We have already given the interpretation of the following text. "And the Lord said unto Moses in Midian, Go, return into Egypt. And Moses took his wife and his sons, and set them upon an ass, and he returned to the land of Egypt: and Moses took the rod of God in his hand. . . . And it came to pass on the way at the inn that the Lord met him and sought to kill him. Then Zipporah took a flint, and cut off the foreskin of her son, and made it touch his feet, and she said, Surely a bridegroom of bloods art thou to me, so he let him alone. Then she said, A bridegroom of bloods because of the circumcision" (Exodus iv. 19-26).

On this event Dean Stanley comments as follows:—"On the journey a mysterious and almost inexplicable incident occurs in the family. The most probable explanation seems to be that at the Caravanserai either Moses or his eldest child was struck with what seemed to be a mortal illness. In some way, not apparent to us, this illness was connected by Zipporah with the fact that her son had not been circumcised —whether in the general neglect of that rite among the Israelites in Egypt, or in consequence of his birth in Midian. She instantly performed the rite, and threw the sharp instrument, stained with the fresh blood, at the feet of her husband, exclaiming in the agony of a mother's anxiety for the life of her child, 'A bloody husband thou art, to cause the death of my son.' Then, when the recovery from the illness took place (whether of her son or her husband), she exclaims again : ' A bloody husband still thou art, but not so as to cause the child's death, but only to bring about his circumcision ' " (*Ibid.* pp. 116, 117).

The reader is referred to pp. 35-37 above respecting this event. The Dean again ignores Jehovah and guesses His seeking to kill Moses into a common case of illness, eliminating every trace of the divine and supernatural from it. He makes Zipporah throw the flint knife at Moses' feet, instead of touching his feet with the foreskin. In a note he designates the *almost inexplicable incident* as ' a story.' He invents circumstances, puts words into Zipporah's mouth, and makes her call Moses ' husband ' when the Hebrew for a purpose says bridegroom."

Of course he discredits the witch of Endor calling up Samuel to Saul, although myriads of such cases occur at the present day. His pages are full of the virtue of the Jews, and of their deserts as the chosen people. The invisible God is acknowledged as in them, and they are near by promise and performance to a Christianity which is a continued, established, and endowed Church of Judaism. Both Testaments are ignored. The Book may not unfairly be regarded as a well-oiled systematic Pantheism wrestling with two revealed religions, and bent upon casting them to the ground.

XLVI.—ETHNOLOGY.

If we find no recognition of the peculiar character of Judaism as it is written of in the Old Testament in works of so-called Theology, so neither does Ethnology, which ought to treat of all the great causes that determine the character and history of races, admit as an explanation the Divine interference recorded in the Scriptures. Oscar Peschel's learned work, *The Races of Man*, treats the Jews as a self-developed people. The theory of Evolution is what accounts for their Monotheism. They were once savages in a remote past, and worked up through polytheism to one God in long ages. And after the Captivity those who chose to return brought back from Babylon enlightenment about immortality, and a modified temper purged of some of the cruelty and revenge which were signal in their ancestors. They were brought nearer to Christ by these additions to their knowledge and their morals. That a purpose even of this kind was served for the best of the race need not be doubted; it was chiefly due to the "blessing of adversity": but the destruction of Jerusalem, and the final dispersion after the Crucifixion of Christ, forbids us to think that the race itself was influenced towards Christianity. And the obduracy of the Jews to-day proves that the core of Judaism is unmodified. Oscar Peschel follows the writers of the Old Church in not taking the Jewish Dispensation for granted; and in ignoring the miraculous march of it, which seems to be the easiest account, and the only account, of whatever has concerned, and still concerns, that interesting, and to the most of thinkers, that mysterious people.

XLVII.—ARCHÆOLOGY AND THE MONUMENTS.

Professor Sayce, that untiring Archæologist, to whom we owe so much light on ancient history and rediscovered languages, cannot be reckoned among the defenders of the Old Testament as an objective revelation, or as part of a special Divine Word. His thesis is that the Bible of the Old Testament has been hitherto at a disadvantage in standing alone: there has been no other known record to compare with it: an unfair glamour has surrounded it, and prevented the same study and attention being given to our Scripture as to any other book. Reverence for its presumed holiness has closed it against true appreciation, which can only be attained where strong prepossession is absent. If you approach it from the first as awful and divine, you are not likely to dare to understand it, at least not in the learned Professor's way.

The cause of this paralysis of attention is now removed; the mind need not cower henceforth in Bibliolatry. The Old Testament no longer stands alone : a number of other documents belonging to religions more ancient than the Jewish, and perhaps ante-dating the Pentateuch, have been brought to light ; the cuneiform and hieroglyphic in which they were written are deciphered, and read by many learned men ; and. so we may be said to have a shelf of Bibles of which Moses and the Prophets are a modern part.

History stretches new arms of power through these great and curious discoveries, and comparative Bibliology comes in view, as comparative anatomy and physiology, comparative philology, comparative mythology, and comparative religion, have already been inaugurated. Soon therefore we shall be comparatively well-informed all round, on subjects hitherto stunted by lacking the tests of relationships.

The gain to history is indubitable : and historians may exult in it. We shall probably learn before long great landmarks and many details respecting the Holy Land and Mesopotamia before the Israelites conquered Canaan. The Bible will be illustrated as regards its geography and its earliest and least historical events. It is good to be learned, and good to be historical, good in a limited, and not in an absolute sense : good according to the use you make of your knowledges.

Now to quote the Professor himself, and do him no injustice. "The Old Testament has hitherto stood alone. Its Books could be interpreted and explained only by themselves. They were what logicians would call 'a single instance.' There was nothing similar with which they could be compared : no contemporaneous record which could throw light on the facts they contained. From 'a single instance' no argument can be drawn."—Of the last sentence we ask, if it were not good to find some instances beyond argument. Something like Ego and freewill that stands alone however many of it there are. Central principles are such. To argue about them is not to perceive them: when conscience knows them as right and wrong, true and false, arguing is historical but dangerous.

But in the Professor's meaning, does the Old Testament stand alone, awaiting a family of brothers and sisters from the monuments, to tell us who is who and what is what, in our Scriptures? On the contrary, according to received opinion which has every warrant, the Bible contains earlier books than those attributed to Moses. In this case we have in the covers of the Book itself, the Sacred Books of three different Religions already, and with the New Testament of one Theophany and four Religions. Here the argument of the "single instance" disappears, and we find a multiplicity in the Old Testament itself, which forecloses the need of any other series to furnish grounds of comparison and illustration. In supplement to this argument, and as a greater multiplicity, the Bible is a congeries of Booklets reaching in nominal authorship over thousands of years; and the consistency and the difference they offer from great distances of time and place is such as must be absent from the "single instance," but is many-voiced in the Bible, and suggests endless comparisons, textual and real; and a Unity as of one God in all.

We need not then go to Babylon and Assyria to increase the pregnant wealth of Bible truth, by which we mean now, self-certification as a basis for further conception. The Books indeed can be explained and interpreted only by themselves, but they are so many and so various, that upon each point of themselves that needs it, the testimony suffices to justify an interpretation sanctioned by the whole. The historical facts contained in the Bible can be attested by the monuments, and can be received without such attestation.

The divine facts are attested by the Fourfold witness of the Word itself.

The Bible language is a whole literature like the Latin language with all its authors: its words form a complete dictionary which admits of no other tongue in its alphabetic series. How if there be an inner meaning to every word? Here is the highest and absolute rescue from the charge of single instance.

We find in the monuments, a narration of the Flood which is similar in many details to the account in Genesis. Other coincidences between the Old Testament histories and the newly interpreted inscriptions demonstrate that Genesis had no monopoly of such legends. They were a floating property in a large region of the ancient world. In this sense the peculiar divinity generally attributed to them in the Bible as its private possession is challenged by heathen monuments. What for instance would we say if we found in a Latin author who had never heard of Jesus, an account similar, even verbally, to the death and resurrection of the Divine Person of the New Testament? Should we say that it is the nature of such legends, which if true must be miracle, to be common to many races; as the flood is reported to find a place in numerous mythologies? In this way should we strip the Holy Scripture of its unique authority, and relegate it to the books of the nations.

There is such a passage in Ovid's *Metamorphoses* in the account of the Death, Resurrection and Ascension of Hercules after his twelve labours completed. He, the Son of Jupiter and Alcumena, puts off the finite heredity of the Mother, and ascends in pure Godhead to his Father. The Poem is full of spiritual contents; and is a lesson for Clergy in the true theory of the Incarnation.

So if we find in Christian lands, and in the best races, a high standard of moral law with a religion to back it; and yet if we find ruder notions of right and wrong in all races, and *idola* or gods even in the lowest; and if we think towards a comparative morality and a comparative religion: must the commonness of these good, better and best things dilute their central examples, and be a proof against their primeval special gift from above?

Comparison seems to work that way: we are in a world of dilemmas. If all truth is thus comparatively true, and good comparatively good, the centre is washed away by the circumferences. Yet we have a refrain in the mind which exults otherwise. "The earth is the Lord's and the fulness thereof, the world and they that dwell therein. For He hath founded it upon the seas and established it upon the floods." Here the overflowing generalities are obeisant towards establishing the earth of the Lord.

In the midst of our opened mounds and treasuries of books and inscriptions, with our Bibles still in our hands, may we not use our new facilities for comparison, as means to recognize what is centre and what is circumference in our stores new and old? May not revelation come from God, although there be many copies of it extant which are partial and questionable? May not a true and good revelation be primary, and echoes of it, and perversions of it, and imaginations and impostures of it be secondary? May not all mythology be a beggarly legacy of a primeval wonder-mind which based on nature and regeneration perceived the deep things of God as we cannot perceive them; which thought creatively and redemptively? Which had all dispensations and thousands of years in its open ideas? In which the Fall of the Recoverer were immanent?

Comparisons between things need not be on a dead level: no science comes out of the Cities of the Plain. Eminence, mountains and hills, are as necessary in logic as multiplicity for syllogism. There is a will in reason, and end, cause and effect are its souls. So in comparing heathen Bibles with Holy Scripture we fall into the condition of the "single instance." For however extensive our Shinar Plain may be, and however many stories go to the Babylonish tower, yet if revelation be sunk in the monuments, the whole becomes one; it is confronted by no eye, and it ceases to be objective to thought, which always demands to be above and internal to its object.

We may, however, assume that the Bibles of the monuments are more important than our Bible; though few will venture this. It is too evidently above while they are beneath.

Can we not then more easily institute comparisons, downwards than upwards? If we begin with our feet and reason from them to ourselves, we shall have no heads to appeal to. If we begin with our heart and lungs, we pervade our system: the central ark of the bosom breathes and burns: the belly and the members expand and pulsate: their life comes from the bosom; and in this way these solidities also breathe and burn. Centrality governs, and outlying things obey.

The monuments in Egypt and Mesopotamia belong for the most part to the period anterior to the Mosaic dispensation: the traces of the Israelites in Egypt are few and doubtful. Archæology has therefore little relation to this part of the Old Testament. Is there any comparative thaumatology which can throw light on the facts here? Jewish history and Christ's life are comparatively recent history; and miracle and God Incarnate are in record here. Within this four thousand years the Jews underwent their drama, Jehovah presiding: within two thousand the Lord Christ made His Divinity and His miracles into the Word. Dominant disbelief is of no consequence to the facts. Neither is comparison at hand with either of these strongholds of supernatural religion. There are no similar records or archives; and the perfection of the Old and New Testaments stands alone as the Word of God in the waste of literature.

We approach nearer to comparative cases before the time of Abraham. In one sense the monuments seem on the plane of the dawn of history in the Pentateuch. But in a material respect, what equality is there between the Bible conserved by thirteen hundred generations of faithful Jews "who counted its words and letters, and considered this a weightier business than ascertaining what they actually meant," and the fragmentary remains of the library of Assurbanipal, with its fire-baked and sun-dried tablets, often broken in pieces; and in the whole having no beginning or end to the collection were it all edited even by the Professor, unless such wholeness be suggested out of the perfect revelation of Genesis. The legend of Gisdubar, save as a curiosity, containing as it does the Babylonian story of the Flood, has no gravity either for archæologist or historian unless as a pendant to Noah's deluge. It attests the prevalence of a flood-story; but it does not attest the Flood, or render it more probable. It lends no support to Bible history; nor reveals why the Flood was written of, nor how it now takes rank as spiritual necessity, with breath of life as natural.

The monuments give no Testamentary light on the first eleven chapters of Genesis from Adam to Noah, but confront us with a forged heathen Codicil. In my work, OANNES ACCORDING TO BEROSUS, after studying the learned Professor's *Hibbert Lectures*, I found that anything generically similar to the account of the six days' creation in the first chapter of Genesis, and to the creation of Adam on the seventh day, was not found elsewhere than in the Word. The end of the most ancient Church is portrayed by Berosus. Its consummation, which he mistook for the creation, was of monsters and abominations, coagulating, breeding, and working in an infernal sea or Chaos. Belus put an end to this state of things by means of self-sacrifice which is recorded and interpreted in my OANNES. The northern mythology in its account of creation similarly omits the Divine order of life found in Genesis i. and ii.; and begins with giant-generation. In neither case do the primeval revelation or the innocent Adams who accepted it, find any record. The reason may be that this state called Adam was inconceivable to the next humanity: it was pre-ëminently "alms for oblivion"; and that anything lay in it, or could come out of it, was beyond belief to those whose once heavenly faculties had been drowned, and their inward breath extinguished, by their damnable persuasions called in the then current language of correspondences the FLOOD.

There is therefore no Adam apparent in the monuments; no Adamic Order answering to the innocence before the fall, and to the rational certainty that Jehovah then moving in manifest creativeness gave gifts ineffable to us to his first sons and daughters. Here then the Bible has no competitor: it is beyond compare, and is a single Divine instance as God Himself is One.

The Word begins thus:—" In the beginning God created the heaven and the earth. And the earth was formless and empty; and darkness was upon the face of the deep: and the Spirit of God moved upon the face of the waters. And God said, Let there be light: and there was light. And God saw the light that it was good: and God divided the light from the darkness. And God called the light Day, and the darkness He called Night. And there was evening, and there was morning, one day."

An Assyrian tablet which according to the Professor " bears a striking resemblance to the account of the creation in the first chapter of Genesis," and which he inclines to think may not be earlier in its present form than the seventh century B.C., has the following:—

"At that time the heavens above named not a name, nor did the earth below record one. Yea, the deep was their first creator; the flood of the sea was She who bore them all. . . . At that time the gods had not issued forth, any one of them; by no name were they recorded; no destiny. Then the Gods were made; Lakhmu and Lakhamu issued forth. They grew up. . . . Next were made the host of heaven and earth; the time was long. The Gods Anu. The host of heaven and earth." . . . The narrative continues:—"The Creator made beautiful the stations of the great Gods. . . .

At that time the Gods in their assembly created. They made beautiful the mighty. They made the living things come forth, the cattle of the field, the beast of the field, and the creeping thing "* (pp. 22-24).

God's first work in Genesis is creation; His first spirit or breath moves upon the face of the waters. His first word is, Let there be light. His first naming calls the light day, and the darkness night. The heavens and earth of the Assyrian tablets have no *names*, none of the division of quality signified by such. The deep was their first creator: the flood of the sea was SHE who bore them all. She is here probably the woman Omoroka, of whom the author treated in OANNES. "The woman Omoroka is the regent of all the monsters engendered in the darkness and its waters. She is the sea, in identity with the regnant Moon: the Moon being the Queen of the heavens, Ashtaroth, or Astarte. The sea in its evil sense signifies the great Hell; and the moon, the self-intelligence which obeys its tides. Her rule is the empire of lusts by persuasions. She is woman in the evil sense; the listener to the serpent of the sensual selfhood. The Mother of evil" (pp. 26, 27).

The Gods are impossible without names. When they issue forth, they are Lakhmu and Lakhamu. What these signify the Assyriologists must inform us. As the progeny of the sea-woman Omoroka whom Belus cut in twain, they are the monsters recorded by Berosus; and Anu, and the next gods, the new generation, still of gods, who could sustain the force of the new or spiritual light. See, however, the interpretation of Berosus in my OANNES. His account is more in connection with the Word than any tablets yet translated from the monuments. It has a remainder of spiritual sense. But the passages from Berosus as well as from the tablets yield no record of God the Creator, or that God made man in His image after His likeness: or that

* *Fresh Light from the Ancient Monuments*, by A. H. Sayce, M.A. 1886.

the Lord God formed man, the dust of the ground; and breathed into his nostrils the breath of life, and man became a living soul.

Hesiod in the Greek mythology has the legend of the ages, golden, silver, brazen, heroic and iron; and also some legend of the first happy race. From this the golden age has been often celebrated in classical literature. It seems to have entered Greece from Asia, and is in some accord with the ages in Nebuchadnezzar's dream in the Book of Daniel. It has on it the fabulous stamp of Greece, and is in no sense suggestive of being a remainder of the Holy books of any nation. Indeed, excepting in the Poets, there are no writings which suggest a scriptural comparison in the literature of Greece and Rome. Nothing like what the monuments yield to us in Egypt, and in Assyria and Babylonia.

Is there then any account attainable of the origin of these monuments of the Old World, and of their relation to the books of the Bible? Has Providence in these days, when such light is wanted, vouchsafed to shew by a new Revelation how the case stands between the Word of the Old Testament and the fragments that are left of what was once *the same Word* in the graves of "the famous nations of the dead"? We answer this question in the affirmative. The earlier portion of our Word, the first eleven chapters of *Genesis* down to the call of Abraham are a portion of an Elder Word, and depict in correspondences which were the modes of thought, speech, and writing in the first times, the rise and decline of two Churches, the Adamic and the Noahtic. Noah, the tenth Church from Adam, was the end of the Adamic, and the Patriarchs were the end of the Noahtic Church. A true Word of God, of which we have the chapters just mentioned, but which contained other books, was revealed to the Noahtic Church in all its natures and races: these were participants in the second great Æon of Revelation. The account therefore is that the Word, as now extant, and as it existed in other books in the early part of the Æon, was known, for the most part, as we now have it to all the branches of the Ancient Church: that it was the ground of their true religion : that it maintained them in life for ages. That when the nations and peoples over which this Word presided became apostate, they still had its letter, and corrupted it by their several dispositions and different geniuses to magic and idolatry: these being two great destroyers of good and truth in the human family. Love of dominion signified by Babylon is the Imperial form of these evils, giving them leave to propagate : and represented by ruling men in Church and State, is Atheism, and does what it likes. With these infernal factors in the world, spiritual depravation of the Word is ensured. A false spiritual world, a false heaven and a false earth, become as it were revealed to the human mind and senses. Every lust of human days ministers to this: sham oracles, dreams, omens, abuse of correspondences, intuitions become superstitions, fanatical persuasions, hysterical diseases in weak members laid hold of by the strong to formulate a whole mythology, as the Vala in Völuspá has given a whole improvisation of the birth of Gods and man to the North in the Edda. Therefore we have no difficulty in seeing that the Ancient Word was revealed to a great group of nations. The identity of parts of the legend of the Flood with the Word itself in Genesis bespeaks that the whole Word unaltered once was in Mesopotamia, and the alterations of it are accounted for by the decline of the Ancient Church, and by the active spiritual parasites of heathenism which then inhabited its ruins, the owls and the bitterns of Holy Writ. See my Work on *Revelation, Mythology, Correspondences,* where I have treated of these subjects, and shewn that where the Spirit of God leaves mankind, Spirits of Hell take the place of it, and that the remainders on the evil side are not materialisms, as they *apparently* are at this day, but diabolic possessions and satanic credal institutions.

This, then, is our answer to the learned Professor's invitation to enlarge Scripture by adding to it the recent lore of Assyria, Babylonia, and Egypt. It gives us ample reason to keep Israel to itself until the spiritual sense of the Word is fully seen, and until Israel can be the third, the highest and the predominant partner with Egypt and with Assyria, a blessing in the midst, and a divine power of ordination and executive discrimination.

If Swedenborg had written in 1894 he could not have given a stronger instance of prophetic answer to a want of to-day, than in his revelation of the existence of the Ancient Word uncorrupted over the nations represented by these Graves and Monuments still pregnant with spiritual death. The learned Professor gives us, to our great satisfaction, materials for a most detailed history of the perversions of early mankind, and he lends us a power, that these also may not come under the ban of the "single instance," of comparing them with the Word of God, which rejects them into incantations and superstitious myths.

We will now submit to the reader some extracts from Swedenborg which show that he was fully aware that a Word, which he calls the Ancient Word, existed among the great group of nations in question, and also that in after ages it had been corrupted and destroyed in their midst. The following quotations are summaries taken from *The Swedenborg Concordance* of the Rev. John Faulkner Potts; a work that should be in the hands of every Biblical Archæologist.

"The doctrinals possessed by the men of the Ancient Church were preserved out of the revelations and perceptions of the Most Ancient Church. These doctrinals were their Word" (*Arcana*, n. 1068).

"The first Ancient Church, signified by Noah and his sons, was not confined to a few, but was extended through many kingdoms, namely Assyria, Mesopotamia, Syria, Ethiopia, Arabia, Lybia, Egypt, Philistia, all the way to Tyre and Sidon; and through the whole land of Canaan on both sides of the Jordan. . . . A certain outward worship afterwards began in Syria, which in time spread far and wide through many lands, especially through Canaan, and which differed from the worship of the Ancient Church. There arose hereby a new church, which may be called the second Ancient Church ; and of which Heber was the institutor " (*Ibid.* n. 1238).

" In process of time the first Ancient Church degenerated, and was adulterated by innovators as to both outward and inward worship, and this, in various places, especially in this way,—that all the significatives and representatives that the Ancient Church had from the mouth of the Most Ancient Church were turned into idolatries, and with some nations into magical arts " (*Ibid.* n. 1241).

" The worship called Babel did not prevail in the first Ancient Church, but in the succeeding Churches, when men began to be worshipped as Gods especially after death ; whence came so many Gods of the Gentiles " (n. 1327).

" That the first Ancient Church was deprived of the knowledges of truth and good, is evident from the fact that its nations for the most part became idolaters, and still had a certain outward worship " (n. 1328).

" The Ancient Church had its last time, when all charity grew cold, and all faith was darkened ; this was about the time of Heber. Then was the Last Judgment on that Church " (n. 1850).

" The last remains of the Ancient Church were in Syria " (n. 3249).

" The Ancient Church established by the Lord after the Flood was a Representative Church. All and each of its externals of worship represented the celestial and spiritual things of the Lord's kingdom, and in the supreme sense the divine things of the Lord. And all and each of its internals of worship had relation to charity. That Church was spread through a great part of the Asiatic World, through many kingdoms there, and although they differed about doctrinals of faith, the Church was one, because all the members in

AND THE OLD JERUSALEM. 197

every division of it made charity the essential. They who at that time separated faith from charity, and made faith the essential, were called 'Ham.' In process of time this Church turned away to idolatries, and in Egypt, Babel, and elsewhere, to magic. They began to worship outward things apart from inward, and as they receded from charity, heaven receded from them, and spirits from hell who led them, took its place" (n. 4680).

"The Ancient Church at its institution was at first without truths; was afterwards instructed in truths; and at last rejected them" (n. 5433).

"The first and second states of the Ancient Church in the regions round about the Jordan and Egypt were like the garden of Jehovah (Gen. xiii. 10). The case was the same with Tyre (Ezek. xxviii. 12-15). Ashur was like a cedar in Lebanon (Ezek. xxxi. 3-9). Wisdom flourished in Arabia, as evidenced by the visit of the Queen of Sheba to Solomon, and from the three 'wise men.' The third and fourth states of that Church, its states of vastation and consummation, are described in the Word throughout in both its historical and prophetical books. The consummation of the nations round about the Jordan or the land of Canaan is described by the destruction of Sodom, Gomorrha, Admah, and Zeboim. The consummation of the nations of the Church within Jordan is described by the expulsion of some and the slaughter of others. The consummation of that Church in Egypt is denoted by the drowning of the Egyptians in the Red Sea" (*Coronis*, n. 41).

"As this Ancient Church, typical of the Church which was to come, converted the representative correspondences into magic and idolatry, Jehovah raised up the Israelitish Church" (n. 42).

"The Hittites were among the better ones in Canaan. Abraham dwelt among them, and afterwards Isaac and Jacob; and were also buried with them. They behaved with piety and modesty towards Abraham. Hence, they as an upright nation represent the spiritual Church, or the truth of the Church. But, as with the rest of the Ancient Church, in course of time they fell away from charity, so they afterwards signified the false in the Church. Still the Hittites were among the more honoured. This is evident from Hittites being with David, namely, Abimelech, and Uriah whose wife was Bathsheba, by whom David had Solomon" (*Arcana*, n. 2913).

Wherever the Ancient Church is mentioned the Ancient Word is mentioned or implied, and hence the whole of the nations and peoples whose remains furnish "the monuments" are simply covered by the Word, let us say, for the general reader, by the Bible or Holy Writ, which was once their Bible, and from which, by their corruption, have sprung the great heathenisms of Asia and Africa, and ultimately of Greece and Rome. Again we say that the comparison can now be instituted between the inspired books of the living Word which are one body from Genesis to Revelation, and which have an internal spiritual soul, and the remains of the skeletons of the Ancient Churches. They are broken bones,—fragments which portray the vanity of this world, but have no spiritual cohesion, excepting in those parts which are identical with the letter of the Ancient Word. These capital pieces are here the skulls. We hope that archæology may carry the truths now revealed into its investigations. They will become fruitful of good historical information, and would in this way, by comparison, instruct the modern world respecting the lusts of dominion and the cruelties of superstition which destroyed the ancient Æons.

The Lord says, "heaven and earth shall pass away, but my word shall not pass away." Heaven and earth have passed away five times, including the "former heaven and earth, and the sea" named in the Apocalypse. These heavens and earths which perish are the dead but still pretentious churches in the spiritual world which are left at the end of each Æon, and are there and then the subjects of Last Judgments. The Word judges them. Its divine truths come into living contact with the "imaginary" heavens, and they sink into new hells. There are imaginary heavens here also, which must be cleared away before the new city can descend.

We see now that the spiritual sense of the Word based upon the verbally inspired letter, instead of leading into philosophical abstractions, goes directly home into concrete history and sits there as a judge, and that the Ancient and even the Most Ancient past comes out of the night of time towards a new day as the mind opens to the Revelations of the New Jerusalem.

XLVIII.—THE BODY OF MAN.

The body is the letter of which the mind is the spirit. The spiritual part by which alone we feel and know that we have bodies, and are anybody, must be omnipresent in physiology and psychology, or the lower reality has no true life in it. The use of the body to the spirit is the end and final cause of our embodiment.

God is a Man and the only Man. Hence the theological science of the human body is its veriest science.

Revelation claims the human body as a subject to be entered by theology. Man is made *for* the image and likeness of God, and when he is regenerate he is *in* that image and likeness. If the body regarded as the human form is for a divine image and likeness, all its organs, members and viscera, are orderly component parts of the design of that building of flesh which is for use in this world as a preliminary temple.

The "beginning," in Genesis, must be followed out in the Word of God; for nowhere else do we find sanction for considering the fleshly frame as a dwelling for the soul, and a designate house of the Lord. We are at no loss for the mention of the principal organs which enter into our revealed constitution. They are ready to our hand, and each endowed with a theological import. The head, the heart, the reins or kidneys, the lungs, the bowels, the stomach, the belly, the shoulders, arms and legs, the hands and feet; the breast, the loins, the generative members; and the five senses; and last, not least, the bones. The Word makes all these parts and organs, and indeed the body itself, canonical; and claims them for natural thought for conduct; for spiritual thought for doctrine, and for spiritual enlightenment about the Revelation which contains and owns them.

If our organism can have a theological use for the mind, there must be a theological gate into anatomy, physiology, and psychology. In other words, the structure and functions of the body can be studied as a branch of spiritual instruction. At present they are studied principally for two objects—(1) as a ground for medical and surgical education, knowledge and practice; and (2) as science for its own sake, to build up the fabric of knowledge, and complete a mental survey of nature. In the Word, however, where the organs are spoken of, we can have no such limited purposes; for we have with us everything that is human. Whatever there is in man, good or bad, is flesh in his body, and the tendency to the leading incarnations of his life and character is given in the seed of that body that begets him. Hence his drama of existence is written and prompted in every organ, nay, in every organic thought. Already out of this fact general principles of knowledge are gathered applying to the human race, and to no other, as that the heart is the word for the affections, and the head for intelligence. These names for spiritual things belong to humanity alone. Comparative anatomy and physiology show comparative faculties analogous to those of man; but no problem of the soul, no regard to theology, occurs primarily in the investigation of animal similitudes.

They are a rich outlying province when the central realm is admitted, and when its truths are at work.

The sciences we are considering, after the labour of thousands of years, consist of valuable stores of carnal facts, elicited to a great extent by scientists working independently of medical practice, and chiefly for the second object before stated, namely, love of knowledge. The knowledge gained is a large estate, and it is a question, What faculty of mind can show right to it by worthy use and administration of so splendid a property? At present materialism is in undisputed possession; and in alliance with medicine, itself endowed and established by State patronage and protection, Matter as a first cause of man is a national scientism almost as the Church of England is a national ecclesiasticism.

The gate whereby Theology enters the sciences of the body of man is already given in the fact that man is to be an image and likeness of God; and finitely to correspond to the infinite Creator. This law of Correspondence, an omnipresent image-and-likeness-law, descends through every degree of his being. It means that his soul is the first given correspondence, reserved in its three degrees, celestial, spiritual and natural; that his spirit is to follow in act and life; that his will and understanding are to be images and likenesses, or correspondences, by behaving as such; and that there is to be a spiritual body within him corresponding to his natural body. If this be so, then every natural organ is full of Uses, and has a spiritual organ within it uniting it to correspondent faculties next above it; and by private degrees of ascent to the soul and the Creator. So considered, theology will be at home in physiology.

The first recognition of this must be effected by leading instances embodying universals. These are at hand, as mentioned already. And consider, first, the LUNGS.

The Spirit of men is embodied in their breath and breathing. What is this breathing but a momentaneous correspondence during wakefulness to thinking? If the reader observes, every intention of thought modifies his breath to suit itself, and to carry to the soles of his feet, and to the crown of his head, the peculiar opening and shutting, expansion and contraction, inspiration and expiration of the lungs. By these ratios he weighs and estimates himself in every thought every second; and proves, or approves himself. This is the chief bodily spirit in man; a true consideration, an entire bodily understanding of his moving case. The second and lesser bodily spirit is the air breathed in and breathed out. This carries the man into the world, and is the sphere of his whole bosom and its loves, his bodily contribution to the Zeitgeist. The correspondence of thought with breath, whereby man breathes good or breathes evil, breathes peace or breathes slaughter, means well or means ill, is the perpetual union of the soul with the body, and is ultimately the spiritual body itself which lives after death and becomes the permanent life and character of the individual. For the spirit has a respiration of its own, the result of the spiritual state acquired by all the respirations of the will and understanding in the natural body.

Here we have in the first new function of our mortal day, in our first breath leading to all breathing, one gate by which the whole body is in close relation to the Author and Giver of Life, Himself the Infinite Spirit, whom we are to "worship in spirit and in truth."

These correspondential functions of the lungs, obvious as daylight, are unknown and unteachable, unless we have a belief in the higher term, the spirit, and an interest in the moving fact that we are always transmitting our ruling love by its spirit, breath, or intellect, into our persons, and making them into its image and likeness.

Theology is in sole possession of this domain of the lungs, which embraces the whole organic body under the whole conscious and more organic mind.

The HEART corresponds to the affections by feeling them

in itself, as we correspond to those we love, and feel with them. They are out of us and away from us, but we correspond to them. The Heart makes love, because by Correspondence of form and mingling it is Love. The affection within it is in its own form, a Heart of Heart. It loves the whole body, and by pulses or beats of love feeds it with good blood. So it keeps alive all the organs of rebuilding and purification. We say that it *makes* love; for in itself it is the highest organ of blood-marriages; in its chambers and beds effecting unions which are to enrich the body with the choicest progeny of secretions, so creating digestion in the stomach, juice in the pancreas, general and universal fluid wealth in the capillaries, and nervous joys thence to the very brains. This is because all these things are images and likenesses of a Love of which they are the children, and to which in USES they correspond in the most bodily, the most spiritual, and the most celestial fashion.

Theology is the sole owner of this heart also, and claims all its sciences, spiritual and natural, as its necessary title-deeds: it must feed upon them all.

So again, if the body is the continent and incarnation of all that we are, the belief in what we are fixes what we accept as the contents of our bodily selves. If we are material stuff throughout, the words breath and spirit, heart, affection, love, survive indeed in language, but have no other than a carnal sense. If the organs have divine or unknowable uses, yet they are of use to nothing we believe in, and their instruction only repeats our flesh. But if the Revelation which teaches us that our spirits are ourselves is our faith, and that love to God and man is their life, then these are the contents which our bodies and members have to recognize in our anatomy, and in our freewill to incarnate.

The Heart and the Reins are united in the Word. The right side of the heart receives the venous blood from the whole body, and with it the new chyle which feeds, and the lymph which vivifies the blood; and these it mingles and unites, and sends them through the lungs, in the capillaries of which they are purified in expiring, and in inspiring. The blood returns from the understanding lungs to the loving heart ruddy and arterial. It is received in the left side of the heart. Introduction and association is the function of the right side : marriage is the function with the left side, and also extends to the whole heart. For the heart is the blood-maker; as love, to which the heart corresponds, is the maker and perceptive distinguisher of affections. The heart enjoys in conjugium the central blood of the body, because it is representatively the lord of life, and the head of the love which is the life. By the strong muscles of its affections it couples its humanities together; and by the same acts and deeds it purifies itself; and through the coronary arteries and veins discards whatever is effete for its intimate circle into the lower service of the body, where it can still be useful and worthy. Thus the heart itself is the mint that coins and stamps the golden blood, and gives fortunes to all its brides.

The REINS or KIDNEYS in their office purify the serum or watery element in which the blood consisting of globules floats. Like every organ they have in them an instinctive freewill of their own which incites them to their work. This is made lively by the expansion and contraction which they undergo as an individual personality of the general movement compelled by the breathing lungs. The kidneys breathe in the serum with the blood which it surrounds. And their whole organic life is a miraculous machinery for attracting the worthless serum with the worthy blood; and while the latter circles easily in its own right through nodes of labyrinthine arteries, the stale serum, angular and lame with chemicals, stumbles down into straight tubes and pits, and is on the way out of the body. It is not the purpose here to pursue in detail these functions, which the reader without some knowledge of anatomy will fail to understand; but rather to indicate that there is a spiritual side to the human form, in which the soul, spirit, or mind, will and understanding are made flesh. Being made flesh, however, these organs, in their functions and judgments, reveal the fates and destinies of the higher faculties, that is, of the man himself, when this corporeal frame is laid aside.

All the physiological knowledge that I have which transcends the text books, is derived from the Treatises of Swedenborg, THE ANIMAL KINGDOM, CONSIDERED ANATOMICALLY, PHYSICALLY, AND PHILOSOPHICALLY, and THE ECONOMY OF THE ANIMAL KINGDOM, which I translated 51 and 48 years ago, and which I now read with wonder. The great Swedish Physiologist, Prof. Retzius, at a meeting in Stockholm held in honour of Swedenborg as a distinguished member of the Royal Academy of Sciences of Sweden, stated that he (Swedenborg) had discovered nothing new in Physiology. This is true in the same sense as that Swedenborg has discovered nothing new in the Word of God, and also as the Biblical saying is, that there is nothing new under the sun. Discovery is one thing, and Revelation, which has many kinds, is another. And I dare to affirm that the ANIMAL KINGDOM above alluded to is a continuous revelation of things previously unknown and unknowable, and that it is preliminary to the *Arcana Cœlestia*, and to the *Heaven and Hell*, which are further miracles of divine light, but not records of discoveries.

The former works are *seeings* of what the designs and uses in the human body are, and Swedenborg, after the amplest knowledge of his facts, is the SEER of them; as he also is of the spiritual world.

Now the seership of the intellect is the highest kind of perceptive induction and deduction; and throughout the organs of the body of which he treated, he read them off through these processes into rational explanations of their uses corresponding to their forms, and of their times corresponding to the ages of man. Where Newton divined one gravitation for this material world, Swedenborg saw a thousand centres from organization to life, all held to the one Centre, the Lord.

Listen to the following from the chapter on the Kidneys in the ANIMAL KINGDOM :—

" As the blood is continually making its circle of life, that is to say, is in a constant revolution of birth and death ; as it dies in its old age, and is regenerated or born anew ; and as the veins solicitously gather together the whole of its corporeal part, and the lymphatics of its spirituous part ; and successively bring it back, refect it with new chyle, and restore it to the pure and youthful blood ; and as the kidneys constantly purge it of impurities, and restore its pure parts to the blood ;—so likewise Man, who lives at once in body and spirit while he lives in the blood, must undergo the same fortunes generally, and in the progress of his regeneration must daily do the like. Such a perpetual symbolical representation is there of spiritual life in corporeal life ; as likewise a perpetual typical representation of the soul in the body. In this consists *the searching of the heart and reins*, which is a thing purely divine " (n. 293).

In a note to this passage Swedenborg says :—" In our doctrine of Representations and Correspondences, we shall treat of both these symbolical and typical representations ; and of the astonishing things which occur, I will not say in the living body only, but throughout nature, and which correspond so entirely to supreme and spiritual things, that one would swear that the physical world is purely symbolical of the spiritual world : insomuch that if we choose to express any natural truths in physical and definite vocal terms, and to convert these terms only into the corresponding spiritual terms, we shall by this means elicit a spiritual truth or theological dogma in place of the physical truth or precept ; although no mortal would have predicted that anything of the kind could possibly arise by bare literal transposition : inasmuch as the one precept, considered separately from the other, appears to have absolutely no relation to it. . . . This symbolism pervades the living body."

The kidneys, ureters and bladder are the lowest of the chemical organs. They administer purification and rejection. Of those persons who constitute this province in the Greatest Man, Swedenborg says: "They are of such a genius that they like nothing better than to explore and search out the quality of others; and there are some who desire to chastise and to punish if only there be some justice in the case. The functions of the kidneys, ureters and bladder, correspond to this. They explore the blood thrown into them, to see if there be any useless and hurtful serum there: and they separate such from the useful, and afterwards chastise it; driving it down towards the lower regions; and on the road they agitate it in various ways. These are the functions of those who constitute the province of the kidneys. . . They explore and search into the quality of others; what they think and what they will; and live in the desire to find occasion to condemn with an especial view to chastising. . . Many of this kind when they lived in the world were judges, who then rejoiced in heart when they found cause which they believed to be just to fine, chastise, and punish. . . . By this passion these spirits communicate with the hells; but by the justice of the cause, which they seek for before they punish, they communicate with heaven. On this account they are kept in the province of the kidneys" (*Arcana*, n. 5381-84).

"From these things," says Swedenborg, "it may appear what is meant in the word by Jehovah searching and trying the reins and the heart, and by the reins chastening, as in Jeremiah. Also by the following, Jehovah that triest the reins and the heart (xi. 20). Jehovah that triest the just, and seest the reins and the heart (xx. 12). In David, the just God trieth the hearts and the reins (Ps. vii. 9). Thou hast possessed my reins (cxxxix. 13). I am he who trieth the reins and the heart (Apoc. II. 23). The reins signify spiritual things, and the heart celestial things : the reins those things which are of truth, and the heart those which are of good. For the reins purify the serum, and the heart, the blood itself. Hence trying, examining and searching the reins signifies these processes applied to the quantity and quality of truth, or of faith, in man. That this is so is evident in Jeremiah : Jehovah, thou art near in their mouth, but far from their reins (xii. 2). And in David, Behold thou desirest truth in the reins (li. 8). And my reins chasten me during the nights (xvi. 7) " (*Ibid.* n. 5385).

The nights are spiritual states of sadness and reproach when our evils and impurities come home to us, and motives and resolutions to a better life can receive strength from above.

In these remarks on some organs in the Body of Man I do no more than indicate the grand future uses of the sciences of anatomy and physiology. A small part of them is sufficient for medicine : a still smaller part for surgery. On the other hand the whole field is a basis for the Theology of the New Church. It is significant that the knowledge of anatomy has been gained principally by anatomical specialists, without immediate regard to the healing art or to any obvious use. Experts indeed are indignant at the thought that the men of the experimental laboratory have for an end the low motive of helping the cure of diseases. Anatomy and physiology for their own sakes is their motive. In Homœopathy, the principal System of Medicine in this century, Hahnemann relies on abnormal symptoms and states as indications of disease : and requires only regional anatomy as a plane of location for his corresponding drug symptoms, that *similia similibus curentur* may be enacted. Schüssler also, the inventor of Biochemical Medicine, has slender need for Anatomy and Physiology in their breadth and facial expressiveness. Armed with his twelve cell-salts he aims to rectify the mineral man, redundant, or deficient, in chemical constitution. He would have us properly crystallised. Beyond this, the general form and make of the patient, and the use of his organs in health, do not interest him. His drug divinations, if angular, are admirable in practice, and mark a peculiar genius for estimating the balance of important weights in the body. Biochemistry seems to be an instinct of the atomic theory striving to enter organization, and implying definite attractions, relations and compositions of atoms as last resorts, all working in life as a mysterious place just above physics. It is singular that Swedenborg inaugurated a Biochemistry in his doctrine that the formal atom of sea-salt is the mineral cross upon which the blood globule is built. He essayed to figure this atom as he had done with the atoms of many other chemical substances in his early work on the *Principles of Chemistry*.

Anatomy and Physiology developed as mere knowledge, will then be a valuable possession for the coming Æon, but at present their hypotheses end in no theory, and in nothing but uncertain metaphysics, with the Unknowable always at hand. The estate passing to spiritual faith as a successor becomes a basis to the new Revelations now given to the world by commissioned Swedenborg.

He has himself given first the physiological light which makes the organs available for spiritual use. He has given a human theory of the uses of each by which it is a piece of spiritual man. And next he shows the magnitudes which amplify organs into whole humanities, as the provinces of the Greatest Man. For even in this world, every society is an organic man; also every kingdom; the whole world too: and in every organic man, all the organs are present to constitute the individual, the social, and then the general personality. The same is the case in application to the spiritual world which is marching upwards to the heavens; and to heaven itself which is continually fed with new members, expects them individually, and thereby and in itself, of the Divine mercy, is continually marching onwards in perfection towards the Lord.

This fact involves two things; first, that every man belongs to some province in the greatest man, and is on his way thither when he dies: he is new food for the celestial brain if he belongs to the highest heaven: for the heart or the lungs if he belongs to the middle heavens; for the abdomen if he belongs to the lower heavens: and he is received for his own province by the constant attention all the way of the assimilating personalities of the Greatest Man.

Dr. John Worcester gives a diligent survey of this awful subject in his *Physiological Correspondences*, Boston, 1889; those who desire instruction should read it. All who die, and who are to nourish heaven by their spirits, and to be there, require to put off the earthly, and to put on the heavenly. The Greatest Man, in passing them to their homes, consists of ministering angels and spirits who correspond to the functions of spiritual purification, adaptation, and fitness; and by instruction, guidance, and trial, the new-comers are led, as new food is led, into the spiritual flesh and blood of the kingdom. They pass according to their fitness through few or many disciplines of association. All that can at present be said will be found in this admirable Book, which tells of the pilgrimage of men from earth to heaven. It flows in a stream of divine order from the first reception of newly departed spirits by the lips of the Greatest Man, to the final blessedness of home in the heart, all the way through personal organs which are love and truth, promoting and correcting; angelic individuals and societies being the only organs here.

The purpose of this section is to indicate that human anatomy and its integral physiology reserve their main use for the Church, in which they will be a basis of spiritual knowledge by enabling the mind to dwell on the uses of organs by which they correspond to the personalities of the individual and of all the incorporations of man from the least to the greatest. This carries the lesser proposition that all sciences so far as they are not applied to immediate arts will be similarly the property of the New Jerusalem, according to that law of the Word, "There shall be a highway out of Egypt into Assyria, and Israel shall be the third with Egypt and with Assyria." Israel is the spiritual Church.

There is yet another realm in which a knowledge of the body is a necessity. No true metaphysics can be attained without it. For it alone makes all thought personal. This is a large subject which cannot be entered upon here. Swedenborg availed himself of his seership into the human economy to lay bare mental secrets which have been inscrutable to the learned since material science began. Speaking of what can be gained from this source he says, " All the things that can be known of the will and the understanding, or of the love and the wisdom ; therefore which can be known of the soul of man, may be known from the correspondence of the heart with the will, and of the understanding with the lungs." This algebra, in which the process is from the known to the unknown, yields the true metaphysics ; from the anatomy of the body reveals the anatomy of the living mind. The result is stated at length in *The Divine Love and Wisdom*, Part V., as it was revealed to Swedenborg. "Those things which correspond to each other," says he, " act similarly, with this distinction, that the one is natural and the other spiritual." By working the above correspondences he has even shewn how the analogue and basis of Freewill is organic in the peculiar blood-life which emancipates the lungs from the dominion of the heart, and enables them to breathe or think either with or against the affections. The body is therefore, as stated at first, the Letter of which the will and the understanding are the Spirit.

XLIX.—THE WELLS OF ABRAHAM.

The Patriarchs preceding the Jewish Dispensation, beginning from Abraham as an idolater in Chaldea, represent the

Lord in His human nature about to make His humanity divine. This, by which the Word was fulfilled and made flesh, was progressive, and took place from the inmost, highest, or celestial degree, through the middle or spiritual, to the lowest or natural. The celestial was represented by Abraham, the spiritual by Isaac, and the natural by Jacob. Love, Wisdom as the rational principle of Love, and actual life or Use, are plain correspondents to these three systemic denominations.

It is said in Genesis, referring to Isaac as the Divine Rational, "And all the Wells which his father's servants digged in the days of Abraham his father, the Philistines stopped them up and filled them with dust. . . . And Isaac returned, and digged again the wells of waters, which they digged in the days of Abraham his father, and which the Philistines stopped up after the death of Abraham; and he called their names, according to the names which his father called them" (xxvi. 15-18).

The Wells of waters of Abraham, stopped up and filled with dust by the Philistines, even at first sight suggest a second meaning. This is clear also in the Word because it is said further on that the servants of Isaac dug in the valley, and found there a well of "living waters" (19). Abraham's wells, spoken of as not in a valley, are more living waters than these by virtue of the signification of Abraham and of Isaac.

The internal sense of this part of Genesis treating of the Lord's Coming through the humanities signified by the Patriarchs is of divine significance, and in the mere virtue of it as communicated in the *Arcana Cœlestia*, it confirms the mind in the faith that the Old Word is as the New Word, a direct Will or Testament of God.

As Abraham signifies the Divine Love in assumption, his servants are truths of love ministering, and the wells of waters they dig are doctrinal knowledges of charity in the field of the Church. They are dug because instruction is necessary about them, and reception or attainment is implied. In the spiritual church signified by the servants such doctrines are not natural fountains, but spiritual obedience to truths. The Philistines filled the wells of waters with dust. This signifies the conversion of these truths into mere hearsays and knowledges; the conversion of them from handmaids of love into matters of external faith. In this case they become a mere system of knowledges, *scientia cognitionum*, and are not commanding truths. "In the Ancient Church and afterwards those were called Philistines who paid very little heed to life, but very much to doctrine, and who in the succession of time even rejected the things which belong to life, and as the essential of the Church they acknowledged those which belong to faith, which they separated from life. These are the uncircumcised Philistines. Dust signifies terrestrial things, that is, the loves of self and of gain. Those who are called Philistines, that is, who are not in life but in doctrine, obliterate interior truths by earthly loves, that is by love of self and of gain, and can do no other than fill up the wells of Abraham with dust. These loves induce darkness, which extinguishes the light of truth from the Lord. The love of self and of gain suffers nothing of truth from the Divine to come near to it. Still its Philistines are capable of glorying in, and boasting of, their knowledge of truths; they even preach them with a sort of zeal. The fires of these loves are what kindle and excite; and the zeal is only the fervour of these fires. This is plain from the fact that they can preach against their own veriest life with the like zeal or fervour. These are the terrestrial or earthly things, by which the Word itself, which is the fountain of all truth, is stopped up" (see *Arcana*, 3412, 3413).

"The Wells of waters which they digged in the days of Abraham" signify the goods and truths which were known and received among the ancients. These truths are at this day obliterated, insomuch that scarce any one knows that they once existed, and that they could be any other than what are taught at this day. They were, however, quite different. They held *representatives* and *significatives* of the celestial and spiritual things of the Lord's Kingdom, thus of the Lord Himself; and they who understood these were called wise ; and they were wise ; for so they were able to speak with spirits and angels. . . . And as the angels were in the representatives and significatives of the Lord's Kingdom, in which there is nothing else than celestial and spiritual love, so the ancients had also *doctrinals* which treated solely *of love to God and charity towards the neighbour*, by virtue of which again they were called wise. From these doctrinals they knew what charity is, namely, that it is the affection for being of service to others without any design of recompense. Also they knew what the neighbour is to whom charity is due ; namely, all in the universe, but still each with discrimination. These doctrinals at this day are utterly lost, and in their stead we have doctrinals of faith, which the ancients made nothing of in comparison. Who knows at this day what that charity is which is void of all self-seeking, and averse to all that is for self's sake ? Who knows what is meant by the neighbour; namely, every individual with discrimination according to the quantity and quality of good belonging to him ; thus good itself—in a supreme sense the Lord, because He is in all good, and all good is from Him, and the good which is not from Him is not good, however it may appear to be so. And as it is not known what charity is, and what neighbour is, so it is not known who they are that in the Word are signified by the poor, the miserable, the needy, the sick, the hungry and thirsty, the oppressed, widows, orphans, captives, naked, sojourners ; by the blind, the deaf, the halt, the lame, and others. The doctrinals of the ancients taught who these are, and to what class of neighbour, and thus of charity, they belong. The whole Word in the sense of the letter is according to those doctrinals. When the Divine passes down to the natural plane with man, it passes into such things as works of charity, with discrimination according to genera and species. The Lord also spake in this same way because from the essential Divine. As in Matthew, " The King shall say to those on the right hand, Come, ye blessed of my Father, possess the Kingdom prepared for you ; for I was an *hungered* and ye gave me to eat, I was *thirsty* and ye gave me to drink, I was a *stranger* and ye took me in, I was *naked* and ye clothed me, I was *sick* and ye visited me, I was *in prison* and ye came to me " (xxv. 34). The works here recounted signify universal genera of charity, and in what degree they are good or belong to good ; and show who are the neighbours towards whom charity is to be exercised. And the Lord in the highest sense is the neighbour ; for He says, " In so far as ye have done it to one of the least of these my brothers, ye have done it to Me " (40).

" By Isaac returning, and digging again the wells of waters which they digged in the days of Abraham his father, is signified that the Lord opened those truths which were known and received among the Ancients " (*Ibid.* 3418).

" He who lays stress on the literal sense, believes that if he gives bread to a hungry person, takes outcasts or vagabonds into his house, and clothes the naked, he shall on that account be admitted to glory, and to heaven ; when yet these are mere external acts, which the wicked may perform to merit heaven. But the hungry, the afflicted, and the naked signify those who are spiritually such; different states of misery incident to man, who is the neighbour towards whom charity is to be exercised " (*Arcana*, 3419).

The averment by Swedenborg of truths lost out of life, and of ancient wisdom departed, cannot but seem unwarrantable to an age which reckons itself new and great in the possession of stores of fact and knowledge in which former ages were deficient. But however clever humanity may be at this time, it has a short memory, and this is becoming shorter and shorter as time, more and more crowded with events, makes one thing obliterate another in our passage. The railway car of change from state to state favours no possession of sense, and we live in an age of its sensations. Now Swedenborg mentions two heads in which the Ancients did surpass us. One will not be denied if it be conceded as a possible gift. By perceiving the correspondences of things the first men were not sensualists, but were in equation with the angels and with the spiritual world, and as men and spirits are both generically the same people, and had then the same language, namely of correspondences; so they spoke with each other by these real hieroglyphics, which were not Cadmean letters, but inward creations to the soul, and outward creations to the senses. Nature, at first coincident with man, was thus intended as part of the Book of God, and the Word comprehended it.

So far those who do not deny primeval intercourse with heaven may accept the position that truths inspiring life, which are now forgotten, were still extant in the Ancient Church. But when we come to the second clause, that the truths or doctrinals concerning charity have existed in the past, and do not exist now, an age so busy with "charities" may well be exercised in examining so apparently merciless a statement.

The clue to its justification is that a true religion is the fountain from which true charity proceeds, and that those who are deficient in this religion, and from mental or hereditary causes incapable of it, are the principal objects of the charity to which the Ancients attended. In the better ages—I do not speak of Churches in decline, but in uprightness—they had the asylums and hospitalities that were needful in their own way; and they gave benefactions where they were wanted. But the other charity was the main thing, and automatically ensured not the short but the ample commons of human kindness.

It is obvious that if charity be another name and state for love, the amount and quality of it is measured not by the number of persons housed, fed, clothed, and otherwise provided for, but by the genuineness of the love which does this work also, and of the religion which enjoins and consecrates the love. And if charity or love needs discrimination with regard to its objects, it is clear that the wisdom that regulates and administers the love must be present and in operation. Without religion neither of these factors exists. And if charitable institutions were a hundred fold as plentiful as they are, without the charity which is love, and the administration which is wisdom, the country would still be restless with a woeful remainder of wants and incurables in all classes.

The charity that is wanting is thus more needful at first for the charity givers than for the charity receivers. There are two great starvations in the modern world: religious starvation, and irreligious. The religious starvation comes directly from the dogma that faith without works is saving. This shuts up the very heart of man, and starves it. Loss of open and true understanding, paralysis of brotherhood follows. Irreligious starvation, of which Atheism is the final name and ground, is pinched and starved by self-satisfactions and their liberalities; it believes pre-eminently in itself and its lucre, and that giving matter, whether money or bread, supports the people, and shall be called from old usage, charity. It would feed the hungry *voter* until he is all mouth with no end to it: a hydatid. The sure debasement and depravation of charity, confining its field of operation to poverty, ensues of necessity from the starved hearts or wilful minds of these two opposite genera of charity givers.

The relief of poverty and material distress is then one thing, and love of the neighbour, the injunction of the second great Commandment, is another. In our day, when there is no faith or inward truth left on earth because there is no charity, Society, for its own sake, lest ruin overtake it, minds its workhouses, and prisons, and private individuals establish almshouses and benevolent institutions to supplement the debt of the trembling State to its members. It might seem as if Relief is to become universal, and that all of us are to be fed by trade regulation. This goal is one solution of the first question, the relief of poverty and of material wretchedness. It is apart from religion, and the lust of power goes to and fro within its still limited den as a roaring lion.

The second thing is the love of the neighbour. This is not a product of legislation or of the State, but as the Second Commandment it proceeds from the First; from the Love of the Lord thy God with all thy soul, with all thy mind, with all thy heart, and with all thy strength. These two loves embrace the Commandments.

All men will admit that you are bound to love only that which is good in your neighbour. It is evident that Jesus Christ, who gave these two new Commandments, sanctions no other love than this. Your neighbour's evil ways, vices, crimes, you are not to love, but only what is good in him; and you are to love this because by your selective brotherhood he and you both become better. Good itself which is God is the First Commandment; good derived which is a good man and every good man is the Second; and good possible in those who are naughty is included in the love of the neighbour. The good of punishment and of separation comes in here when needed. Good possible you may long presume to exist though your eyes have not the magnifying glass of sufficient charity to see the small germ of it that may save *what is left* of an unfortunate character. One germ that does not hate will do it.

Because there is in the world a new Religion based on these two Commandments, and it is received intellectually by a few, and because John, or Charity in act, has tarried till this second Advent in some simple hearts irrespective of new religious knowledge, therefore we cannot say that there is none of that Love of the neighbour which is enjoined by the Lord. If there were none, the Lord would not be here, He would have no remains to vivify, and the world would die. But it is the doctrinals of Charity which are absent; and being designed as the commanding and public, *truths* of the Church, they are nevertheless not to be found in it. I do not here speak of the New Church as an ecclesiasticism, but of the National Church, in which, according to Swedenborg, the true Religion should be made known.

If we look round upon our Societies, the superficial appearance is that the world grows steadily worse. Unparalleled enormity of crime in private stalks abroad as a moral principle; as a conviction. Suicide is epidemic. Murder reddens every newspaper. Insurrection against all establishment, *and notably against individual freedom*, is universal. Malignant pulling down of old things, and effacement of old landmarks of right and wrong, are sops to restless multitudes maddened by demagogues. The classes of Society are rhymed and marshalled by the rhetorician against the masses. The black heaven is starred over with atheists, banefully constellated in parliaments and ministries; and they are mighty men, men of a name. His Holiness the Pope is at one with us here. On March 2, 1894, he told the members of the Sacred College, in referring to the condition of the Church, that the need of making its beneficent action universally felt was urgent. For "all the old conceptions of honesty, justice, authority, liberty, social rights, and social duties have been overthrown." This has taken place in spite of the Catholic Church, in spite of the other Churches, and of the Nonconformities. A religion has died out: the consummation of its Æon has come. That consummation is written on the walls of our dying century in lust of pre-eminence at any price, in new greed and dishonesty in all classes, in luxury demanded for, or by, everybody, in power conferred especially on manageable ignorance, the clay of the demagogic potter; in the notable absence of religion from journalism; and in the deadness of ecclesiastics on all hands to the signs of the times.

Where then is there any sign of that love of the neighbour which loves only what is good in him; associates with that good, brings it out, and being its brother, fosters and supports it? Ask anybody you like who is not professedly godless, and he will endorse the above statement, even although he reserves reasons to mitigate it.

Evil also associates with evil, and the evil of the companion, who is no brother, and no neighbour, is the charm and wealth of him. The present society is the first standing army of the bands and regiments of evil. The most opposite lusts shake hands, and hating each other with deadly hatred, yet form great battalions, medical, legal, ecclesiastical, proletariat, to destroy the good of the neighbour.

These things are known in the city, in the Church, in municipal life, and are accepted with a shrug of the shoulders, and a placid humour about the situation. Being patent and universal, there is no need to discuss what is an admitted state of things, and no worse for one person than for another: only keep thee, my comrade, from present legal crime! It may not be legal crime long, and then you can enjoy its virgin *parterre*.

But if social silence and concealment make it difficult to know that there is no love of the good that is in the neighbour in our world of society,—for the sure process is that at a certain stage evil is called good,—yet another magnitude of object-lessons restates the case most expensively. How of the relations of nations to loving that which is good in each other, and nothing else? First, Where is the love? Let armaments speak. Let fear speak; fear which occupies the seat of love rejected. Europe is dying of its battalions: industry and homes are dying with it. What nation in modern times has ever loved what was good in another nation because it was good. Emotions of admiration for chivalric exploits have been, but they are not born of love and they lack its substance as not being sanctioned by Christ's Religion. We pause indeed over splendid passages of history, but they are not to the point of admiring righteousness in them. The smallest causes exasperate nation against nation. All the facts demonstrate that these large humanities in varying degrees hate each other, and that this, with their self-love, creates larger and larger armies and navies, with destruction of each other more fiercely in view every decade. And as in private hatreds, and political hatreds, so they can form alliances between totally opposite and warring evils, for temporary menace to other peoples, the most hated for the moment. These are the national friendships of evil.

This year an interviewer sought M. Zola for his opinion specially on Anarchism : What could be done to meet the newness of the case? The French Realist confronted the fact that demolishing the present society with dynamite transcended crime as being on the top of a diabolic temple, and there transfigured into duty and conviction : in short become a New Faith. Recognizing this, he said, that the only counterpoise he could suggest was a New Religion ; were such a thing possible.

There are two solutions, the one of which prepares for the other. "Resist not the evil one," is a way of stating the first necessity. We know all these bad things alleged against us ; we are in the " science of knowledges" about them,—*in scientia cognitionum*. In our scientific age they can be classified just like the species and genera in zoology or botany or mineralogy. Yet we do not believe and confess them to be evil otherwise than with the mouth. We do not accept it as a truth of our personal salvation that they must be repented of, and put aside ; and as a truth of our personal damnation that we persevere in them. And if we acknowledge something of our "evil one," our heart's self, we do not use the insight to accompany the accusing conscience from one misbehaviour to another. Perhaps we—

"Compound for sins we are inclined to,
By damning those we have no mind to."

We do not, as Sir T. Brown says, "dive into our inclinations" with a purpose to overhaul and imprison them. This must be done; and if the Church, somnolent with faith alone, and under the opium of the atonement, cannot waken sufficiently to warn us, then a new responsibility rests on Journalism, for which Carlyle predicted this use, to take the pulpit of ecclesiasticism into its offices.

Ceasing to do evil is the preliminary to learning to do well. After this, in whatever field of life it takes place, a plot of ground becomes more and more prepared for the seeds of the New Religion. Its seeds are the truths which can be refreshed into vigorous life by the wells of waters unstopped by Isaac from the dust with which they have been filled by the Philistines. The wells of Abraham! Forget not the translucent Word. The way to work the neighbour's good is then to cease to work him evil. So the Lord becomes present in the faculties, and reveals as a new field what the best thing of the neighbour's mind is; for when you begin to love him in this sense, the fire of it makes a light of charity in which you see almost all of him as a new creature. You see the worth of him, and the sin of wronging him. What beauties love reveals to a man in his sweetheart when first he loves her. Carry this to the value you would have of your neighbours if you loved them as the second commandment enjoins. But this is not a given natural condition like the other love; but is strictly dependent on the keeping of the first commandment of love to the Lord.

The immensity of the field of loving the neighbour, namely, divine charity, can go as duty into a small compass, and therein embrace all humanity with affection's own arms. The kingdom is to come, "as in heaven, even so upon the earth." "To the above," says Swedenborg, "I will add this memorable relation. In heaven all who perform uses from affection for use, by virtue of the communion in which they live, derive as their portion that they are wiser and happier than others. And to perform uses there with them is to act sincerely, rightly, justly and faithfully in the work proper to the calling of each. THIS THEY CALL CHARITY. Acts of adoration in worship they call signs of charity, and the rest of offices they call dues and kindnesses. They say that when everyone does the work of his own calling sincerely, rightly, justly and faithfully, the Community subsists and persists in its good; and that this is to be in the Lord, because all that flows in from the Lord is Use, and it flows in from the parts into the community, and from the community to the parts. The parts there are the angels, and the community is their society" (*Divine Love*, n. 431).

Here comes the use of being able to talk with angels, and to learn how practical these brethren of ours are in regard to honesty, and how wise we shall become when we accompany their footsteps towards ever new uprightness.

Descending from these altitudes, we notice that no prominent man, either ecclesiastic, or statesman, seems to have any perception that a religion, once a spiritual power, but now falsified in half the civilized world, and rejected by the other half, implies a material alteration in the peace and stability of mankind. And yet facts show that the loss of religious influence over a community has alarming consequences. The French Revolution and its Goddess of reason is a proof and a prophecy to this effect. And it is only a few weeks ago since a savage mob at Valentia assailed a body of pilgrims on their way to Rome, and did bodily violence to many; including dignitaries of the Church : this in Spain, now, like France, beset by Anarchs; and with its Old Religion, once a power, now dead within it. The greater the dominance of a religiosity in the past, the greater the revulsion when it is found out, and its influence is at an end. Whatever things it has protected and held upright will come to the ground, unless a new power at the same height, namely, in the religious sphere, supplies the needful spiritual pressure.

To pursue our point, the most ostensible though not the leading anarchs are defiant Atheists. They are proof on the smallest scale, namely, in the individual, that the highest and greatest pressure of the past cannot be taken off, and the man-serpent not swell with all his self against his abhorrence of vacuum, and with all his venom for the loss of his old life, and the direness of being his own god.

To a spiritual view it is clear that all the evils we have characterized are due to an end of the Church,—to the consummation of the First Christian Æon. Minds accustomed to exact observation in natural things should know that there are mental dynamics and pressures as well as physical. You cannot diminish respect for so secondary a power as rank and station in any country without calling up brutal manners with angers and dishonesties in the lower and once respectful strata: their earth will quake from diminished pressure. You cannot cashier one chamber of legislature, and leave the other unchecked, without the survivor, whether higher or lower, becoming a pit of passions with its worst men stirring them, and restraint of the nobleness of probity gone. Reasoning from such common things, it is easy to see that by leaving out God who governs the world, and by discarding the Word declaratory of His existence and righteousness, you debauch out of the mind the highest custom of reverence and obedience, and that the residual lord of himself explodes sooner or later, individually and socially.

So a dead Church cries out in the rational mind for nothing less than another and a living church to keep the race of man to divine order. Even Comte saw this, and believing in his way in Æons, he invented the church of humanity, whose religion it is to worship our noble selves past and present and especially future; and let it be added in "positive" justice, to behave ourselves with increasing propriety age after age to justify our creed in our own godhood. This recognizes the necessity of an Æon, though without a God to begin with, or an immortality as an end.

It is not however what we want. It is not a pressure on *us*, because we may be taller than it is : for it turns out to be our Tom, Dick and Harry exaggerated by apotheosis.

But as we have seen in these pages throughout, we have not to invent a religion. It has pleased the Lord to make His Second Advent in the Word of both Testaments which in their spiritual sense reveal His Godhead ; and also declare that man's regeneration, his good character in the divine sight, is the condition of heaven in him here and hereafter. This, in those who accept it, and strive to live it, supplies again the pressure of responsibility, justice and judgment which has been lost by the inanity of the Old Church. The new Revelation has in it the sure and certain hope of the regeneration of the world. The dogma of justification by faith and imputed righteousness gives the world up as a city of the plain of uniform sin perpetually forgiven and perpetually sinning till the day of judgment. The doctrine of the truths of charity applied to life regenerates the individual man, and gives him a character which can bear the light and heat of heaven, and by power of inherited good and continual regeneration this will realize *on this earth*, where no Last Judgment can ever take place, the kingdom of the Father who is Christ.

But when shall these things be ? Well, they are already, in the people who accept the new commandments in life as the only means of salvation. But when shall they be in the world, and as a New Earth answering to the New Heavens ? Plainly, only as the majority which *votes* for charity by enacting it, is confronted by a minority which embraces all our old "evil ones," and by its love makes inroads upon these unfortunates and begins to turn many of them round. We do not now however speak of numerical majorities and minorities, because not of opinions but of lives. The number of charities that are in a man counts. Christ had infinities of charity in Him. When the entire universe voted for evil, and One Man stood against it, that universe succumbed and sank down. So miracle is again involved. And does it not seem impossible that into such a world as ours a veritable Religion should again enter as a conqueror of our Hell and Death, without great and successive miracles? The divine part of it has come by mercies ineffable, and as God's work greater than miracles; for miracles are over-rulings of ordinary levels by higher reasons. But in the divine there are no miracles and no corrections. It is our human that needs and scans the miracles. And as the first Advent came with such, so the second Advent comes, but with spiritual miracles instead of natural. The natural miracles in both Testaments are given, and they are the loving clouds and veils in which the spiritual miracles to which we shall awake seem to be reposing. In consequence of miracle, great multitudes followed Christ, many sought to touch Him; He healed all manner of sickness and all manner of diseases in them : He fed them in their thousands with natural bread of His creation : He healed individuals, and restored their lost senses: He raised the dead. He gave the power of healing and casting out devils to His disciples and apostles. So these miracles are to be repeated on a higher plane. And it will be a discipline in the Word to receive divine instruction of who are the blind, the deaf, the palsied, the fevered, the possessed, the raging men among the tombs, the halt, the lame, the poor, the sick, the hungry and the thirsty; the naked, and those who are in prison. The truths of doctrine become the active eye or intellect for applying exact charity to those who are spiritually in the states signified by these incapacities, will be the Lord's miracle workers; and the descent of the New Jerusalem to the earth in successive multitudes of the hungry and thirsty, will be the miracle. It may take place in long ages, or it may come rapidly,—the Marriage of the Lamb. It is sure to come when His Bride has made herself ready. From a desk of small work it seems to me that the turning-point will not be so long in time. The evils permitted to-day are such in enormity and magnitude, the hopes of the Devil and Satan are so mighty, the invasion of humble and simple souls appears so imminent, that the supreme gravity of circumstance seems to be reached, and the Divine may be about to bow the heavens and come down.

If this be attended by national humiliations, a way will still be prepared for conscience and its Author again to reign; for Patriotism to look to Godliness and not to glory.

L.—PERSONAL IDENTITY.

Wherein does personal identity lie? We answer, it is the name of each individual as I,—I containing in perpetuity all that the man is, was, or will be; and all that he can be. It is by no means to be confounded with memory, but is an instant witness of individual existence communicated to mankind. As conscience with men, where it exists, is an abiding monition of right and wrong, so consciousness, which is identifiable with *Ego*, I, is the bare subject at the other extremity of the person. It is a sense, and lives in the sensual nature, which itself is an everlasting factor in man.

It is not the same with the memory of the past, for in that case it would be incomplete unless the whole thick dictionary of memory were carried about in its hands. It is the smallest of things; the personal point, *hominis punctum naturale*. Conscience is the still small voice speaking from God; *Ego*, I, or consciousness, is the small shrill voice pleading one's self. In it a man always re-asserts, not remembers, that he is, and that I am he. It is not needful that he should be conscious of the former stages of his existence to constitute him an individual man: his early childhood he has never known; his *ego* then existed, but not the mind that could claim or express it; but the bystanders knew that he had it, and would jealously appropriate it by his all-peculiar self-will. Of the rest of his existence in detail his outward memory preserves but little, but his *ego* grows stronger in this oblivion, often in consequence of it. Look at an old man, and see how little allowance he makes for childhood and boyhood: his friends, to make him tolerant, have to remind him of the forgotten fact that he was once a child and a boy. Of love affairs among the young, how he can call them "stuff," until some good wife reminds

PERSONAL IDENTITY. 229

him that he was once made of that stuff, and went through its play.

Memory therefore is not necessary to personal identity; not even one grain of it; though indeed much of it accompanies the man, and is the memory of his various faculties, welling up, like the faculties themselves, from his basic *ego*. But the *ego* is no faculty, but for him an ever-present point. It is not however an uncompounded thing, but is the whole concrete man, body, parts, and passions, from moment to moment. In other words the man is continuously himself. He applies it to memory, as to all the rest, and says, I did this, I thought this, I loved this, and so forth. It is the bond and bound of his nature.

You identify a man by his person, and by your memory, and his own; but he identifies himself by his *Ego*, and by nothing outside it. He is, and knows it.

Personal identity is often in apparent abeyance, as in dreamless sleep, but leaps into its central seat the moment the sleeper wakens. It can be in apparent abeyance in madness, when the mind is sometimes divided in itself, and the man is beside himself, and reflects more than one *ego* on the broken surface. But this is disease, as it were again a sleep. Seldom however does the madman give up his *ego*, but fastens it to his disordered faculties. If he seems to give it up, another *ego* indistinguishable from his own claims to dominate him, and he is said to be possessed. Sometimes a voice unlike his own speaks through his person, and the personal pronoun may not be used, as is often the case in narrative writing; but some *ego* is understood by reference under the third person. These are collateral cases, and have little to do with the matter in hand.

The chief difficulty that has been felt arises out of the common identification of memory with personality. Of this we have already spoken. Many a thought and many an act among the smaller elements of this life is utterly forgotten by the man, and yet it is plain that each such element has contributed to the formation of his character. Volitions and deeds of larger import may be likewise forgotten, and yet the person is laden with them and responsible for them; and of wrongs done it is no justification before any law that they are not acknowledged by the perpetrator. The question is whether he, a personal *ego*, did them, not whether he recalls them. Here we transcend the first statement of *ego*, and find that it is to be identified also with acquired character. Waking or sleeping, well or ill, sane or insane, this never leaves a man, because it is *the* man: the only definite article of him.

The *Ego* is therefore a progressive entity, and gathers more as life goes on: gathers it not only or chiefly into memory, but into essential substance, by its own power converting it into such.

"But the greatest demonstration that memory is not the root, is furnished by death, and the life beyond it. At death the natural brain, which is the seat of all memory and mind here, perishes, and all thought and recollection subsisting in and through it, is impossible: that is to say, without a natural cerebrum and cerebellum it is impossible for man to think naturally or to utter a word of any natural language. These brain organs are gone, and no event of the past life can be recalled naturally, though it may be represented for the purposes of adjustment, not from the memory, but from the character. This latter is permanent, indeed everlasting; and after death spiritual faculties, organs and tongues in which it is enshrined in the good, and incorporated in the wicked, and which have been forming here on earth, carry forth the character or *ego* into its result. The persons have no recollection ultimately of who they were on earth; if they had they would haunt earth still; but each of them has the personal *I* as his possession: and no sense of any break in it. This is personal identity, and all that is requisite to complete it. The possession of character in this is entire. It carries no burden of the past, but a statical moment is the whole of it. Time is gone.

What is this miraculous I, so small that no thought has seen it; so embracive that it is the mortal and immortal man? John Morley, a man of thought, has made a guess at the answer, and though wholly wrong, is not far wrong if he will let himself be put right. He regards personality, the *ego* itself, as a delusion. It is impossible with such a despotic presence as yourself to get quite away from the truth. Personality or *ego* is not a delusion, but the opposite to it, a real appearance, and if claimed as absolute, then for the claimant it is a delusion, but a permanent one. Felony committed on it does not alienate it, for were it abolished, there would be no character and no man. Where from disorder it is even fragile, the man is mad and out of reckoning.

But whence comes this true appearance which is personal life? We can only say that it is from God, and is His seal on every human soul. Yet still it is an appearance. The world's misunderstanding is that man is alive on his own account; that his life is his own ; that for his time he is an absolute being. The correction is that there is only one life, namely, the divine life; and that man of himself is dead ; but his created form and faculty is an instrumental recipient of the divine life, and in perpetual reception of this, most involuntary reception, man is alive. The appearance is communicated to him that his life is his own in order that he may be a man ; and the knowledge, through Religion, is also communicated, but by instruction from without, that his life is not his own, but his Maker's, in order that knowledge may by slow degrees end in practical acknowledgment of the real truth. Thus appearance and reality can co-exist in him.

A word more about Memory, which we may seem to have slighted. There is an inner man and an outer ; a spiritual man and a natural. Each of these has a distinct memory.

The deeds done in the body are represented in both memories; but with no failing in the spiritual. They are constantly translated thither from the natural memory into a living record; into the book of the man's life. This Swedenborg, from revelation, calls "the internal memory." Things are not there as mundane events, but transformed into states of good or evil; as constituents, or, it may be, fixations of the character. By them man is judged; they are not his recollections but his ruling love; they are his veriest self. This memory therefore is his finite I am, his *ego*, his love, his formed character; and whether he be a good man or a bad man he is receptive of a personal identity in it, and loves either himself, or his Creator, with an everlasting affirmation of his own being as a separate Ego. The Angel still talks of I with an after-confession of Not I, but Thou, O Lord: the Satan asseverates I with appropriation of a divine gift to himself.

A right conception on the subject of personal identity may enable some good friends, but self-puzzled thinkers, to believe more easily in the fact of personal immortality.

At the end the question of the natural man in the doctrine here propounded will revert continually, Who is Who? To which we reply that in the spiritual consideration to which the subject leads, the final question for each man is, not Who he is, but What he is. From this what, this *quale* or qualification, he receives hereafter a real name in which his identity abides; and therefore he is never a nameless entity but a deeply nominated man. By this, his spiritual fellows on the good side know him and hail him as Adam knew the creatures and named them. Substance of name is here given instead of shadow. Moreover, let us add for the consolation of our clinging nature, loath to part with mortal times, that all memory of the past as it was transacted in this world is immortal, though not reproducible at will; that the whole natural mind is indrawn as a sleep, and kept as an ultimatum and foothold; and by representatives in series of any length the man can be let down into it, and brought face to face with all his former states; but for divine uses; therefore when God pleases. So even in this memory identity has a central throne, and the man is again himself for ever, and for ever. He is forced on trial to say, I was it all, and I did it all, and *I* result. Unfailing mercy meets him there, and makes the best of him. And then for the most part natural memory ceases into long oblivions.

LI.—THE CHANCES AND LIKELIHOODS OF SCIENCE.

Inasmuch as Jehovah God has created and made the world and all good things that are therein, and that He governs all good and bad things by His omniscience and omnipotence, for divine ends, the question of finding out and knowing His works and ways, which in their ultimate result are the world, proposes itself as the question of questions for science.

What scientific mind, and what *præsupposita* in it, can enter upon this knowledge? The world enters our senses in infancy as a theatre of disconnected sensual facts. Things occur, inextricably connected with our human affections. The first experience of solidity is a mother's breast; the first warmth sensed is a mother's warmth. Human knowledge is the beginning of knowledge; and this fate pursues man in every career through all action and speculation. Himself is his field and his ring-fence, and what he gradually makes of himself is his possibility. All his knowledges are his intentional action and reaction with his fellows; all are his ruling loves and good or evil ambitions in unsuspected forms of thinking: all are ways of advancement " steeped in affections."

For the most part the sciences occupy the field of sensualism first given in infancy, but with infancy no longer permitted in it. The first humanity lies dead around the scientific cradle. A bird of larger brood has shouldered it to the ground. Yet the field of sensualism is vast and of itself ordinate, and faculty after faculty of knowledge can be developed through it. The world can thus be accounted for from end to end by *amour propre* working by means of the reasons, the *pros* and *cons*, of sensual things. Sensual intuitions start up readily on the way; new sciences, and cunning arts, are born; and man is full-fledged with new faculties of his own creation : new broods of intelligence.

The result is imposing. "Men run to and fro and knowledge is increased." It is an immense pyramid with no point. Or if it has a point it is a culinary one; an end of making the mind gloriously comfortable in the kitchen of nature among its own Egyptian flesh-pots.

The sensual immensity of things is however on any showing worth all the trouble that can be honestly bestowed upon it; and if man will not and so cannot now make use of his God-given powers, the secondary powers that he himself engenders are left to him, and he has work for them. Sensual facts, and their inferences, inductions and deductions, remain, and are the plane which is explorable. It is a big study, bounded only by the "flammantia moenia mundi." The Atheist, Lucretius, has given us these words, and they mark a practical limit for knowledge, as they contain, by correspondence, a true doctrine of the girdle of space ; and almost divine its "cherubic" character.

There is in fact a great gulf fixed between the possible knowledges of godly science, and of godless science ; a gulf for the most part undiscernible at present ; because the better and nobler science is scanty as yet; is not recognized where it appears ; and the light of it is darkness to the ways of the voluptuous senses. The warmth of it also is hateful to them as destructive of their progeny.

But not to rest in general propositions, let us take an example from human physiology. The body of a man is simply the house of his soul, with all its faculties, love, intellect, reason, senses, incarnated in it in this world for his time; and the organs the body contains are derivations from these sources, and principiates from these principles. All the currents in the body, and it is a cosmos more final than the great world, are influx and reflux, carrying and representing spiritual ends of life, and realizing them momentaneously. In this body the man's life is building up the human form which will be his for ever. Starting from these faiths of certainty, God-given, and making them into the scientific faculties through which perforce, and not perchance, you view the human body, you will have a Physiology, sensual indeed, for the body is of sense, yet not limited by the senses, but descending by degrees of order from the soul, and with each faculty sought for in it, and when the science is attained, represented in it. The "*flammantia moenia corporis*" are then the doors by which the life enters, and this life constitutes the body for knowledge as the image of God.

In the meantime, before this faith is given you, the *dead* body has to be explored by all common and uncommon manipulation, and the facts of form and connection must be elicited from age to age; for the sensual sciences must be learnt first, or real objects for thought would not be present, and the mind would not be in its *nature* which is its earliest basement and existence. Observe however that nothing but mere facts, and the knowledges close above them, belong to this field, and that nature like a cope of stone bounds it in. It may be cultivated into surprising minutiæ and details; but reasons and principles are out of its legitimate scope. At the highest and lowest it is pure naturalism. There is no bridge between it and the sphere in which all that accounts for and inhabits the body is situated. No anatomy or sensual physiology touches the love, intellect, reason, imagination or senses, in, for, and from which the body exists, as any other than atom-work and matter first materially and then sensually energizing. Such science, if it insists on exploring these things on its own account, does not proceed many steps before it denies the soul. Indeed, at this day, this is the general mind of physiological and so-called psychological investigation. Nothing can come of it but ingenious surface after surface proclaimed as depth and height: as it were cock-crowing of a morning which is deepening midnight.

Of course it is obvious for the theist to say, What evidences of design are here! What textures of realized plan! In a word, what amazing organization and maintenance! What divine Wisdom! Truly there is nothing to cavil at in this; and God is manifestly at work in it all to those who believe in a God. But such Theology is a head with no body to it: with no middle truths to bring it down to human care of intelligence. The plan, design, organization, is for something. What is it for? Obviously, it is to build and launch the vessel of a man. And what is a man, but a capacity of loving and being wise if he pleases by means of intellect, reason, imagination, sense, heart, hands and feet; by all his soul and all his strength? No physiology and no psychology solves its accounts without showing how these ends are prepared for and rendered reasonable in the human frame. Without this achievement, the living man is left out, and though God is posed, it is as an organic Designer meaning something by his elaborate work, but what that something may be, is physiologically in darkness. The "argument from design" explodes on these terms. The body is a fortress which has abandoned its keys to nature and evolution. The above question therefore brings back the necessity for the missing links, the missing "middle truths"; so important in all solid reason and thinking. What then is the preparation in the human structure for the faculties which the man gradually gets and uses in his natural lifetime? They are himself, incarnated in him from top to toe. If they were not in him, as the main and only things in his organization, we should have no right to look for them in the genius of his body: Being in him, and being him, we can ultimately be bound to look for nothing else. Behind brains, spine, heart, lungs, bowels, liver, kidneys, genitalia, there is no view but into man's soul and spirit, and their attributes, faculties and functions. To discern these in the organs, is to see what the organs are, and what they are made for ; and by placing the middle truths, to replace the argument of design, capable of completion as long as science and intelligence live ; and so to reclaim the fortress of the human body as an incarnation of the soul: to reclaim it from being self-made, against which David warns us, "Be ye sure that the Lord He hath made us, and not we ourselves."

Is it possible to effectuate such a psychological physiology? It is possible, on two conditions ; a knowledge of the forms, fluids, functions and organic capacities of the body, *so far as this can be gained* from the dead subject, supplies for elementary science the realities of structure and the channels of influxion. Personal observation on our own living bodies gives the first life to this *corpus* of knowledge. We know that the brain thinks and wills, that the lungs breathe, that the heart beats. These knowledges are put into the *corpus*, and it lives so far. Observation extends these knowledges to all our external functions. "The light of the body is the eye." It sees and notes what we are in its ocular measure.

But the mind has to be shown in its incarnation. For this object no sensual knowledge is other than a basis. The mind *as answering to the body* is an unknown entity ; nor can it be known excepting by new truths about it which are *revealed doctrines*. These make the mind as definite and structural as the body itself; they reveal the mind as a frame of spiritual organs with a spiritual order in them. When these truths are admitted and received, there can be parallelism and correspondence between the two realities, the body and the mind; the embodied mind and the mentalized body can coalesce in one doctrine.

To exemplify this is beyond our limits. We can only adduce our familiar instance that the understanding and the will are to the mind what the lungs and the heart are to the body. The one pair of organs performs the life-function mentally which the lower pair performs physically. The union of the soul and the body is the agreement or correspondence between them. It is a bare statement, but can be studied out in the psychological and theological writings of its author, Swedenborg. The whole mind, shown by him to be organic, in similar statements or doctrines stands over against the whole body, and claims it as its instrumental image; as the mind claims the face as its working expression or image; but veritably-structurally.

Here we end one illustration of the "chances and likelihoods" of merely sensual and material science penetrating beyond matter and the sense of it even into the proximate mental sphere above: and we may make the *point-blank* assertion that no chance and possibility of the kind lies in its powers, or opens to its ambitious future.

The immensity of natural science, and its increasing difficulties, vote in our favour. If science had struck any great central point either of doctrine or humanity, material of real confirmations would be co-extensive with it, and difficulty and size would be a decreasing phenomenon; whereas the reverse is the case, and the human frame and its contents, Man and Mankind, are more unintelligible to the present men from day to day. Their incessant business at present is to undervalue and brush aside these contents.

A science that is advancing on the right road would also have a conscience of admonitions of relevancy and irrelevancy pursuant with it, clearing it of useless accumulations of particulars, and warning it from mean fields of search; it would build with unhewn general stones as fit for temples; and not with rubble facts. It would not mistake its huts for temples. This, we say, is a department for the intuitional conscience; a true Episcopal realm.

Such function at present is not performed ; and science is squandered in accumulating dust, to choke "the Wells of Abraham" with it as the Philistines always do.

Take another brief illustration of "chances and likelihoods" from cosmical science. It also works on the godless track. Matter, space and time are its feeders, and mechanics and mathematics are the end of it. Now in spite of telescopes and other wonderful instrumentation, and of geological exploration, nearly the whole realm of heaven and earth lies beyond the senses, and not within reach of natural reason. The firmament with its suns is a woof of imponderables invisible and incomprehensible, as it were the nerves of a creation susceptible and unitary from end to end ; an inconceivable system ; dark with excess of light ; and, for science, cold with incredible heat. No natural-rational account of its maintenance is possible. Imagination droops under the weight of bare sense. Science, piling up knowledges, accumulates the arrear of difficulties, but does not desire their solution. What is the solution ? A world above nature with another heaven and another earth to it, out of space and time, in which the Divine Love is the sun, and the Divine Wisdom is the light of it. A world in which God is enthroned, and from which He creates by material correspondences the framework of Nature,—suns, planets, and their spheral spaces. For this knowledge a doctrinal or teaching Revelation is needed ; for of that higher world no man of himself knows anything. Such a Revelation stands over the world below as the Revelation of the mental faculties stands over the organs of the body ; and it tallies with the great cosmic forms and forces, as things corresponding to those which it makes known. God is the centre of it, and God is Love, and love is heat indeed, and God is Wisdom, and Wisdom is light indeed. The Revelation of God descending from these two principles into science, meets the suns and systems which are its subjects, and by the Divine life, infinitely one and infinitely manifold, supplies the ends of nature, intelligizes its causes, and substantiates its uses or effects. Love, intellect, reason, imagination, sense, are vivified thus by Revelation; are humbled, ordained, and corrected by it: and the presence of God with nature is rationally proclaimed. No fact is disregarded ; for sensual facts are the basis; the ultimate guiding lines into which all Revelation fits; the Revealer being himself the Creator of all these sensual ultimates. They are the knowledges, memorial and irreversible, which teach us to walk ; and revelation coming down to us at last, is the way, the truth and the life in our natural pilgrimage and scientific wayfaring.

"Chances and likelihoods" for science in this field also have no existence apart from a doctrinal revelation.

There is one subservient faculty which may be singled out as having a strong sensual relation to science, namely, the imagination, to which the world is a Poem. The first fire and light of the senses come from it. We may call it their infancy and delight tending to their manhood. It is deficient in science now because men are afraid of it, having no reverent faculties to control its waywardness, and keep it within the cosmic lines of definite knowledges. And yet without it science is lacking in its primitive genius ; in its happiness of suggestion ; in its appetite and stomach for hypotheses. Revelation alone and its commanding influence, can prescribe its lines ; and tame this wild horse into a real Pegasus, with legitimate scientific wings. For considering that the Works of the Allwise are for our speculation, imagination is not a faculty to be dreaded but cultivated by the reverent mind ; under whose pressure it will put off gradually the erroneous proclivities of sense, and penetrated by the higher reason, be transfluent with orderly intuitions, and ultimately itself wear the guise of spiritual insight.

Among the circumstances of the present mind we notice its addiction to sensual things below, and its repugnance to them above. It knows that they are the marks and characters of reality wherever they occur, and demanding them for this world, it gets rid of the other world by denying them. But senses and external objects of sense, that is to say, the human form and a sensible world, are as much the necessity of spiritual as of natural existence; and without the appearances of space and time, of Cosmos, there is no foothold for human beings. Ideas also, thoughts and affections, are clothed with forms and shapes for ever, even to the highest and most intimate degrees, for finiteness exacts this as a necessity. Love cannot be seen nakedly, but it is visible to man as a Man and as a Sun: Wisdom cannot be seen in itself, but it is essential Man, and the light of Man; and there is a visible and tangible world answerable all through to these centres. This is a matter of Revelation, and cannot be realized without it. Here also Science on its own ground has no chances and no possibilities.

Neither has it any such in regard to the internal series of human history, which is contained in the spiritual sense and Revelation of the Word alone.

The inference from these remarks is, that psychical physiology to be completed, requires the descent into it of a revelation of the organic mind, faculty by faculty: and that cosmology requires the like information and infilling from the revealed attributes of the World-Maker and World-Ordainer. The Science of Correspondences, now given and possible for man, is the supply of the missing link in both these cases. And it is the supreme and noblest incentive to the prosecution and exact knowing of all the legitimate and useful natural sciences. Intuitions and arts now inconceivable will be born of it; for both worlds were made for it, and are at one with its genius. *Similia similibus intelligantur.*

LII.—SOME PRIVILEGES OF ATHEISM.

To the Christian the rights of man are limited by his duties; no power is his own in an absolute sense, but each has an owner and proprietor other than himself; the man is a co-proprietor; and his ownership is subordinate to that of his Master in him. The Atheist is sole lord of himself; he is himself his lord. This latter estate has some privileges, and carries them out. Being his own, he can do, and does, what he likes with his own.

Each several Atheist is in himself a seed, and is limited by the size of his own will and courage. Original Atheists of governmental capacity invent far-reaching powers applicable to the fields of their life and action. And Atheism is social and congregational, as what is not? It becomes therefore a world in itself, with a government, laws and institutions. In this world, being absolute, it is a godless god, and may do all it can.

Like every seed, its first and abiding aim is to transcend its own limits, which are as wide as matter, but with a felt narrowness co-extensive with the width. With a philosophy of its own, it beats against the bars of death by the creed of a social in lieu of an individual immortality. With peculiar arts and sciences it works to lengthen individual life to any degree beyond the present span. It would not discard a thousand years as a proper enjoyment of this world. And here some of its bodily privileges come in. Judging by the rule of Autocracy, it is a present king in Medicine. This is exemplified in experimentation on the poor, to educate the life-prolongers in their work for the poor and the rich. Being, as we postulate, absolute, that is to say, within the sphere of the mutable social conscience, and having its own, and all our lives, for an end; it is in its own right, lord over the animal creation, and may do to the subjects of it whatever it considers will conduce to its arts towards individual immortality. All within social permissions, which mean at first laws of the land, fellowship with profitable Christians, and at last through Atheistic ages, respectability, whatever that may mean, as a residual terminus. If cutting up men alive, as Erasistratus did, could presumably lengthen the average of human life,

Atheism can perform it with a free hand. The social conscience is the only limit here. None but an injudicious Atheist would vivisect his own reputation. No one but an unsocial Atheist would injure the reputation of his clan.

Yet, as regards the disposal of Life, Atheism has no more undeniable privilege than the right of Suicide. The circumambient social conscience may limit this right somewhat, but it is there for occasions, and the Atheist has only to balance the inconvenience and pain of the mortal immortality around him, against his own propensity, and to determine accordingly. To be, or not to be, that is the question. His life is his own absolutely, and the end of it is his own : if his will is made up, there is no power to say him nay. Others may kill themselves in madness or intolerable states when their God is not audible. He can end himself in ordinary, because he prefers it. Who is there to give the reason to? "There are no bonds in his death." There is nothing after it.

Atheism has also an indefeasible right to patronize any and every religion for the simple and the vulgar, on the way to their emancipation into the atheistical light. It can be a church-conservative, and make the lower orders powerless for mischief to itself by keeping them in the darkness of religion.

Next, Atheism, besides its care for its corporeal body, its dignities and pleasures, looks after its own soul which also is its body. It cannot do without a soul in present Society. Looking round for a soul, it finds one made to its hand in various religions, and lays claim to it. To conscience, and the virtues which lie under it, and spring from it, it lays strong claim. It is under no restraint of commandments in annexing the good things of the world, and conscience is the best of all things socially. Atheism appropriates it in this sense, and walks proudly in the light of its fellow-men, and of all men. This conscience with its virtues is mutable from time to time, and Atheism lives in its rigour when respectable, and in its relaxations and indulgences in looser times. Being a law to itself there is no denying this, and no helping it. So Atheism has a time-soul. Its privilege here is to acquire it, and to turn it to social gain.

Atheism demands a society not too remote at a given time from the present codes. This it finds ready to hand in the society around us, and which, though no product of atheism, it is not prevented from appropriating as its soil. For what principle prevents it from appropriating? Expostulation is out of place with the masters of legions, and atheism, not being an internal potentate, does not, except through pressure from without, expostulate with itself. It therefore adopts property, marriage, family, country, the laws and the State, as social needs, and calls them its own. And the more readily, because being now creations of its mouth, it has only to bide its time, and utter them differently, or repeal them, according to its new wills and lights. Being itself its author and its throne, it is clearly absolute from age to age in these material things. So Atheism stands in social costume with the privilege of appropriating from a wide world of religious modes, and putting on from time to time from their stores what is becoming.

Atheism has also the privilege of providing itself with Goodness; a mystical quality which it must possess. Here its supplies are large. With its faculty of appropriation,— for it is the great *Proprium* in all men,—it is the realm of present free trade with all religions, and claims all their goods, bartering in exchange for their commodity freedom from the religions themselves which have supplied the old corn and wine. It will keep the goods as long as it wants them, and Nature will be its greater source for the next supplies.

Atheism, being its own Truth, leans on nothing but itself for truth in the general acceptation. It does not borrow

SOME PRIVILEGES OF ATHEISM. 245

this from religions, but is a light unto itself. Here in its avowal of its name its honesty shines. Nature is its truth, and Science its high priest of nature. It loses nothing of respectability by declining scientific commerce with religions, for nature of itself knows nothing of them, and science is a neutral field of knowledges. But it has its compensation in a privilege of hypotheses and fancies all its own. With these it fills its world : fills it so that no room is left for theologies. These hypotheses it has stamped from of old with its own absoluteness, and they are in general currency. Such bills of sale are the eternity of the world ; the infinity of matter, space and time ; the materiality of mind ; the production of life from nature. These are its instruments by which it brings within its grasp a multitude of corresponding particulars. Their realm is its fairy gold minted for its autocratic treasury into certainties. For Atheism would be poor without its facts, and these are they. It comes thus into the privilege of speculation and belief : and appropriates eternity and infinity as peculiarly its own. For who sees an end of its space, or notes a beginning of its time.

Its absoluteness privileges Atheism to demand a *Cultus*. For what other ground for Cultus or Worship has any religion than the affirmation of a supreme Being, and the Atheist, —individual in small things, and collective in great things, —is a supreme being, an absolute self? His privilege therefore lies in the worship of himself. For hypothetical endowment and establishment here, all the absolute little selves make one general unselfishness ; like finite inches making up spatial infinitude.

Atheism is neither King nor Priest, neither Order nor Law, excepting as it is circumpressed by these passing expedients : but the Atheist is an essential politician. The hoary mountain of religion oppressing his breast makes him glow and smoke and erupt, and the ground reverberates with him. He is ruminating a world of new ages in which he himself will be all in all. No one as he is privileged for the work of change, of abolition and demolition. The old world is a tradition of mummeries; its states and institutions are the sum of them. He stands among them, but is not of them. He holds no principle or affection which respects them excepting as temporary needs ministering to his honour, glory, and gain. He is a typical reformer privileged to put on the present as a garment, and to tear it to pieces when he can. His following in all the above privileges is vast, unbeknown to itself. For the wind of Atheism is a strong wind, and can carry away churches and states that are not founded upon the opposite Rock. And in the present non-foundation, Atheism has its day of genius, and a large privilege of hopes and expectations in the politic secular belly of accidents, occasions and opportunities.

LIII.—THE FERTILIZATION OF FLOWERS BY INSECTS.

Thinking much of the train of observations of the illustrious Naturalist, Darwin, on the above subject, the wonder occurs that they were not made before; for the facts are as patent now as the flowers and the insects always were. Can it be that the common human eyes are holden for an appointed time; and that as there is a time for everything, there is a time naturally for opening them?

Note here a higher realm of life and organism conjoined by ministry to a lower. The lower is enriched by it, gifted with new colours and varieties as if so much light and chemistry were born of the warmth of the conjunction. Nor only that, but the plant-systems are perpetuated and extended in area where otherwise they might die out. Male and female flowers would oftener be abortive, and engender no seeds, if there were not winged go-betweens to carry the fertilizing spur from the one to the other. It is a provision for fixed

THE FERTILIZATION OF FLOWERS. 247

natures which to a good extent cannot meet, or help one another. Also for interblendings which ensure strength of progeny. The plants know nothing of their providence, the insects. The insects are on their own work intent, and mean nothing by their uses to the plants. But both parts reap the benefit of the unconscious good in the coming season. There is mind in the distant background somewhere.

The matter does not begin here, for the vegetable world at large is a ministry for the mineral, converting its surface into new substances and varieties. The shedding of leaves, and the universal death of trees and plants, conjoin mineral and vegetable in a common mould from which natural life begins, and without which the planet would be a bald stone. The trees and plants themselves are like the birds and insects here; movable or removable, where the ground is immovable. Accordingly, through their decease and fortunes, every unctuous spot has some vegetable inhabitant, great or small: iron Gellivara has infinitesimal lichen on its apparently naked ore, and the ore, a film of iron mould to make this possible. Marriage here! The precipices grow pines in their rifts, the crow dropping cones into their crannied mould. It is hard to say where such ministration ends. The crust of the earth keeps the hearth of the under world warm; makes a walled house of it, and precludes the escape of its heat into space. Fire, if fire be the terrene centre, is banked up into perpetual fire by the solid globe. Against its nature, it becomes the footstool of fixtures.

These are facts and parables from nature. Facts because they are true circumstances. Parables because they point away to universals and stand under them.

We can dwell on very few of these, but with gratitude to Darwin for the initiation.

Society may be a first illustration. Wherever there are ranks and orders in a common body the analogy of things at rest and things in movement obtains, and those at rest are ministered to by those in movement. Irrespective of the problems of good and evil, this is the case in the social field. The upper strata are superposed upon the lower in planes of services or uses. Capital wandering over masses of men, and looking out for sinews and capabilities, fertilizes labour, and gives it forms, colours and varieties which the working mind would not have otherwise; gives it, because capital is itself a mental order, a discipline which the insect cannot give to the plant; and in the discipline, a unity which makes armies of industry out of mere individuals. This is fundamental to Society. Other suggestions from the Darwinian beginning are easy. The ordinary services of man to man, and of one rank to another, follow the same lines. They all lie in the fact that a moving and designing upper plane gives a lower plane a help and a chance which it has not in itself. It is a set of endowments strictly descending and communicated from above, and awaiting reception from below. Divers orders or degrees are the modes and means of the beneficence of Society, as it were so many falls and forces of mutual service. And the ultimate service is that the lowest plane is the foundation and the basis. Service to it is therefore the due of the whole. The highest social service is example, a winged thing which brings men's minds together, and puts the senses of the lowest and the highest individuals in rapport with their own internal things, conjoining interior faculties otherwise remote from each other, and impregnating and fertilizing natures, so that by good sense they produce good works. It is needless to dwell on this theme, because, with Darwin's unveiling clearly before us, Society is one great expansion and illustration of this law of the service of the lower plane by the ministry closely above it. And so on, to the top; which descends through all; and not only through all, but also to all immediately when occasion requires: for the Queen can enter the cottage in person, as the Monarchical State from its height comes to it as Law, Order, and Security. Immediate therefore as well as mediate is the inflow of uses where there are tiers of membership with a head to them. Due honours and dignities are one useful result.

It may be thought that a whole class or plane does not stand in analogy with our so-called male and female plants, but the analogy, though strict, does not follow literal lines. The lower stratum becomes procreative and receptive mutually all round by the influx of the higher. This develops mutual events into the power of satisfaction. The natural man is made up of wants, bodily, and the rest; and the social planes are enriched and vitalized, say fertilized, in them by the planning wealth of the higher. The social dealing of man with man expresses this reciprocal relation. It would scarcely exist if society consisted of only one degree in any of its faculties.

So much for the field and garden of men in one consideration. It has also its earthworms continually worming and animalizing its soil with a view to the upper services.

But the individual mind stands also in analogy with the Darwinian parable. Think of what its faculties gain by the descent of the higher into the lower. The naked eye becomes a lens and a telescope clothed upon by the mind's exclusive optics. And so forth throughout the round of the cultivated senses. The free mind of art and invention wanders over them, seizes their points of limitation and infirmity, and its vitalizing genius extends their scope through instruments that carry them into the depths and recesses of a nature unknown to their naked organisms. In a word they see, hear and touch in a new sense from the mind above them.

It is always the truth of a higher mind which vitalizes the good things in the stratum of a lower. The latter left to itself would remain an obscure life of casual and unconscious change incapable of reciprocations with itself, and in itself infertile; passive, like a lower class with no planned work given it to do. We need not go through the mental faculties to illustrate so obvious a truth, though the working of its problems has not perhaps sufficiently engaged the attention of metaphysicians. But we know by common observation that the mind lies in planes; that sense, observation of sensual things, induction from these, constituting sciences, imagination, reason, intellect, and faculty of conscience, rise one above another as at last a hierarchy of degrees. We also know that in just order the higher influence the lower, and that the highest have as their mission to supervise, control, and often to subjugate the lower, and keep them to their places. The lowest deal with the present moment, they see, hear and touch it. The whole of the upper influences have wings beyond its time, and do not rest in it. Mounting the scale, the higher you ascend the whole mind is taken up into a present simultaneous with the future. The inner man may be said to live justly, if not in, yet for, the future: it is present in his cogitations. Here the Darwinian Parable recurs. The passive things are visited by the active of which they at first know nothing by themselves, and they get their own life from its life, and as the mind is alive and habitual, they expect its advents, and would die without them.

In this garden all the healthy and profitable flowers call aloud for their bees and their butterflies. They plead, My Lords, help us. But *en passant*, a cardinal thing is to keep the mental pile of faculties to their order of stratification, and not to allow them to shift their places; for whichever is constituted at the top has the powers of the top; the descent and the force of it: for instance, if the conscience is put below the senses, they become its instigators, it is sensualized by them, and acts out their mortal behests. It is all a thing of order and placing, and the natural parable still holds of it whether for good or for evil.

The same remarks apply to the affections; they too are in planes one better than another, if we please to give the highest rule. The other faculties are but their truths or

THE FERTILIZATION OF FLOWERS. 251

images. They penetrate all, because ultimately they are all in all. They are selfish at the bottom : the infant loves his mother as his convenient milk. Winged instruction, itself coming from affection, supervenes in time; and objects of natural love are discriminated. The young creature feels that there are others in the world besides himself, and takes apparently from without the germ of a moral being. But each plane of these natural loves called affections is content with itself, in other words is passive, until the plane of induction above comes over it, and warms it with the beginning of a new life. Truths, as we said before, are the winged things in this garden, which when they are obeyed, make the affections rightfully alive; and hence the gardening or Eden-making here lies in the obedience of the natural affections to these truths of life.

Divine things are not averse to this true fable. The Spirit of God hovered upon the faces of the waters, and Creation followed, a creation from death towards divine life. The Word makes frequent mention of such broodings ; and where the man is receptive, there is no state so helpless and dead that has not God helping and awakening it, and giving his image away to it as hope, life, and ideal. Without this inflow, whether received or not, there would be no existence ; for man as a mechanism is dead in himself, motionless and powerless ; but he is allowed to feel life as his own, and lives in the feeling. The gift is final and inalienable, and not subject to natural death. In fact, death is the beginning and basis of it, and not the end or abyss. For without death or fixity, which is nature,—are not her laws fixed,— the immortal man would have no *ressort*, no individuality to lean against, and when he died, he would slip into nothingness. Fixation is therefore the beginning of him, and it is insinuated from this first life into every conscious state to which he ever attains. The internal sense of the fable here is divine help. Every faculty is brooded over, and from being dead is made alive. Be sure also, following the parable, that orders of subordinate ministrations are in attendance to convoy and convey the help where the death is most urgently felt. He Who provides these succours for the lilies of the field, teaches thereby that He provides them for all willing mankind. He provides them immediately, but mediately also by the higher and lower brethren in either world. For all words now, following the Word, come from without; to the simple by wise simple teachings; to others, by other monitions from more recondite sources. Ministration of the higher to the lower is thus universal for men; and ministration or service from the Highest is the perpetual ground of it all.

So far the fact, parable and myth of the great Naturalist holds good throughout. We say advisedly and repetitiously fact, parable and myth; for the natural world is all these three in every detail. That nature is a fundamental fact all men allow, and the idealist acts upon it like other men. That nature is a teaching parable few allow, because few care about it as such, and therefore will not go to the school where they can learn it. That nature is a divine myth fewer still will own. Yet as nature proceeds from an Infinite Love and Wisdom, it images His attributes as men's works image the minds of their authors. So the age of Mythologies is past, because nature as a given fact will become our Mythology. But this, by gradual stages; and future Darwins unearthing pregnant hieroglyphs will help to found this spiritual-natural science.

We have somewhat anticipated that other realm in which the planes of mutual service,—the higher ministering to the lower, and the lower substantiating the higher,—are still exemplary necessities. Close above nature and resting upon it there is a spiritual world which contains all the departed from the beginning of times, and it is linked to this world by consanguinities of affections. It has part of its life in our very wills and hearts. It is a world potential and capable of presences beyond all mortal imagining; transfluent on its

DARWINISM CARRIED OUT. 253

heavenly side from the One Lord throughout; and ministering, as was mentioned above, under His direction to our humanity. It too all lies in planes of inductive affections, with divine truths embodied also in ministries apportioning and uniting them. Use and service are the keynotes of the heavens. They are to our world what just and orderly Society from above downwards is to itself, and what the kingdoms of nature are to her order and maintenance by creation. Infringing no freedom, if they find us dead they would fain make us alive. All that is good in us, all the secret thoughts and inspirations of our minds and hearts, pass through them on the way to us, and are held by permission momentaneously in their hands. However high they are, we are their brethren, though our time-state is immeasurably below their spiritual state. The interval, however, between them and us is filled by a love and mercy which is adequate to these necessities. Its wings as of the Holy Dove are over us, and foster in us the heavenly implanted by the Word in the earthly.

LIV.—DARWINISM CARRIED OUT.

It is remarkable that Darwin, so acutely observant in regard to one plane of fertilizations, should not have generalized its facts to the next orders of nature above plants and insects, and inferred that birds and animals also function in imparting fresh potencies to the lower series and to the atmospheres and cosmos around them. He has indeed shown this of earthworms, but there must be higher forms of it. For nature repeats herself with variations suitable and correspondent to all stages. Not much is observed in this field save that the excreta and exuviæ of living creatures, including man, enrich the ground, as dead leaves and trees also enrich it. These are farmers' truths. We may also note the treatment of seeds eaten in pregnant berries by birds, in which the bird serves as a hothouse. But the fertilization of flowers by insects is so much higher and more active than these functions that one must expect that in the lives above insects other and important planes of service are indicated. They are somewhat visible in the destruction of noxious insects and even reptiles by birds; also in one tribe feeding upon another; and in the limitation of the procreant animal world by many "selective" means. This is a purging *ministerium*. But what we intend is not so visible, and therefore easily scouted by the senses. All natures have their own spheres about them, and these bulge out into space. They keep the tracts the creatures inhabit modified and comfortable for them by emanations from themselves, and so by mediations: even the breathing of living organisms by its motion and modified air, and the more subtle pulsation of their hearts, have this result. There is vegetable air, and air almost non-vegetable. In spring and summer and autumn the air is variously filled with effluvia from the varieties of the seasons. In the Mammoth caves the air is almost mineral. Those who have sensed it, know. There is also animalized air from the effluvia of many animals together. But this is not the sphere of which we are in search. It is a subtler influx impinging upon external ether, and sending through it the impact of the character of the animal itself: letting nature feel in her depths that the creature is her ward and domestic. There is a scientific view extant, that every vibration penetrates through space to indefinite distances, as a blow is diffused in sound from a vibrating drum. To those who hold this theory the present subject may be commended for amplification. The view of the benign effect of good animal spheres commends itself to me for a practical end; as a plea against the destruction of animal life, wild and tame, and especially wild, wherever it can be prevented, or avoided. Kill nothing good, except for good use; kill nothing recklessly, lest the murder destroy a harmonic medium, and make "a gap in nature." Avoid extermination as a horror. I am prone to believe that the cruel and wasteful destruction of the buffalo has deteriorated the climate and serenity of the United States, and that the murder of the seal in the sea and on its islands, and of the walrus and white bear, makes the polar cold more intolerable and inhuman; that the extermination of the whale, "the king of the sea," will unship a Zooarchy, a spirit in the waters, and ordained by a divine Neptune.

Darwin might have drawn some of these conclusions, and lent his weight to the practical recommendation here indicated. He might have done so had he, like Swedenborg, believed in Ends and Uses as an evident chain and harmony in things. Not believing in this, but in the force of life, availing itself of circumstance, his fruitful "fertilization by insects" yielded no inferences; and in his hands it remains as a comparatively solitary and thus piteous fact; when yet the two worlds of matter and spirit, earth and heaven, are ready to accompany it with a shining train of corroborations.

"The Lord's Kingdom is a kingdom of Uses."

Confirmation of the above position which deals with the invisible may be had from the earlier stages of the earth in regard to development of life upon its surface: in particular from the huge animal forms which then inhabited it. The ground and the waters teemed with these monsters, and a series of organisms led up to them and succeeded them. We ask, why was this? The question involves for its first answer that a divine end existed for such creations. It is illegitimate unless we may affirm that final causes produce all the effects in nature. A further answer is that all previous forms are preparations for the human form; for Man. How are they preparations? Analogously as the human fœtus is a series of organic stages leading to the birth of man, to the perfected infant. Nature in this respect may be regarded as a scaffolding of instincts, as one organism with man at the summit. The special services or Uses ministered by the advancing lower to the higher are a scheme of planes in a manner opposite and complementary to the services of the higher to the lower. Not much can yet be seen or said upon them excepting in the merest generalities; for they are not scientific but primarily theological entities, which however may ultimately enter science from above. However, they are not yet in it. As we have already hinted, they are ministries of life with its instincts and magnetisms pervading mother earth and nature, and suiting her or making her good for coming implantations. They are to the general system what the mould and the soil are to the vegetable. They are ground raised higher towards life, rendered quasi-living, and made moveable, so that the brood of life finds ready a floating nest from life to be reared in. This is a function not depending so much upon decay, as in the vegetable case, as upon perpetuation of exterior and lower movement; as it were a lung-function; for the lungs move all, and thus effectuate all things even in the body beneath them. The eye for this function lives from faith in God as always regarding ends, and therefore doing nothing in vain; and also as placing end within end in a wise or everlasting series. It is a heavy argument, and of right overbears science. It is also to be observed that the vegetable has a like preparatory magnetism with it for the cosmos; the mould being only its material ultimate. Such heavy arguments, against which there is no appeal, are indispensable for the religious mind. Another of them is brought to bear in the religious doctrine of the inhabitation of the planets by men, women and children. No telescope confirms this, and there are strong scientific reasonings from material heat and cold against it. Yet nevertheless it is heavily true from enlightened religious faith, because the human race, and a heaven formed from it, is the purpose of the creation, and God does not make suns and systems for anything less than the omnipresent end of ends.

To this it may be added for argument that universal nature is telegraphic, teledemic, telepathic and telephonic;

words derived from the root τελη, distant, and implying that the world and all that is within it intercommunicates, and is effective from the first cause within itself. Of this there are many suggestions if not as yet scientific proofs, in the harmonies of time, in the *Zeitgeist*, which makes each epoch, physical, organic, mental and affectional, in keeping with itself. This Time-spirit is subtler than heredity, and is continuous from the centre of things to the circumferences, and from the past into the future. To be operant it must pass through things on its way, and carry their essentials along with it, and control them. It is the regulative will of a providence that makes for unity, and in this embeds all things by something derived from each singular. The smallness of the animals contemporary with man is an illustration of it; they are shorn down to adequacy with his existence and purposes by the severe necessities of his sphere which bounds them and hems them in. These however are recondite considerations, in their origin theological; and will no doubt be limited and thus extended as religious thought is opened.

So USE is the third with love and with wisdom in the Divine Trinity ; and "the gems of purest ray serene in the dark unfathomed caves of ocean," are in its reserve and intention; and "full many a flower that is born to blush unseen" has a life, property and prophecy in it which breathes to a future when the desert shall blossom as the rose.

LV.—SUN WORSHIP.

Some Biblical Commentators have imagined that the adoration of the sun as the apparent source of the maintenance of life in nature is the earliest and most obvious form of idolatry. There are however reasons which contravene this conjecture. A first reason is that idolatry is now proved to have proceeded from the decline and corruption of the

Ancient Church which was a revelation co-extensive with the ancient world. That Church inherited a knowledge of representatives from the Most Ancient Church; and the representatives imported that all the good objects in nature are representative of divine qualities from which they creatively proceeded, and which they signified to the earliest men. All nature, as we have often said, was perceived as a theatre of correspondences. When this perception was lost, and the residue of faith in it weakened, in inevitable succession to it, the mind regarded certain objects as divine, and was prone to sink the Creator in the creature, selecting such things as had been the most holy representatives for especial adoration. But this was a process of many ages. The two states of faith, the ecclesiastical and the idolatrous, were gradually mingled, until the latter became central, and overcame the former. We are therefore to consider that the representative Ancient Church subsisted, especially in Egypt, long after images had been apparently worshipped, and that the One God still came through them to priests and people in what on a superficial view we should regard as idolatrous times. Swedenborg, our only authority on this subject, alleges that the record of the end of the Ancient Church is the destruction of Pharaoh and his host in the Red Sea; also the destruction of the nations in the land of Canaan. In the former case the whole sojourn of the Israelites from Abraham to Joseph, and to Moses, was still in the epoch of that Church, and Egypt, however perverted and perverting, had not utterly ceased to be a branch of it. Idolatry there had not yet extirpated its remains. Some traditional rituals of Egypt were genuine enough to be transplanted into the Israelitish and Jewish Church, which was then imminent for mankind.

The Ancient Church had no Sabean worship, no adoration of the sun as a representative. Its gods in Egypt, as the sun-god Ra, were in human forms, or sometimes in animal forms compounded with human, and which in the Ancient

Church signified human affections and faculties. They were not peices of dead nature, large or small, not sun, moon, or stars. They were human myths, not otherwise solar. For they were descended by degradation from the worship of Jehovah Who made man in His own image and likeness which is divinely human. The Church which succeeded, the Jewish Church, went down into Egypt to take up its religious scientifics for incorporation into the new dispensation. But the idolatry of Egypt, the worship of its symbols as in themselves worshipful or divine, was expressly forbidden.

It may therefore be seen here that in Egypt, as well as in Chaldea, Babylonia, and Assyria, and afterwards in Greece, the primitive idolatries regarded human and animal forms, thus things of life, and not dead nature. These forms still suggested Man and God. And the same anthropomorphism still subsisted in the worship of heroes and ancestors who were deified after death, and often became synonymous with the more primitive gods, and nominally supplanted them. In this there was still a worship of spiritual forms. The veriest fetishes, idols of wood and stone, pointed to humanity.

The case became different when inorganic nature in whole or in part was worshipped. Such worship no longer regarded representative symbols with a possible inhabitation of something spiritual as its mediating gods, but evidently lifeless existence itself as divine. This is a worship of nature as a creator and a cause. It is not Pantheism, for the human God Pan was in Pantheism. Chaldea and its neighbouring countries were the seats of nature-worship, and when it was established, the worship of the sun and moon was an obvious stage : Baal and Ashtoroth came upon the scene. This seems to ·have been a final stage of departure from a detailed revelation : a worship of the presumed essences of time and space. Fire, in itself a destroyer, was at length the most sacred, not emblem, but substance.

This view may be important in the history and classification of idolatries, some of which were mild and semitheistic; others gross, and culminating in a rigorous anti-theism. Among the latter, Swedenborg, to the surprise of some lovers of the sun, declares that the worship of that delightful luminary is the worst kind of nature-worship. It is a position so little obvious at first that it requires to be defended. We essay this after Swedenborg by showing that it swallows up all human conceptions of Jehovah, and cancels the last representatives of the ancient religion by absorbing it into nature. All forms and rituals perish before it, and matter is the be all and the end all.

Something of this is exemplified in a common and growing creed of the learned to-day, that all the mythologies are resolvable into solar and astronomical myths; and that light and heat, sun and moon, day and night, are the esoteric contents of the ancient theogonies and theologies. Such a creed marks out that the worship of the sun is not a primitive but a final state of the anti-theistic mind.

For in itself the sun in its form is not an emblem of the Creator. No mind can associate love, wisdom, intelligence or life with a globe of fire: it has no prosopopeia, no face to express these things, and no arms and hands to carry them forth. And therefore the more pressing it is upon the senses, the more sternly it must be rejected as seeking an entrance through them into the holy of holies. The moment a man dies the Sun is gone, and he stands face to face with another order of things from which natural heat and light are absent, not a ray of them possible in fact or thought, and in which their fostering, so needful here, is non-efficient. Not a vestige of them can enter into the spiritual world.

The Word proves Swedenborg's declaration as to the heinous nature of the worship of the Sun. When the Lord God brought Ezekiel in the Visions of God to Jerusalem, and showed him the abominations which the elders of the House of Israel do in the dark, every man in his chambers

SUN WORSHIP.

of imagery, the image of jealousy was in the entry, alienating God from his sanctuary. In an inner door by which Ezekiel entered other great abominations were seen, " every form of creeping things and abominable beasts, and all the idols of the house of Israel portrayed upon the wall round about." To these the odour of the cloud of incense went up. Then the Lord said also, "Thou shalt again also see other great abominations: And behold, there sat the women weeping for Tammuz, Then said he unto me, Hast thou seen, son of man? Thou shalt again yet see greater abominations than these. And he brought me into the inner court of the Lord's House, and behold, at the door of the Temple of the Lord, between the porch and the altar, were about five and twenty men, with their backs toward the Temple of the Lord, and their faces toward the east; and they worshipped the sun toward the east" (Ezek. viii. 1–17).

The same declaration is proved out of the following in Jeremiah where the end of sun-worship is seen. "At that time saith the Lord, they shall bring out the bones of the kings of Judah, and the bones of his princes, and the bones of the priests, and the bones of the prophets, and the bones of the inhabitants of Jerusalem, out of their graves: and they shall spread them before the sun, and the moon, and all the host of heaven, whom they have loved, and whom they have served, and after whom they have walked, and whom they have sought, and whom they have worshipped: they shall not be gathered, nor be buried; they shall be for dung upon the face of the earth" (viii. 1, 2).

Swedenborg's words are, "The activity of the natural sun is not from itself, but from the living force proceeding from the sun of the spiritual world. If the living force of this sun were drawn back or taken away, the natural sun would collapse. Therefore it is that of all the forms of the worship of God, the worship of the sun is the lowest; for it is quite dead like the sun itself, and hence that worship is called an abomination in the Word" (*Divine Love*, n. 157).

In that world however there is a Sun, as we have often said above, and there are heat and light. The Spiritual Sun is for the heavens, and the Lord is in it. Yet neither can it, a globe of spiritual fire, and a living sun, be worshipped, because the Lord, Whose apparent mansion that sun is, is a divinely human mind, a human form within it, and as such alone is the object of all worship. His sun is the veil under which He can appear to angelic senses; His human form divine is the reality under which alone He can be loved and perceived by Angelic minds. A corollary from this is that the worship of the natural sun in this world is the last resort of sensuality, which in the character imports the final rule of the love of self.

LVI.—THE HUMANE SUN.

The mighty work through the dead sun consists in the exclusion and preparation of dead nature as a first theatre of human life. Considering whose obeisant creature the sun is, its operations in a secondary sense may be called humane, just as the heat of fires and stoves, and the light of candles, by reason of their use, and as proceeding, from man, though dead, are also humane. It is important to plant this heavy conception upon science when it comes to deal with the agencies which are visibly at work in and from the central orb. Do not be afraid of the lessons of the sun. A just theology tempers it, and puts reason into it.

The Sun itself is one thing, and its proceeding is another. Its heat and light come down through firmaments of ether in to us noiseless passages, and chaos and darkness are met and abolished by them. Close around the sun there is indescribable activity, as it were of the commissioning and starting of these travellers and messengers on the highways of finite space, which are tracks of divine uses to the planetary worlds. Such innumerable goings forth cannot

THE HUMANE SUN. 263

but be attended with courages, partings and emotions with which the glowing surface pulsates and respires; for the sun, which is dead, still images Him Who is living. The apparent unrest is on the surface. The outfit for this host of messengers, which are mundane heat and light, involves the first surprises of matter when by alienation from the central fire it is, analogically speaking, frozen into substances which have names on earth. A perturbation in first matter but not in the sun. Immeasurable jets of such substances are observed; the beating and breathing of the uses of the secure, serene and pacific Sun. To the first thought it is a volcano; but there is no Vulcan here, but Apollo in all his significant splendour; if we may use these good myths. For the sun has no furnace and no anvil, but radiance is its nature, and it has only to ray to produce the substances which it gives away. Perhaps they occur freshly at every distance from the centre. The spectroscope shows that on our earth its terminal beams are charged with many of the matters which we know here. We infer, it may be hastily, that they also exist as such in the Sun. But is not their alienation from the Sun their separate creation?

Of the body of the sun we know nothing from present science. Nor of the weight of it. Nor whether it has weight at all. Centrality may have a quality in it which stands for weight in a world of gravitating weights: a close dead analogue of the creative will making itself felt in universal physics: a form of forms. The sun's weight or importance lies in its imponderables. The pivot of worlds seems answerable to no claim or pull of its offspring but that of instant active service. The sun itself is hardly visible to the naked eye, being hidden in a blaze inferior to itself. There is no reason to suppose that any of the material elementary substances as they are called exist in the body of the sun. They would be dissipated there, and be resolved into what the sun is, the central universe of fire.

And what is that fire? It is not a fire of combustion kept up from without, but, under the divine auspices pure or autocratic fire. Combustion begins from the surface of the orb where separation occurs, and specialized things, not subsisting there, are produced and ignited. We have already used the word frozen in speaking of the first creations from that heat of heat: for the solidity of nature may be regarded as the congelation of substances at a distance from the sun. The sun regarded as fire is therefore essential or as Swedenborg says "pure fire," the intangible and irresistible substance of all terrestrial subjects. Do not conceive the idea of fire as of what is flimsy or baseless; it carries the whole dead creation in it and on it and is the might and weight of nature.

Another thought we draw from this. The perturbation of the surface has no place in the solar centre. There are no elements there to be resolved: the pure ($\pi\upsilon\rho$) fire is not mixed with these: it subsists in its aloneness, and there is nothing like it or second to it in its cosmos. Doubtless it is an architecture, a palace of uses to the whole world; an indefinite programme and order of details: but to none of these can we assign lines and currents of solids or fluids in any oceanic or planetary sense. Only we know that the pillars of the edifice are for ages of ages: enduring so long as the divine uses performed from that footstool-throne are required by its group of children, its earths or satellites. That is the limit of the existence of any particular sun. But the thought before alluded to is, that in all this work, the substantive sun remains peaceful and humane, and being constructive through deity in its outgoing, it is not destructive to itself. A proof, if you please from design, of this, is found in the distance at which the rest of the creation is placed from the sun. No habitable globe can fall into it, and undergo the resolution involved. The sun itself revolving has already thrown it forth. Destruction is prevented in the very plan, and permanent construction ensured.

The circumferences attest the pacific intention in the centre. We may name our majestic luminary in itself Physical Peace.

The sun is a plane of cessation: the Spiritual Sun proceeding through its degrees has at length ceased into it, and nature, dead nature begins, the spiritual now accompanying it *from without*. It begins from its peaceful womb. But being a divine operation, equated to everlasting use, it is of a substance and on a scale above human thought excepting in bare general acknowledgment of an ardour betokening the infinite and eternal. It is a shadow and correspondence of the attributes of the Almighty, humane because God is human.

This is not science; it has theology pressing behind it, and yet it is in its measure true of the sun. Better and greater thoughts will come to the subject from spiritual intuition and reverent natural consideration. I have set forth my own imperfect view affirmatively, yet not dogmatically, for I would have it to be amenable to all the fresh light and heat of wisdom and love that can be given from time to time.

The centre of the earth seems at first sight more inscrutable than the body of the sun, for it is buried deeply under our feet; crusts of matter wall it in; it seems to be hidden in darkness as the sun is hidden in light. But both sun and earth centrally are beyond *scientific* thought. Speculation about the earth's inmost region is of little account. Mythology has made it sometimes into a hell; sometimes into the abode of the disembodied to which the grave was an antichamber. The temperature gradually increasing the deeper the descent is made in mines may point to a central heat of great intensity; and volcanoes, and their connection with each other in spaces of time, may induce the same conclusion. The fire, like the sun's, may be either something we know nothing of, or a relic of the first heat of the planet when sent forth from the sun. But the only way through the darkness seems to lie in the science of correspondences, and in the revelation of man to himself. For he is a microcosm, an earth in miniature. Without a revelation he does not know his own centre. Without a mind having faith in the revelation, he does not admit the concentric globe of his faculties. His senses and his understanding and his animus, which are his surfaces, he believes to be his substance. But the order from within outwards is that his love, whether good, or evil, is his centre, and that his other faculties are circumferences animated by this *amour propre* or *proprium*, and are active forms of it. The love here, unthought of and unsuspected, is a central fire in the man. The earth by this analogy is an obverse image of the sun; a lowest centre of terrene heat and self-combustion the opposite to the supreme unwasting solar fire. It may suggest itself as a prison of centres in chaotic conflict. But it is futile to pursue the unknowable further. Not that we need despair of knowing whenever such is useful for human regeneration. Intuition can be given, with confirmations from the facts and analogies of man and nature, and the earth may become transparent to guided seership when the humble man of the Church consents on any measureable scale to see into himself.

LVII.—SPACES AND NUMBERS IN THE WORD.

The measures of space signify according to extensions in the heavens. Length in the Word denotes good: breadth, truth; and height, the degrees of these. A broad land is the extension of truth in the Church. Length of days is increase of good in the mind. Elongation or distance is disagreement and aversion. Height is degree as to good and then as to truth: what is high is what is internal: height is the measure of inwardness. Heaven is high, and the Kingdom of God is within you; the highest kingdom the deepest within.

SPACES AND NUMBERS IN THE WORD. 267

Also all numbers in the Word are correspondences, and among the deepest in signification. Forty throughout, as we have often had occasion to mention, signifies temptation : forty years in the desert ; forty days in the wilderness. Six is combat of good against evil, and of evil against good. Six days shalt thou labour ; spiritual labour is such combat. Seven is the holy or the profane. The seventh day is the Sabbath of the Lord thy God ; in it thou shalt do no manner of work. While it lasts do not revert to the past labour of which it is the period ; the next six days is for another labour. Rest in good and in its peace. The reason why seven also signifies what is profane, is, " that the same things which are doing in heaven, when they flow down into hell are changed into opposites, and actually become opposite : hence the sanctities signified by seven, in hell become profanities." Thus in the Apocalypse the great red dragon had seven heads, and upon his head seven diadems. The beast which came out of the sea, had seven heads, and upon his heads the name of blasphemy. The great harlot, with whom the kings of the Earth have committed fornication, sits upon a scarlet beast, full of names of blasphemy, having seven heads.—The number ten denotes remains: so also tenths. Remains are goods and truths stored up by the Lord in the interior man. Man receives the remains of good from the Lord from infancy ; the remains of truth afterwards, and without remains man could not be man. They are let down into his natural mind during his regeneration. They are memories from mothers, fathers, and instructors in what is good and true, stored away in the inmost nature, and they serve for the uses of conscience when the opportunity bringing tenderness comes. All spiritual life is from them, and by them man communicates with heaven. From these two examples it may be seen that all numbers in the Word signify things and states, and their qualities.

Few themes in the Sacred Scripture have excited more

derision from the sceptics than the attempts of reverent commentators to assign a meaning and value to these which are called mystical numbers. The coherency, however, of the above explanations when they are carefully traced through the Word, proves their truth; although the subject being so abstract and inward, is beyond the grasp of the natural-rational mind. Might we say it is the higher arithmetic and mathematics of the internal Word? God is said to have made all things in "number, weight and measure": in that case this applies to all spiritual things especially. Spiritual things are real forms and organisms; more real than those of nature. In nature the facts of number invade the thoughts of the sciences in many directions. Chemical substances are engineered upon them as bricks are made into architecture. 'Atoms become buildings according to them, and inhabiting properties flow from them. Each compound is a polity of atoms, and the action of it depends in its fitness upon their numerical adaptation. Music and tone are ultimately grounded upon number of vibrations. The reconditeness here is undeniable; nor could it be resolved into sensual explanation unless we could see the atoms in their forms, and how they oppose, marry, conjoin and interpenetrate. And even then the dynamic end, and its influx into each several creature, upon which all individuality and working depend, is inscrutable. In the meantime the fact remains that natural science has numbers among its bases; and also that they do produce the separate varieties of natural things and qualities: of which crystallography is a large set of examples. So in like manner it is that numbers in the Logos are very recondite, and that the unaided mind seldom touches the true meaning of them; which is the substantial form. But here also the fact remains that we have now a valid inductive explanation of their meaning though no vision of their origin; an explanation proved to be correct by its consistent rendering of the inner language into a sense that is luminous throughout. No other explanation than this is required to prove our attainment of the Assyrian or the ancient Coptic tongues; and to the real student of Scripture, where the field from which the induction is made is immense and unitary, Swedenborg's interpretation of these hieroglyphics is, for our service and use, complete.

LVIII.—THE ANIMAL KINGDOM AND THE EARTHLY BODY.

When man once and for all, and first in his nurse's arms, has made permanent obeisance to the law of gravitation, with the compromise presently by the privilege of Freewill of standing upright, his body and what is in it becomes an earth unto itself, its attractions are its own, and are not determined by the centripetal attraction of the planet. The living body always rests for important ends on the bed-rock of the earth-body, and material weight is in its physiology. " Quot libras in duce summo inveniam?" is the question the earth asks of Hannibal: how many pounds weight shall I find in the supreme leader?

So the earth-body has the earth for its dominant centre. The living body however has as many centres as it has organs, and the organs again consist of nothing but atomic centres. By the weight or importance of its use, each centre, great or small, attracts what it requires from the health and wealth of the system. Attraction,—drawing to you,—signifies love of some kind, whether in stones, men and women, or angels. And love signifies internal freewill. If then you desire to think of any organ, how it can supply itself with what its life needs, like a lamb seeking its mother's milk, or a lion at dawn going to a well of waters, think of it as a self. Think first that a love proper to it rules the organ ; then that the body with the other organs is mutual, and that as the organ sees and wants, so it gets what it loves, what it uses, and what it is useful for; that is to say, if the frame be in a healthy state.

Thus the whole body gravitates to the earth first, because it wants the earth to stand on for ever, and the earth attracts and pulls it to itself, because the earth wants the organ and union with it as its final cause, which is the human race. These two wants satisfied from birth to death, and afterwards, the heart thenceforward can bring its full freight to the door of each organ of the now independent automatic man. In such case, the blood wanted hastens to the organ which it knows is expecting it: the organ is a freewill and special love of this very blood as its commerce of Use: it attracts and draws it in: and the work neither slumbers nor sleeps; for the organ breathes the ordered blood when the lungs breathe the air; expanding with each respiration to inspire it, and contracting to close the momentaneous account, and to make the work and the eating keep pace in the day's uses. Such is the free commerce of the body ordained in the projection of its Mercator, the soul.

As there is no interfering terrene gravitation within this living monarchy, so neither are there any earthy or chemical matters in its dominions. All undergoes a human change. Effete fluids and solids and gases are degraded out of chemistry by judicial life. Corporeal building materials, such as salt, flint, lime, phosphorus, potash, soda, iron, oxygen, hydrogen, carbon, nitrogen, may be called bio-chemical if you please, but they do not subsist within the functions as they are known in nature or in the laboratory. They have left chemistry as the organs have left terrestrial gravitation and attraction; they yield up their affinities into the higher bonds of affections. Freewill, Man, has touched them; they are chemical no longer until they are of no use to man's properties; and then they are virtually cast out. But even so, they have caught life, and remember it as its soil. The freewill that acts and elevates in the supernatural daily metamorphoses, daring to stand upright by the balance of two-sidedness, confers the seals of kingly power throughout the organic commonwealth and republic, by the ordinance of inner and outer, higher and lower, more and more excellent in service, from the head to the heels, and from the brains to the toes. The rule is that the highest is most excellent as the highest, and the lowest most excellent as the lowest.

We speak here of the human body, but whatever is said of mere life applies also, so far as independence of chemical and physical law is concerned, to all animals; and also to vegetable life. Even the plant dominates the chemical.

The organs have their outward limits on their surfaces, and their inward limits in their least organic forms. These latter are the individualities of which they are composed; their persons. The liver in its inmost ends in least livers, the tongue in least tongues, and the brain in least brains. It is the old doctrine of *homœomerla* applied to living bodies, thus an animate atomic theory. In this way the organ is demarcated from the common groundwork of the form, stands on a separate identity, and is a population of centres of attraction answering to tides of gravitation.

Physiology is better served through the wholes which constitute the subject, than through the ultimate cell-work which is universal under the frame, or through the products elicited from the fluids or solids by analysis. The latter analysis is nothing if it does not destroy the first integers which life works to build and to construct. Death is the humane province of chemistry; life, of organization. Life in man has swallowed up a measurable amount of death and made it ghostly. So, thinking further, the career for physiology is greater before modern chemistry entered it than since. It is more amenable to insight belonging to the body itself; insight which stands upon the rock of doctrine that Man himself is the presence of presences in all his parts, organs, functions and uses.

Food departs into scientism, and becomes invisible to the

Higher Physiology, when we think of it as nitrogen, carbon, oxygen and hydrogen. Air, which is superior food, strengthens, invigorates and renews the body. We now learn that its nitrogen contributes to our muscles, and its oxygen to our blood; for nitrogen is yielded to the chemist by muscle, and oxygen combined with carbon by breath from the lungs. But it has always been known that fresh air in health braces muscle and makes muscle, and that fine air makes breathing easy, and keeps health warm. Nothing new is taught here by chemistry, but new substances *out of the body* are handled by the chemist. I am not now thinking of medical interests, but of those of the higher physiology. In this humane branch of insight it is a loss of direction when thought which should be organic demolishes instead of constructing. For instance, the greatest object in respiration is respiration itself: it breathes the man's body into consciousness; and afterwards into every conscious action, and every organic function. But thinking of oxygen, nitrogen, and carbon, the air is the first victim to chemistry: then the breath of life from the lungs is forgotten; then the office of breathing the air in and out locally, obliterates the notice of the general office, which extends to the whole man. This comes of the first false step, which consists in accepting dead transitional gases as guides through the spiritual labyrinth of the lungs. Human Physiology by this showing can be more easily based on integral air, and lungs breathing it in and out, than an organic cell-work, the province of the microscope, or on gases born of the retort. Large facts of outward nature group themselves more willingly round this instructive field of experience redeemed by common sense.

It is a law of scientific memory that limits are its food. When they are obliterated by analysis, as sentences may be destroyed by seeking the etymology of their words, records and landmarks fade from the mind. A new importance attaches to the next set of limits, accentuated as they will be by novelty and the jealousy of innovation. So sciences can propagate themselves which are conditioned on undervaluing and then forgetting the past; and a greedy oblivion soon solaces the restless mind. In *Epidemic Man and his Visitations* I treated at some length on a Doctrine of Oblivion, and gave as an instance that Harvey, in his own mind first, and for the scientific world following him, destroyed the memory of what was rightly known of the heart's central supreme functions of blood-making and blood-circulating by which it corresponds to the love in man, by making hearts to be mechanical pumps for only the lower circulation of the blood through the body.

If the food which is out of the body, and the air drawn from the atmosphere, are estranged from better thoughts by being dissipated into chemicals, much more so are the living things of and in ourselves. Blood and brains valued chemically and materially are troughs of scientist sensuality, and inquisitions for hideous practice. Knowledge about these sacred forms elicited by violence, is worse than destruction; it is devilish knowledge, and begets devilish stupidity, and hatred of mental good. Such 'research' is a final antagonism to the Love which creates and to the mind which can comprehend living creatures.

In studying physiology we again observe, that the forms taken and accepted as they lie in the cold, impartial corpse (honoured in being reverently approached for its secrets), are the first field to enter. They are so much dead letter; so many dead languages to be pondered over as classic treasuries and monuments of a past history. Each organ is a language. Then obviously the more loving, living and spiritual the physiological genius who interprets, the more his life can enter these void properties. But he must be gifted from above. Not otherwise in the average human image before him, itself once ensouled, can he see the lineaments and instruments of his own soul.

The higher physiology will save the mind from the graceless oblivions here spoken of. It will gather up the remains

S

of the perceptive and intellectual past, and enthrone the truths of the ancients upon the experience of the moderns. But science follows the fortunes of good and evil. Truths lived in become hereditary virtues with lasting places. Their commands and charities disregarded, their importance is obliterated. The plainest things to a good mind are pestilent interferences to a bad one. Oblivion is sought as a relief from the truths which have been rejected. Good remembers its own evil, but evil must forget good, and must obliterate its genius. So you can interpret our age by the truths it is forgetting, and has forgotten. I have seen in my long life that its physiology and medicine, though tricked out in terribly red expensive facts, are both of them senile and appointed to die, and that a sign of the end is that the better memory maintains no way in them.

LIX.—A PIECE OF MORAL PHYSIOLOGY.

As an example of the selective power of the organs over the blood which they use, and of the supply of this power everywhere by the brains and nerves, I select the case of two organs which lie just above the kidneys, namely, the suprarenal capsules. The reader will omit this section if he has no liking for anatomy, or no anatomical plates. I dare to insert it because it is weighted with what will generally be called a moral correspondence. The use of the above organs is obscure to physiologists. They are of large size before birth, and continue large during early life, but wane afterwards. They are both promoters and controllers in the field of generation. For generation has two realms; 1, the generation of the body itself, to which the foetus contributes *proprio marte*, developing as it were by its own force; and 2, after birth, the generation of the species. Thus in the earliest time of all when they are largest, these kidney capsules call out the best blood of the body, back its circulation, and stimulate the growth of the little embryonic body through its own seminal virtue and courage. After birth, in a lesser degree, owing to diminished size, they stand for some years over the proper seminal organs, and by diverting their blood upwards, they forestal premature sexual development, which is a thing possible to occur very early in life as a wasteful state. They reserve for subsequent purity, when they are smaller and smaller in size, the true generative power, now, under the love of the sex, about to be emancipated, and in which the mind and body become not only productive in personal vitality, but also reproductive. And true to themselves throughout existence, they still have the offices of controlling and promoting. Small, and subject to freewill, they select and rescue some of the finest blood which is descending to the sexual organs, and restore it, fertile and eager though it be, unspent to the higher powers. Thus in the beginning of their lives they control and promote the germ of individual life; and implant deeper than memory a suggestion of purity and the design and good of it in the frame, whereby they foreshadow manliness and womanliness as the two strengths of life. This is a deep ante-natal endowment, fabulous of the life after death, when the children that are born are the virtues of love with wisdom added to the married pair. When puberty is reached, these same organs plead their primeval Vestal vow, with the lamp of life in their hands; and are virginal handmaids, in their pure blood looping imagination upwards towards the higher places of conjugial thought. None but a Seer could make the first journey in the body, and see such spiritual ends and purposes for true life in its organs. This happened because he saw without reasoning that the body of supreme purpose is the loyal kingdom of the soul. Therefore on this subject consult Swedenborg's *Animal Kingdom*, n. 443–441, and Worcester's Book mentioned above. The whole subject of foetal existence in its spiritual sense is a record of wonders, and is now committed to the rational mind.

LX.—BREATH.

Let us consider for a moment not what breathing or respiration is but what breath is. It is not mere air, but air humanized. It has travelled in the deep parts of man; and the breath of life is not the air breathed in, but the air breathed out. The air breathed in is dead until it is associated with life in the chest. But the air breathed out is *our* breath. Now the Word makes breath canonical; that is, uses it with a spiritual sense, and we accept the instances of bodily organs mentioned in the Word as involving inspired declaration of their uses or meanings. The first instance we mention is in Genesis, when precedent to the spiritual creation of man, the spirit or breath of God moved upon the faces of the waters. This is repeated in one uniform sense throughout the Old Testament. We have a crowning instance in the New Testament when Christ breathed upon His disciples and said, Receive ye the Holy Breath or Spirit. His breath had His divine powers because it had undergone contact with the virtue of His Divine Body. Descending from this, as a principle of guidance, does not love breathe upon the beloved, and is not such breathing the act of inmost tenderness and yearning? Does not pity breathe upon the sinews of pain, and long to relieve them? Does not aspiration breathe upwards with a sublime breath, and does not meanness breathe downwards? These are examples of different breaths of life, and come from the spirit within outwards, and partake of it. And spirit is the name for them, το πνευμα in Greek: a bodily word and a spiritual at the same time. So we begin to see the contents of breath after it has left the body; especially after it is voluntarily breathed from the affections and their purposes. It is a great subject, and demands volumes. Such breath must be taken literally from the state of mind which is breathing, and nothing lower be thought of: no air, no gas: but life communicated where received. Even the breath of cows gives life away to sick human creatures.

This life in breath enables us to see what animal breath does in the preparation of a climate for man to breathe in ; and what a murder of climate it is to exterminate good and wholesome life, however wild, on the planet. It also shows the reason for the great embryonic animal kingdom which preceded the creation of the first race of men. The vegetable and animal breaths of these ungainly trees and creatures who were the primeval inhabitants, captured the dead material world into familiarity with the first possible breaths of lives, introducing spiritual movement into it from without, and impregnating it with the waves of natural animal affections. The natural man was thus created into a world ancestral with breaths corresponding to his own, and the Lord God breathed into his nostrils the breath of life, and he became a living soul.

LXI.—ASSYRIAN REASONINGS.

" And they digged another well, and disputed also over it." This signifies the internal sense of the Word, and whether there be such a sense. . . . Many disputes at this day go no further than this. But so long as men remain in debate whether a thing exist, and whether it be so, it is impossible to advance to anything of wisdom. For in the very thing debated about, there are innumerable particulars which cannot be seen so long as the thing itself is not acknowledged ; all these in such case being unknown. Modern learning scarcely advances beyond these limits of debate, whether a thing exist, and whether it be so, and this excludes the understanding of the truth. He who merely debates whether an internal sense exists in the Word, cannot possibly see the innumerable, the indefinite things contained in that sense. He who disputes whether charity be anything in the

Church, and whether the things of faith be not the all in it, cannot possibly know the innumerable, the indefinite things which are contained in charity, but remains in total ignorance of what charity is. So also in regard to the life after death, the resurrection of the dead, the last judgment, heaven and hell; they who only dispute whether these things exist, stand out of the doors of wisdom, like persons merely knocking at the door, and cannot look into wisdom's magnificent palaces; and what is surprising, they fancy themselves wiser than others, and wiser in exact proportion to their skill in debating whether a thing be so, and especially in confirming themselves that it is not so. The simple, however, who abide in good, and whom such disputants despise, can perceive in a moment, without dispute, much more without learned controversy, both the existence of the thing, and the nature and quality of it. They have a general sense of the perception of the truth where the learned have extinguished this sense by habits which incline them first to determine whether the things exist. The Lord speaks of these two classes when He says: "I thank Thee, Father, that Thou hast hid these things from the wise and intelligent, and hast revealed them unto babes" (Matthew xi. 25: Luke x. 21; *Arcana Cœlestia*, n. 3428, on Gen. xxvi. 21).

Perhaps it arises from this ground, that the noble science of the human mind is lost in the sands of metaphysical and moral philosophy, and is useless, yielding no guide for life. It consists now in great part of analyses and classifications of the tools employed in the above intellectual debates and discussions, and of how they exist in themselves as abstractions from words. It omits the consideration of uses and functions, and especially of religious uses and functions, which show in act,—the only way of showing—what all the faculties essentially are. On this subject Swedenborg says: "The world in general, including the learned part of it, is in utter ignorance as to the most common and obvious [mental] propositions, as that the rational mind is distinct from the natural mind, and that it is good and truth which constitutes the rational, and which also constitutes the natural. Still less is it known that the rational flows into the natural to the intent that man may be capable of thinking, and of willing accordingly; and as these propositions are unknown, this influx must needs be of difficult apprehension" (*Arcana*, 3314). In consequence of this, the order of the mind is unrecognized, and the servants in it are admitted into its places of rule; the senses sit upon its thrones, handle its treasuries, and spend them upon its useless curiosities, scientifics and discussions. Yet the mind first and foremost is a hierarchy, and all its good uses flow from its order and subordination. Were the canons of its uses perceived, and established monarchy accepted, the senses would be the basis and footsole on which it rests and is supported, and then other senses all the way upwards would be added to the loftier tiers of faculties, realizing them all; for without senses they are nothings: and man would perceive his mind substantially as he perceives its outcome, his body and its organs. But where the senses rule, all the rest is unrealized; robbed of its substance and consumed by their tyrannous greed. After which, good and truth, love and wisdom, affection and rationality, are but sensual scientifics and "become air." The internal sense of the Word treats throughout of the organic faculties of the mind as they are used and abused; of what is first in order; of how this faculty should be master in such a field, and how that faculty should be reduced to be its servant. It is not possible however to comprehend anything of the scope of that sense excepting as an inspired Divine Philosophy commanding the priestly and kingly uses which reign over and in the mind.

The Word also treats not only of the mind's faculties as they are in their just order by creation, and thus appoints and secures their places ready for use, and, preliminarily forbids each from going beyond its sphere, but also reveals their higher functions when they are regenerated by the influx of the superior faculties into them, by which they receive new powers and capacities. It reveals what Egypt and Assyria become when Israel flows into them, and is all in all with them. For instance, the common rational mind dealing with worldly and sensual things,—the natural mind in its entirety —by the influx of an intellectual faculty above it from a spiritual origin, becomes spiritual-rational, and enters by divine acceptance on a realm of perceptions and judgments to which in its former state it was incompetent: it becomes the organ of the spiritual in the rational. When this takes place throughout the adult lifetime, all the lower reasons, ratiocinations and persuasions of the individual *proprium*, by which it criticized and impugned holy things, are gradually rejected and purged out of it; as if the old peccant and quarrelsome reason itself were swept away; and what Matthew Arnold handsomely calls "the sweetness of light" illuminates it, and gives it new and truly reasonable eyes, of humility, with its insights from the interior Word. And so of all the other faculties; and most of all of the rulers of all, of love and the affections. These in their natural state are wild cattle, and wild sheep; regenerated by love to God and the neighbour, they are the flocks and herds of which the Psalm says: 'All the beasts of the field are mine, and the cattle upon a thousand hills'; the hills of celestial and spiritual elevation. There is a coming philosophy of the mind in all this; but it is purely practical though transcendent; and it is all based on order, on the opening of the lower to admit the higher; on the submission of the lower to the informations of the higher; on the gradual elimination of natural objections and obstacles as at-length clear nothings; and in short on the unimpeded transflux of the Word through faculty after faculty from love and charity at the summit to love and charity as the basis.

On this subject we have the following :—" The end of creation being an angelic heaven out of the human race, thus the human race, therefore all other things which have been created

ASSYRIAN REASONINGS. 281

are mediate ends, which, because they relate to man, look to these three things of him, his Body, his Rational faculty, and for the sake of conjunction with the Lord, his Spiritual faculty. For man is not able to be conjoined to the Lord unless he be spiritual; nor is he able to be spiritual unless he be rational: nor is he able to be rational unless his body be in a sound state. These things are as a house. The body is as the foundation, the rational is as the house built upon it: the spiritual represents those things which are in the house ; and conjunction with the Lord is being at home in it" (*Divine Love*, n. 330).

While on the subject of this order and influx, it may be well to point out also that all the faculties should be inviolate throughout, for a special freewill belongs to each of them. The senses, when good servants, have their inalienable rights, and are justified as purveying the wide informations of the kingdom of first appearances. They enjoy home-rule if they are a peaceful home of natural good, and in their domesticity observe their own order, subject to the order of the whole mind. The sensual imagination rules by influence in them, being as a faculty close above them : it sharpens them beyond themselves, and by its delights gives them life. The mind proper, the beginning and centre of man, the rational mind, the organ of common sense and its judgments and determinations, is still above ; and preserves its own sphere in the order; but influences by no force of violence the imagination, controlling it to its just limits, and making it an initial way of truth, a rational imagination, the mother of good views and allowable theories and guesses ; and above all a seeing and observing eye in the perpetual acts and habits of life. The senses with sound strong reason and imagination and facile fancy in them are treble senses, and see what the five of themselves, be they called poets, never felt or saw. The intellectual mind ranges wider, for the spiritual world is with it; regarding as primary the *uses* of the lower minds, and entering into the immeasurable commerce of which use is the field. The service of man is the best ground of its perceptions. The spiritual mind regards spiritual ends in uses; regeneration of the individual and eternal life. The celestial mind reigns in the perception and practice that love united with wisdom is the end of ends; and it influences the spiritual mind to carry its truths to good, and to impregnate its uses with love. This rule of mind over mind, each freely submitting to its superior, is the human form, the image and likeness of God, Who is the creator of the order of the organs, and Who endows them beyond themselves, by perpetual planes and inductions of free fellowship from above. This, however, is as the mind should be, not as it is. Each faculty has the power of obstructing and stopping the influx, and limiting the man to all above its *proprium* or self. A man may be sensual without being rational, and rational without being intellectual, and also intellectual without being spiritual; he can love truth more than good; and in each such case the gifts descending from above come from the lower source.

LXII.—HEREDITIES.

The inheritances of character and disposition from parents to children have been studied with some diligence in this scientific age, but from the natural and not from the spiritual side. I am not aware that any writer but Swedenborg has traced the important bearing of the subject in religious beliefs or states. It is the groundwork of the history of man as a personal agent.

The human family at no time and in no place has been a mass of merely aggregated individuals; but from the beginning has existed in Churches, and in the outlying remainders of Churches commonly called heathenisms.

These religious bodies or churches, divinely instituted and organized, have been subject to the inevitable conditions of inheritance from fathers to sons. We have seen already in frequent detail what the succession of churches was. Each of them declined from its first Word, its first communicated Revelation and its first innocence, as it were from infancy to old age and death, by the development of hereditary seeds of evil and falsity. As Swedenborg observes : "The church decreases and degenerates by departure from its primeval integrity; and this chiefly in consequence of the increase of hereditary evil, every succeeding parent adding some new evil to what he himself inherited. Every evil actually committed by parents induces a new aspect on their nature, and when often repeated becomes natural, is added to what was hereditary, is planted over into their children, and through them into their posterity, and gives birth to an immense increase of evil in the course of generations. This must appear plainly to those who attend to the evil dispositions of children, and trace their resemblance to their parents and forefathers. It is a great error to suppose that there is no hereditary evil but what was implanted by Adam, when in fact each individual by his own actual sin produces hereditary evil, making addition to what he received from his parents, and accumulating the new sum in all his posterity, which is in no degree moderated save in those alone who are regenerated by the Lord. This is the primary cause of the degeneration of every church " (*Arcana*, n. 494).

Also further: "The good into which a man is born, is derived to him from his parents, either father or mother; for whatever parents have contracted by frequent use and habit, or are tinctured with by actual life, so as to render it familiar to them until it has the appearance of being natural, is carried down to their children, and becomes hereditary. Where parents have lived in the virtue of the love of good, and in so living have perceived their proper delight and blessedness, supposing them to conceive children in such a state of life, the children then receive an inclination to similar good. Where parents have lived in the virtue of the love of truth, and in so living have perceived their proper delight, if they conceive children in such a state of life, the children then receive an inclination to similar virtue" (*Arcana*, n. 3469).

These are the desirable goods of nature or birth; but not of the will or the understanding: in one sense they may be called, with an extension of the common meaning, good nature. But Swedenborg again remarks: "Natural good is such that of itself it is not willing to obey and serve rational good as a servant serves a master, but it is desirous to have command. It requires to be reduced to compliance and service" (*Arcana*, n. 3470).

These considerations, if pondered, lift the subject of heredity from family proclivities into the sphere of the highest and lowest history of mankind, and confirm on psychological grounds the doctrine of the church, that man now, *considered in himself*, is nothing but evil and its ever convenient falsity. There is no escape from this conclusion. And the better a religious man is, the more he must be conscious of it as a rational experience. Also his unceasing knowledge and conscience of it is the condition of his advancement in the regenerate life.

The religions of the world, and their decline, are therefore the grounds of all the studies we have attempted in tracing the process from above downwards, from revelations to mythologies, from divine churches to fetish worship on the one side, and to atheism on the other. They involve not civil and moral states, but the direct relations of man to God. And the passage traversed hitherto reaches from Jehovah to graven and molten images, and from the inspired Word to the human philosophy which denies and supplants it. The outward destinies of nations, unconsciously to themselves, depend, now even rapidly, on the "downrush" of their heredities; their characters grow heavier from being more charged with evil; and they tend, unless they alter, to the doom which has already befallen the corresponding nations of the past. Every fresh outward power they possess and call their own, hastens the end, just as enormity of wealth and genius in wicked hands, inwardly, and at length outwardly, consigns the man to a sure place in the estimation of even a corrupt society. For evil is at last the accuser and doom of evil. Therefore decaying churches enact themselves ultimately as social, political, and national history; and inheritance of spiritual evil acted out into sin from generation to generation is still at the root.

Observe however that inherited evil is not sin unless you love it and make it into deeds, and that inherited good is not good for you unless you enter its formless gift with mature principles of wisdom, and lift and detail it from natural towards spiritual good.

The inheritances of the past, including the love of power, and the love of money, have therefore been the essential disendowment and disestablishment of all the churches to the present day. The capacity of standing as open doors for the divine light to enter has been withdrawn from their priesthoods, which are in serried opposition to its instructions; and as in the past, the remote laity remains for the new revelation and the new city. The Christian and more outlying heathens will be summoned to receive the endowment and to constitute the establishment. Of course we are now speaking of divine and not of national or parliamentary churches, which latter especially have the advantage of being for the most part benignly secular, and of being unconsciously in the influx and current of a new church and its new ages. By disendowment we understand the loss of the goods and truths of heaven from the Word, and by disestablishment, the consummation of a church, and its supersession by a new dispensation.

LXIII.—DREAMS AND VISIONS.

The Word, the heathen mythologies, and the course of life, supply a store of materials for enlightened thought on the subject of this chapter. Sleep is one part; the passivity and abeyance of the sensual and bodily life, and the emancipation of the inner mind for a time, is the other. The latter is the awakening of higher faculties, the opening of some spiritual sight, and the perception of objects which the corporeal senses are not adequate to receive. It is not sleep, because the interior man is in increased wakefulness during such sight or vision.

From what has been said of the perceptive Man, the celestial or Most Ancient Church, named Adam, before "the Lord God caused a deep sleep to fall upon the man, and he slept," it may be evident that his normal sleep partook wholly of his character, and that it was a state which does not exist at the present day. No evil heredities marred it. No resistance to divine influx and its immeasurable gifts obscured or distorted it. The soberness, temperance and chastity of the industrious day were consummated in it; and accordingly it was the floor and groundwork of celestial dreams. These dreams consisted of representatives of heavenly things, and this because of the law that angelic discourse when it flows down to man clothes itself in correspondences, which became an understood biblical hieroglyph in those primitive ages. The discourse in itself was ineffable to even these first men on the earth, no vocal or perceived language to them; but the representatives and correspondences created by it as dreams on the tablets of sleep, were intelligible as generalizations or common perceptions, and were attended with delights and instructions. What the intellectual heaven of the day did not give, the affectionate heaven of the night supplied. The day was inspired by the night, and the night was committed to use by the day.

Swedenborg was led through providential personal experiences, which are the only ways of leading, to attest this primeval state by dreams, and by what happened thereafter and thereupon. He says: "It has often been given me after certain dreams to discourse with the spirits and angels who introduced them; they relating what they had introduced, and I, what I had seen. . . . After awaking and relating what I had seen in sleep, and this in a long series, the angelic spirits said that what I related coincided exactly, and was the same, with what they had been discoursing about; and differed in nowise excepting only as representatives differ from the things represented. . . . And they said further that the same discourse was capable of being turned into other representatives—into similar and dissimilar ones in indefinite variety; and that they had been turned into those I had experienced because they were agreeable to the state of the spirits about me, and hence to my own state at the time. That in fact several dissimilar dreams may descend and be presented from the same discourse or from a single origin, because the things in man's memory are recipient vessels in which ideas are varied and received representatively according to the varieties of their form and the changes of their state" (*Arcana*, 1979, 1980).

Here the upper part of the drama is intimately phonetic for those who can so receive it, but becomes hieroglyphic, or as we may say, telegraphic,—using the syllables "graphic" in the sense of giving forth pictures, figures and forms,—at the lower end.

To show how the contents of the memory are employed in this teledemic influx, Swedenborg says: "I had formed the idea of a certain person that his *forte* was natural truth, gathering this from the actions of his life. Now the angels were discoursing of natural truth: and therefore this person was represented to me; and what he said to me and what he did in my dream, followed in an orderly way of representation and correspondence from the discourse of the angels with each other. But [between the discourse and the representation] there was altogether no similarity " (*Arcana*, 1981). Here we have an insight into the conversion of the memory into spiritual cyphers; a clear origin of the meaning of ideographic hieroglyphs; and some guide for the individual mind to the meaning of certain of its dreams. We may also recur to what was said respecting the diversities of statement about the Lord in the Four Gospels; as that the Divine Inspiration was given to four minds for various application to the thought-imagination of the universe of men addressed in the Word.

The state of dream-influx was universal in the earliest men, and by virtue of their perceptive genius they understood their dreams, which were a divine schooling other than their waking lives. Every one at this day recognizes what a power and ecstasy a happy dream is; and how it seems to bless the day, and many days. Speaking personally, I have had three or four such dreams in my life, and they have been of cities in this world. Why I knew not, but they uplifted me. Cities correspond to the doctrinals of truth. I may hope that such dreams were a forecast of some affection for such doctrinals. Also I have repeated a part of Swedenborg's experience respecting individuals who stood for my mind as types of certain qualities; and have found on waking that those qualities from my memory were bodied forth in the apparition of these people who thus represented the qualities in the dream-language. For it may be discernible from this ground of thought, that the life of this natural world, its places, events and persons, are taken upwards into inner faculties, into another memory subject to and possessed by another reason; and that there they are used as representatives and hieroglyphs in an inner series of ideas pertaining to each individual mind.

It is submitted therefore to the reader that the origin of such representatives as are found in Egypt and in general in the monuments of the ancient nations, is elucidated by Swedenborg on spiritual principles consonant to reason, and which the learned may accept if they elevate their minds to comprehend them. Let it be observed however that the dreams here in consideration are in no analogy to the ordinary experiences of the night, which are mostly phantasies depending upon the unrest and unhealth of the day. Even these have a spirit-origin, but the uneasy body is the plane on which a lower influx operates.

Sleep is a type of the state in which genius, which is rational influx from within, and inspiration which is spiritual influx from without, can be given. It is in one sense a compulsory gift, though welcome to weary man. Submission of the mind and the body takes place in it. The vigilant selfhood is no longer in the front; and consciousness, when dreams occur, happens beyond personal help or management. You cannot banish dreams. In this respect it is like the ground of the higher moments or felicities of genius, and of the infallibilities of inspiration, in which the outer man is passive, and does not interfere with the tide in the mind, or attribute it to himself. This rare passivity to influx is also represented in what sleep does for the body and the mind. It pours new life into their vessels, fatigued by the sordes and strifes of the day; and a reason obviously is, that though the man's nature is all there, his wasteful personal self does not actively resist the beneficent " restorer."

And dream-states also, for the thoughtful man, supply some facility for a belief in a spiritual existence. Whilst we are in them, we are a part of them, and believe in them; or do not generally question them. They present to us something of a world full of objects such as we see in the waking state: a kind of Berkleyan universe, which is substantial as this world for the dreamer. This experience can easily be set aside, and dismissed as a dream, by those who please; but it seems to furnish a suggestion towards the mind having a universe of its own attached to it, independent of the fixity of external things. It makes it easier to conceive that

T

space and time and death which seem to be everything, may, when we die, be nothing; and yet that we may then enter upon a world of states to which no sense of reality from outward objects is lacking.

Visions stand somewhat in the same category as dreams from being representative. Like the successive Churches they are in a series. They existed normally as laws of its nature in the Most Ancient Church; and the representatives then communicated were the golden currency of celestial thought, the pieces of which in their divine value are still maintained in the Word we now possess. The standard is invariable, the same yesterday, to-day, and forever. They existed in the Ancient Church in its prophetic books which are now lost. They reappear in the Israelitish and Jewish Church in the Prophets, and plainly foretell the Coming of the Lord. They stand forth in the Christian Church in the Apocalypse, which is a prophetic vision of the consummation of that Church, and of the descent, endowment and establishment of the New Jerusalem. They are adequately, yea intellectually, completed now in an open vision of the spiritual world through Emanuel Swedenborg. The things "heard and seen" by him are, however, "not visions properly so called, but things beheld" as he testifies, "in the most perfect state of bodily wakefulness."

The word, visionary, is mischievous to the mischievous natural man when it is applied to spiritual sight, being easily extended by him to all high informations beyond the lines of the corporeal senses. The Poets are some aid here, and Shakespeare speaks of "the vision and faculty divine." And Milton is full of a perception of the sublime nature and use of this faculty in the Word. In it we read, "where there is no vision the people perish." To discard vision because we cannot attest it in our own experience, is to immerse ourselves in our negative understandings. By this we agglutinate one of "the high capacious powers folded up in man," and which can be unfolded now for our enlargement and guidance, or rebuke. For all the visions of the Word have descended for our daily use; and the very obscurity of them apart from the light of their spiritual sense, has kept the Church in the attitude and endeavour to discover the mystery which has at length been revealed. "I saw in the visions of the night one like the Son of Man coming in the clouds of heaven." In this vision dark and obscure to the natural man, and therefore said to be "in the night," the "clouds of heaven" are the literal sense of the Word, which, when it is opened, reveals the glory of the Lord, the Divine Humanity, in the spiritual sense.

LXIV.—THE PLAGUES OF SCIENTISM.

The countries described in the Word are as we have seen in the internal sense spiritual countries, distinct regions or faculties of the human mind, which itself in the spiritual world is the only map that is known. Regarded in this light it is simply on the one hand an ouranography of goodness and truth, and on the other a gehennagraphy of evil and falsity. These two opposite realms of mental states are each in a divine order of immeasurable detail, in genera and species, embracing all spiritual, and all infernal life. The human form is necessarily the expression of them, with a cosmos of inferior correspondences surrounding and representing it in both cases. The human form is the substance and reality; the world around it is of appearances answering to it. The appearances are realities because they correspond. The countries in the Word have each their signification from this ruling correspondence.

From this it is obvious that all the things in each country, the persons, places, rivers, mountains, and all the animals and trees and plants, partake of the general signification of the land described. They are its particulars. And each variously follows the country in which it mentally lives. The horses of Egypt are sensual scientifics ; the horses of Assyria are discussions whether good be good, and whether truth be true. The horses of Israel are divine doctrinals, and their understandings. The mind or humanity involved is the only place of them : the mind as an immortal man-form.

Bearing this in mind the willing reader will not be surprised to find that in the internal sense the calves of Egypt are not calves, but denote a particular state of the scientific faculty in the natural man : for if Egypt is science, its calves are also of science. Moreover the plagues of Egypt signified the insurrection of scientific knowledges belonging to the Church against its spiritual truths and goods represented by the Children of Israel, and the oppression exercised upon them by Pharaoh. The waters turned into blood ; the fish dying in the river and polluting it ; the frogs brought forth by the river, and coming up on Pharaoh and the people, and covering the land ; and then gathered together in heaps so that the land stank : the dust of the land becoming lice in man and in beast ; the swarms of flies covering and corrupting the land ; the murrain on all domestic beasts ; the ashes sprinkled towards heaven by Moses before Pharaoh, and become a boil and blains upon man and beast, upon the magicians, and upon all the Egyptians ; the hail mingled with fire throughout the land that smote all that was in the field, both man and beast, and every herb of the field, and brake every tree of the field ; excepting in the land of Goshen, where the children of Israel were. The locusts that went up over all the land and darkened it, and ate every herb of the land, and all the fruit of the trees which the hail had left. The darkness that could be felt in which they saw not one another; neither rose any from his place for three days ; but all the Children of Israel had light in their dwellings. After which Pharaoh rejected Moses, and saw his face no more. Then at midnight the death of the first-born in the land of Egypt, from the first-born of Pharaoh on his throne to the first-born of the captive in the dungeon ; and all the first-born of cattle.

THE PLAGUES OF SCIENTISM. 293

These events in the internal sense are an intelligible series strictly pertaining to Egypt in its relation to Israel; that is to say, to the natural mind oppressing and subjugating the spiritual; and they happen in the world to-day as they happened representatively in the time of Moses and Pharaoh. For a detailed illustration of them point by point see the *Arcana Cœlestia*. For Egypt here signifies the destruction of religion and the Church by sensual scientifics, attempting in every degree of the mind, by intelligence gathered out of self-love and the love of the world, to root out the Divine Being from the affections and the intellect, and out of all knowledges which plainly teach the simple man the existence and goodness of his Father. The Lord said unto Moses, "See, I have made thee a God to Pharaoh." And at last Pharaoh said to Moses, "Get thee from me, take heed to thyself, see my face no more; for in the day thou seest my face thou shalt die." Here the sensual scientific man rejects and makes an end in himself of the spiritual man. To see his face then,—day = state,—is to be in hell with him.

From this it may be plain that perverse Egypt, as once an initiating body in the Ancient Church, now, at the end of that Church, denotes the insane attempt to rule by scientifics over the mysteries of faith, and failing in this, to deny all that overlies and outlies the natural senses, and to betake itself to its own magical persuasions and idolatries: for there are idols of the heart and mind as well as of wood and stone, and the innermost idol in the scientist shrine is always the glory of the selfhood.

It is to be observed that Egypt especially signified religious scientifics pertaining to the rituals of the Church, and not the knowledges of science as we understand the term. The Egyptians had physical and astronomical science and learning; but they valued these from a religious ground, and did not advance in them from the curiosity which prompts their magnitudes to-day. Their ritual and ceremonial sciences, however, were powers in their hands such as do not exist now; and their magic, then a most real infernality, by miracles which followed the miracles of Moses, hardened Pharaoh's heart and placed him between two gods. These sciences were not therefore of the rituals which form the order of the present Church. It may further be said that modern scientism,—I use the term to distinguish it from true science,—also has its abundant rituals, but which belong to the egotistical intellect, and to no church. These are careful educations and trainings that the body and the senses are the whole man, as it were catechisms for noviciates; glories and exaltations and apotheoses of violent and trivial knowledges, as it were barkings and howlings, the liturgies of the self-worshipping selfhood; anticipations of omniscience and omnipotence in the materialist future, as it were prophetic enunciations of the messiahship of self; and at length utter apocalypse and persuasion that "the kingdom of man" is at hand, and that the collective scientist is God.

What then do the calves of Egypt signify specifically? On this subject Swedenborg says: "The sons of Israel made to themselves a golden calf, and worshipped it instead of Jehovah, because Egyptian idolatry remained in their hearts, although with the mouth they confessed Jehovah. Among the idols of Egypt the principal were she-calves and he-calves of gold; for a she-calf signified scientific truth which is the truth of the natural man, and a he-calf the good of that truth, which is the good of the natural man; and gold also signified good. This good and this truth they effigied by he-calves and she-calves of gold. But when the representatives of celestial things were turned into idolatries, and into magic, then in Egypt, as elsewhere, the representative effigies themselves were made into idols, and began to be worshipped. Hence the idolatries of the ancients, and the magical arts of the Egyptians."

This assertion of Swedenborg that golden calves, male and female, were among the prevalent idols of Egypt, seems, as a general statement, to be hardly borne out by the researches of Egyptologists. Kitto in his *Cyclopædia of Biblical Literature* figures an " Egyptian calf-idol," which he copied from Cairo, but which was not made of gold. The Israelites, Kitto says, during their sojourn in Egypt, were accustomed to the image of a sacred calf carried at the head of marching armies, " as may be still seen in the processions of Rameses the great." Swedenborg's remark is evidently based upon the Word, and not upon the monuments. A conjectural explanation of the discrepancy, if it exist, may be, that Egypt dealt with Israel in its own coin by golden lures to idolatry. We know that the bull was dedicated to Osiris and the cow to Isis, and that Apis was represented as a young bull—a he-calf. The Israelites were a shepherd-people, and it is at least likely that the Egyptians approached their minds with that part of symbols which would delight them, and that the jackal-headed, ibis-headed and hawk-headed deities were not among these presentations. And that the Israelites at that time loved gold may be evident from their " borrowing the gold and silver vessels of the Egyptians " when they went out of Egypt, and when after the death of the first-born, the people of the land were eager to be rid of them at any cost. Then as now the Israelites had their price.

With respect to the golden calf made by Aaron at the request of the people out of their ear-rings, the ears in a good sense signify obedience and hearkening, the rings conjunction with good, which is gold : in the present case, disobedience and lust to idolatry, and its evils. When the molten calf was made and fashioned with a graving tool,— the making of it by fire is the corruption of the will, the fashioning with a tool the falsification of the understanding, —Aaron said, "These be thy Gods, O Israel, which brought thee up out of the land of Egypt." Here the commentators, with Swedenborg, cannot err in asserting that this special idolatry came out of the lessons easily learned by the people in that land.

The Word itself testifies to a close connection in the internal sense between the calf and scientific and magical Egypt. It is said in Jeremiah, "Egypt is a very beautiful she-calf, destruction cometh from the north, and her hirelings in the midst of her are as fatted he-calves": where a she-calf denotes the scientific truth of the natural man; the hirelings, who are he-calves, are those who do good for the sake of gain; which in itself is not good, but is the delight of the natural man separate from the spiritual. This is the delight in which the sons of Jacob were, which is in itself idolatrous; and therefore it was permitted them to make it known and to testify it by the adoration of a calf (*Arcana*, n. 9391). The prophets abound in passages in which a calf has a good and bad signification in the sense described.

"They made a calf in Horeb, and bowed themselves to what is molten, and changed glory into the effigy of an ox that eateth herbs" (Psalm cvi. 19, 20). "They add to sin, and make to themselves a molten thing of their silver, idols in their intelligence, the whole work of artificers, saying to them, they sacrifice a man, they kiss calves" (Hosea xiii. 2). "The unicorns shall come down with them, and the calves with the strong, and their land shall be made drunk with blood, and their dust shall be made fat with fatness" (Isaiah xxxiv. 7). "The fortified city shall be solitary, a habitation let down and forsaken, there the calf shall feed, and there shall he lie down and shall consume the branches thereof, and the harvest thereof shall wither" (Isaiah xxvii. 20). "Rebuke the wild beast of the reed, the congregation of the strong, among the calves of the people: treading down the payments of silver, he hath dispersed the people" (Psalm lxviii. 30). "They have made a king and not from Me, they have made princes, and I have not known; their silver and gold they have made idols, that it may be cut off; thy calf hath forsaken, O Samaria, for it also was from Israel, the smith hath made it, and he is not a god, because the calf of Samaria shall be made into pieces" (Hosea viii. 4, 5, 6).

What may again be noted is, that this biblical language in the internal sense is as definite and immutable as any of the languages which the learned spend their lives in studying. And further, that although everything in Egypt denotes scientifics, yet there is no sameness or confusion in the terms, but each symbol or ideograph carries a distinct signification in the series according to the subject treated of. All things in the spiritual Egypt of the Word are wanted to make up the entire Egypt. The scientific faculty which is the mind of the natural man, the clear beginning of him, is a realm or universe, peopled with all external and internal objects, and the management of that realm has countless exact issues for good and for evil. The science-man is a whole man with every organ in him, from the crown of the head to the soles of the feet. The Word, if we may use the thought, looks at Egypt through Israel, at the natural through the spiritual man ; and hence it contains things concerning Egypt which are not written, and scarcely hinted at, in the hieroglyphic remains. The Word contains the real history of Egypt : its full inheritance of representatives and ceremonials from the Ancient Church ; and then its perversion of these Church-powers through long dynasties of idolatries and enchantments until Egypt is no more.

From the signification of Egypt as science, a presumption is raised that it was indeed the earliest of the cultivated nations. For scientifics ending in knowledges are the proper beginning of the spiritual mind, which without them we may say has no basis, no bones, and no definite human form. And a people that specially represented religious scientifics would stand as the primitive schoolroom of the Ancient Church which as a divine Æon followed the extinction of the Most Ancient Church.

Finally, if you desire to understand Egypt, study its true hierology in the spiritual sense of the inspired Word. It is necessarily and inevitably a religious study.

LXV.—FUTURITY VERSUS IMMORTALITY.

The spiritual world makes history because every nation has its ancestors connected with it, and either above it or below it; and from its own free determination, it receives its life from these invisible but immense kingdoms. Were their pressure estopped, the human will and understanding would be at an end, and the race would be extinct. God rules man indeed from Himself, but angels, spirits, and demons are also His ministers and administrators. An irrelevant word occurs to me here. A school of materialists holds that there is something selfish and shocking to morality in the desire of heavenly happiness for the individual; that he ought to work for the good of future generations, and not otherwise for his own good. The same of course applies to an age; it ought to work for the next age; and so forth. And the most future age of course has the greatest claim of all. Somewhat as a great man still among us, holds that numerical voting-power should increase the further the poor people are from the centres and opportunities of instruction and intelligence. Let us not thus have our "eyes in the ends of the earth." The people directly and remotely above us are the future ages at which we have to aim, to go towards them here, and join them at last, and increase the joy of their power. They are or should be *our* future ages. The people beyond us in the coming time are not our future at all. They will have their own lives given, and the battle of them given. And if by the regeneration of our hearts, which is our salvation by the Lord, we transmit to them a new and virtuous heredity, we have done the veriest best for them by our useful lives, and in this one essential embracing two points, the present and two futurities, we can safely leave our descendants to take care of themselves; having our little historical example also before them. If on the other hand, we take the downward road, each of us makes one demon the more to tempt and injure the family heredity frail in us all. Thus no one can work selfishly for his own salvation, but in battling for it and attaining it, he clears and purges human nature, and like his Master, Christ, inevitably works towards the saving of the whole race of man.

It is possible that the materialist tenderness to posterity has in it a large self-love, the very quality which is the serpent-egg of all known immorality. As thus: It is intended to compensate for the annihilation of the individual. To transmit this latter falsehood to human beings is to bind them in our special chains of disbelief; to dominate discovery and experience in their highest meaning and possibility. It is to dictate "the way, the truth, and the life" to those who are to come after us, out of our own present pates. The fruit must be immobility, the sameness of ages; the sap of time stagnating in the branches of the world-tree. Ultimately the death of all new knowledges and sciences in particular. For the very spirit of knowing is killed by it. We are the men, and wisdom dies with us. Posterity lives only upon *us*. To eat our flesh and drink our blood is its meat and drink. On the other hand the knowledge of God creating the conscience, and hourly purging the individual life, enables us to die daily; in the inner sense to have no care for the morrow, but to let its things care for themselves; and to leave posterity unbound by heredities which it is our constant business to abjure and eliminate. There is no self-love in this, but freedom from our dead oddities, from ourselves, Freedom transmitted to our children's children.

For our dear posterity, which the positivists would bind us to endow and establish, we have a typical lesson to learn in the land of Egypt which inherits the sepulchres of its past. By grace of dryness, a notable quality, its Pharaohs, dead and gone, have delivered their wealth of monuments, mummies, and selfhoods, to the future, and that future an Egypt which has no existence. And following this example, the inventors of our own dead dogmas, of which the pervert

Egypt of the Word is a standing representative, bequeath their monuments to the life of a posterity of which whoso dreams, let him dream. If we are wise we shall visit these simulacra carefully, as insalubrious, and as the abodes and breaths of doleful creatures. If we are foolish, we shall inhabit them, and aim to consign our next generations to their valleys of tombs, their sands and their wildernesses.

LXVI.—BEGINNINGS.

Everything has a beginning, and that beginning a ground before it; but no beginning has an irrelevant or inadequate ground. The arts and sciences of life all commence from small germs, and proceed often to surprising maturities. We must not conclude from this slender initiament that they grow in savage soil; but rather that the ground is tender, and has been long preparing for them, though not aware of them. They are not developments but implanted lives, not accidents but organisms, not protoplasms but square seeds. No new beginning is a development, though it seems to develop itself from circumstances. It always develops itself according to circumstances, but never from them. Real initiation is not in the nature of *things*. Originality has long and exact lines of ancestors above and behind, and also below; and it is original in conscious people because they feel and think themselves origins, and the claim is allowed by the supreme Giver, and contentedly endorsed all round. Yet the beginning is not in them excepting as the beginning of a child is unconsciously in the father, who knows nothing of the organism which proceeds by him.

The same is the case with the development of important nations, which seem at a certain time to put off a rude or barbarous state, and to enter upon a historical career of greatness. They were not decaying when they were unnoticed or seemingly unimportant, but slumbering and to be

BEGINNINGS. 301

awakened. They had in them the stuff or matrix which was fitted to receive a new impregnation. A condition of their infancy was that they knew nothing of the career which was to come to them. ' When Abram was led out of Ur of the Chaldees as one of the heads of a pastoral clan, and became the Patriarch Abraham, he was chosen for a quality in which the Jewish Dispensation could be implanted, a quality of reverence for external rituals which was unique, and which no men of the surrounding nations possessed. ' They were better than he; but they had not this needful quality; and so, as a ritual church was to be established, Abraham and his descendants, for that purpose of use, were the chosen people. But they themselves, with their father Abraham, originated nothing, but were only the fitting ground in which the Jewish future could become a seed, be vitalized and be enacted.

This is a typical instance, but it is also true of the modern nations. They similarly have emerged from rudeness, and as we call it from its grossness, barbarism; but the barbarism was full of industry, even of the industry of war. It was instinct with active will and understanding, and so far was not in the lines of decay. It wanted; nothing but impregnations, square seeds of the future, and they always, if good, come from above, and beget an advancing race: and if predominant, ensure it a long, or what is the same thing, a useful future. Their inheritances as they proceed become larger, more honest and more polite. When the crude races from which we have sprung naturally were born as nations, there was nothing in them of the history through which they have lived, but it is given to them year by year, according to their faculty of reception, as an unintermitting life. Our analogy of the seed flatly contradicts this in appearance, for does not the seed contain its future plant, and evolve itself into stalk, flower, fruit, and seeds by the heat and light of the suns of spring and summer? We reply, there is an end behind it which does it all, and is the current and present ancestor of its specific stages. The spiritual force, call it the unknown or what you please,—we call it Providence acting through the spiritual world,—is the agent, and were it subtracted in any step of the process, the plant would cease to be. It is indeed never subtracted, though circumstances may render its operation nil. And so it is with nations and races of themselves,—they are as grounds. Good seed is sown in them, and they are as gardens; but not of themselves. They are their own gardeners, but not of themselves. Ages give them new seeds leading to new fruits or uses, but not of themselves. The original bareness of their ground may thus be covered and forgotten in their fruitfulness and beauty; their ages may bloom in panoramic variety; but there is a supreme Husbandman sowing each stage of origins and beginnings, Who is the end and the cause.

And consider gardens from another point of view. All our modern garden-flowers are from wild stocks: perhaps we ought to say, almost all; for there may be among them, still illustrious, "most ancient" flowers which we do not appreciate. But for the others, manifestly they are what they are "not of themselves." Man is interpolated as the beginning of them as garden-series. He is with fruits also as a new originator. His will and understanding are put into the unconscious plants, flocks and herds, and they are raised to a level answering now to his annual expectations and desires. Still not of themselves. The gardener is a spiritual being; and the influx of his affections into skill and science is a new creation for the plants. It is a great fact and a great metaphor in one. Use to Man is at the bottom of it. The existence of gardening is thus a parable of what one good man in a kingdom may be, and of what One Divine Man is in the world.

Each life to a spiritually-minded man furnishes proofs that in the gifts of the mind every man is a receiver and not an originator, a steward and not a proprietor. To the earliest days in which life was merely an inspiration and an

BEGINNINGS. 303.

expiration, baby words came as a tiny seed from without. After that, words were divided into knowledges and the expression of them, and then first things were named and summoned, and baby affections were opened. The young child had this done for him, and did not do it for himself. If he could have attempted to effect it he would have spoilt the process, by interfering with the consummate agent, and foiling the mortal instrument. By and by some early bent discovers itself in the child, some doll with an unknown future state is nursed. The future state, though it be a line of kings, is nothing, but the doll is the beloved and the all. If the issues of this were foreseen, known, and attempted to be manipulated and managed, the doll would be ruined and cast aside. But the ruler of childhood gives ignorance of the future as shield for the delights of the present. The genius that makes the doll alive, and the affection that embraces it, are both of them gifts, and as such are watched and protected with sacred tenderness by the mother, to whom also this tenderness is from the first a gift, new, self-evident, unaccountable. At a later stage life-purposes begin, and a special opening of the understanding is given for each: the purpose and the understanding together constitute a new genius. Some science flows from it, nourishes it, and strengthens it; and works embody it. All these are superadded gifts to an organism made and prepared to receive them. Looking back upon them, you discern now, even from the dim past, that they were consciously prophesied and prepared for. But you also discern, that whenever the issues were happy, they were not your own, and that the more impersonal and unappropriated they were, the happier they were; and the more inspired by a power not your own that made for their joyful usufruct. Accidents often seem to be in the origination of the gifts: but these are not accidents, but rapid moments of impregnation, pleasurable or painful.

What are called conversions, when they are real, or when

you do not make them magically out of yourself, are among surprising gifts; altering gradually a whole life, and subordinating the series of it to a new Order and Ruler. The constant cry they utter, and the claim they make is, that they are not from the man himself. "Non nobis Domine!" The conclusion is that Life is Influx; that all epochs, accidents and chances are in the contemplation and play of it; that man is the responsible receiver and not the origin or proprietor of it; and that the more devoutly this truth is acknowledged, the greater is the personal individuality of the man, and the greater the security for him of large affections and inspired understandings.

LXVII.—SPIRITUAL RULERS.

It may be noted for the natural mind to which such considerations are new, that love, wisdom, goodness, truth, charity, faith, though usually reckoned as mere attributes of human beings, are substances and forms, namely in the lives of those human beings; and determine the characters and deeds of men and their entire humanities. Conscience is the recipient organ and commanding agent of them: a gradually warming and enlightening conscience; ultimately a spiritual conscience. Life on the one hand embraces all the details of our daily existence; so many and so concrete, so filling every hour with varieties of works, that the mind at first resents the supereminent singleness of its own only principles upon which life should proceed. They are regarded as nothings, though heavenwise they overhang and mate themselves to everything, and whether for good or evil become everything. To take an instance. War is a solid fact with its armies and strategists, its battles, successes and defeats. But the only essence it is at last confronted with, lies in the righteous judgment, Whether it is a just and absolutely necessary war. Almsgiving, commonly mistaken for charity, is a common occurrence, but charity, the truth and good of charity, supervises it, and judges in each particular gift whether it is wisely given, and whether it will do good, or harm. Successful speculation and business in general are another field of instances, and these affairs are judged as honest or dishonest; moral principle being of their essence.

Love and hatred are both supervised by mere goodness and truth: as, do we love and hate persons, or do we love their good and what is good in them, or do we hate or love their evil and what is evil in them? All these three things are possible, indeed common: but the good and the true decide upon the *quale* of our love and its inevitable actions. Do we eat too much, or drink too much, for our conscience to approve? These random instances are sufficient to show that love and wisdom, good and truth, charity and faith are, or can be, daily life; and that as judgments and justices they are co-extensive in immeasurable detail with all the things of life: that they are a supereminent universe made in the image and likeness of God and man, and that a heaven corresponding to the educational earth, with all its details in a higher life, is their final name. They, or their opposites, are all the deeds done in the body.

LXVIII.—GOLD AS SOCIAL SUBSTANCE.

A word on the precious metals by one who does not follow the national and international dynamics which lie in the adoption and alteration of standards of value. Is there not a Divine Providence in the creation of gold for the service of human society? The mere name and fame of it is a birth of men in stony places, and a builder of cities and inhabited provinces in far continents. And of itself it is a noble metal beyond the wear and tear of the chemistry of time. It is beautiful. It is amenable to amalgam with other metals, and easily recoverable from the condescension of embracing them: they can be called off to other unions: gold remains unblemished. It is bred in rocks and revealed in atoms in watercourses; and the believer in the atoms is led by them through faith to the mines. It is always good. I know not whether there are different kinds of gold, but some is yellow and some is red. If there are varieties, they are rather loves and amities of variety than differences. Genesis says of Havilah, "the gold of that land is good." It is the first word of gold in the Word, and echoes the declaration of the sixth day, that "God saw everything that He had made, and behold it was very good." In that Adamic Æon there was *auri sacra fames*, a sacred hunger for the good of gold, and an innocence unconscious of the evil.

Gold is rare, and the appetite for it unbounded, and its scarceness combined with its other qualities crowns it with value of use. There is perhaps just enough of it to be the handiest of representative values, while it has also real value from imperishability, beauty, tradition of gifts from love and friendship, tradition of religious gifts and services; tradition of royal crowns and noble coronets. It represents the human mind in its best affections and worst passions from all ages. The seal and die of God and Cæsar are both upon it. And its practical utility is as much clearly providential as its other prerogatives. By its scarcity it drives value home. If it existed for us more easily or in other quantities than it does, it would either by its deficiency be only a jewel and ornament, or by its redundance make food and raiment and habitation compete with it in representative power, and so to speak outweigh its purchases in barter. As it stands it is the last blow in cancelling debts, and a perpetual readjustment in the interest of honesty and equality. At the same time it admits to the extent of proved and settled public credit, supplements, such as other metals, notes and all paper bonds, for its own convenience, until it can travel; and restricts or refuses these whenever it is itself in straits. It is therefore the universal solvent of promises to pay; and the more honest the people are, the promises themselves become more good or golden. Discount is the measure of uncertainty, dishonesty, distance, or other inconvenience.

No other substance but gold can minister thus. Diamonds are too rare, and destructive of value in division. Silver is too abundant, and silver kings if they could would swamp the treasuries of the world, and make them bankrupt in the moral and spiritual arts of purchase. And mere notes endorsed by men or companies with no answerable gold behind them, would require universal honesty ; nor only that, but universal wisdom, to undertake no works that will be found ruinous and unjustifiable ; and a foresight that would amount to a supernatural prevision.

So gold, like a merciless and merciful ruler comes to the front by its divine right ; and calls us up, as no other hungry divinity can, to show our property in it as the gauge of our existence in the body and in society. Have not our good Jews a relation to this precious gold, this love of theirs, something like what they have to the Old Testament ? They are perchance the bottom and basis of an insistance upon gold as ultimate value. So-called Christians indeed love the same metal well, but they believe in paper longer than the Jew does ; and would carry on larger business in it alone were it not for the Rothschilds and others to whom gold is the *ultima ratio* of transactions, and the key to the kingdom of solvency.

LXIX.—THE DIVINE CYCLE.

" Our Saviour Jesus Christ," says Paul to Timothy, " has brought life and immortality to light through the gospel." This opens up, in strict connection with the subjects now treated of, the question of immortality ; for question is made of it by many of the learned. The Lord brought it to light, for it was not in light when He came. He gave it life ;

for His life was the light of men. He is the resurrection and the life.

Had the world then been without the belief in a life after death before His coming? It is an opinion in the Church that the Jewish Scriptures contain no recognition of the immortality of man before the Babylonish Captivity, and that the Jews brought the notion of it from Babylon. It may indeed be that the Jews themselves read nothing of a future state in their inspired writings, but applied them wholly to this world; but to the Christian reader in the light of the gospel there are thousands of passages in the Psalms and the Prophets which transparently announce the perpetuity of the life of man, and the existence of a heaven and a hell. Judaism in the Church can indeed degrade them into promises of prosperity, and threatenings of adversity, limited to the world and the body; but they can fairly be read quite otherwise.

There is however a meaning in the presumption that the Jews brought the idea of a future life from Babylon. All the ancient nations had a greater purview of some immortal condition than the children of Israel, to whom the present life with its good things was the *summum bonum*. The genius of this people above all the world was secular-religious. That genius marked them out for obedience to ritual, in barter for length of days, inheritance in Canaan for all generations, plentiful harvests, election as God's peculiar people, and in the end universal Messianic dominion. Such satisfaction with the blessings as they held them of the present life, closed their perceptions against spiritual things which became nothing to them, and made the deathbeds of Patriarchs more into last wills and testaments to their descendants who were gathered round them, than into pious voices from the first steps of the ladder which reaches from earth to heaven. For the Jews were secularists *plus* a secular Jehovah. With the other nations it was not so, but with all their later idolatries they had a belief in the life to come dependent upon the life man leads here, and it is impossible that that belief, self-made and unverifiable as it was, did not influence them to something of good. The Egyptians had explicit ideas of this mortal life weighed in the balances of divine justice, and doom according to the state and preponderance of virtue : no arbitrary judgment, but a portion allotted according to acquired character. Osiris did not judge the man, but the man's life judged itself. (Rawlinson's *Herodotus*, vol. ii. p. 256.) This fact stands out even through the confusion of metempsychosis, which also has a spiritual side to it. The other nations known to the Jews, perhaps excepting Babylon, from which the Jews were least likely to bring the notion of a future state, had survivals of belief differently from the Jews, who also, until they had finally secularized themselves, were incapable of being made the vehicle and subject of the mere ritual of a church. Abraham, as we shall see presently, had to pass clean through idolatry, and to accept Jehovah as a local and national god, one, and the most mighty, of many, before he stood as the chieftain of the Jewish Dispensation. Jehovah for him was his warrior, in successful conflict with the gods of the Canaanitish nations.

The view held by learned biblicists, and accredited generally to Bishop Warburton, that the Jews first heard tell of immortality from beyond the pale of their own religion, is in evidence that that creed existed in the world before their time ; and the question occurs, how did it take its rise? We have seen that the condition of the world from Adam to Moses was no bare theism or monotheism in which the Father and Creator had left man to acknowledge a god as an abstraction of his own mind ; but that a series of Revelations and consequent vessels or Churches extended through those ages, and were the connections of God with man. Also that all the nations after Noah or the Flood were branches of the Ancient or Spiritual Church, which succeeded the destroyed Adam or Celestial Church. The most ancient tradition and the new organ, conscience, worked together to impart and confirm a belief in personal immortality in opposition to the sensual fact of the mortality of the individual and the race. From these two sources of real information, each regenerate man knew in his best hours, and acknowledged always, that his life here was a natural preparation for a spiritual life; that mortality, or birth at the bottom of the scale, must precede immortality. The Greek axiom, that whatever has a beginning must have an end, was with him a godly and not a physical, scientific or logical truth. The end the beginning has is its purpose, of serving as a basis for the never-ending stages or imperfections of an unending life. This, not in the beasts, but in all souls that have *the capacity* of knowing the Creator. Immortality lies therein both for those who are in good, and for those who are in evil.

"It was usual with the ancients to say when anyone died, that he was gathered to his fathers, or to his people, and they meant thereby that he actually came to his parents, to his relations and kinsfolk in the other life. They got this form of expression from the most ancient people who were celestial men, and who during their abode on earth, were at the same time with the angels in heaven, and thus knew how the real case was. They knew that all who were in the same good meet and are together in the other life, and likewise all who are in the same truth. Of the former they said that they were gathered to their fathers; but of the latter that they were gathered to their people; for father with them signified good, and people signified truth" (*Arcana*, n. 3255).

But in the Most Ancient Church, Heaven present was a perceived fact. The ministry of angels, open vision and every-day seership, were implanted in the natural life. There were not two worlds in the sense of disconnection, but in the sense of order necessary for promotion. Communion between the two was as between parent and child, the Lord being the parent in and through all in the higher degree, and the child in and through all in the lower. The sense of death was eliminated, save as a putting off one state in order to be clothed upon with another. This primeval state of revelation, communion and personal inspiration, is the root of all that was known and thought of a future state until the coming of the Lord. The Ancient Church inherited the memory of it from the Most Ancient; and the ancient nations, so long as they had any human remains, carried it down as a fading tradition. In Greece it was an argument and a decoration of discourse. In Rome a governmental, political, and oratorical copy.

The belief however was kept casually alive and latent by dreams and visions, whether productions of literary imagination, or of real experience; Homer and Virgil both took their heroes to the shades, and reported of destinies there. And Cicero, in the *Somnium Scipionis*, has given a noble view of the destiny of patriotism in the skies. Moreover the ghostly experiences of all races in all ages, superstitions as they are called, and facts as they are, have kept belief in that other life from which the phantoms hail, alive in the fears and awe of all people, savage and civilized.

At the beginning therefore Revelation was the only source of the knowledge of a spiritual world ; namely, by that world actually revealed as a current fact, and factor for life, and for the conduct of life. The race was then known not to be naturally but conditionally immortal. It was saved from its own suicide by the raising up of successive Churches by which a new life was given from on high. So futile is the modern thought that the individuals can all die, and the race survive. Both would perish if there were not a Saviour foreseen from the first for both. And the race here would probably expire first before the so-called ghosts above.

Revelation in Christ is again the source of all our faith, charity and knowledge touching a future state. Apart from His revelation no man can have any certainty of his own survival after death. He can balance the sides of his advocacy *pro* and *con*, and find no end, "in wandering mazes lost." Abandon the Christian religion for information of faith, and there is none to hand. Accordingly our much esteemed Emeritus Professor F. W. Newman, with a candour irreproachable, says: "As soon as I ceased to trust the Scriptures of the New Testament as a divine revelation, my acceptance of a Future Life *as a dogma* at once fell away. But knowing that so many holy souls had devoutly believed it and that ostensibly it had ennobled their devoted lives, I held to it with a loose hand, feeling assured that if the Supreme Lord judged it better for them and for me, He would bestow a second life, as freely as He had bestowed a first life, without our asking; but if on the contrary for good reasons of His own He did not grant it, then I was sure that that was best for us." My friend here, without ceding his doubt, refers touchingly to the Communion of Saints on earth, as he understands it. I cannot but agree with him that no man can solidly find out a future state for himself without an express revelation on the subject; and my wonder is that such a mind as the Professor's should not see that the Supreme Lord in whom he so implicitly believes, is able and sure to furnish such a revelation to His children not only to instruct them about a future state if it exists, but about Himself and His perfections, which no searching can find out; a revelation which He can make by a condescending Word, as easily as He can create man and the universe. To me a speechless God is an incredible god; and a God who commits himself to be manufactured by human faculties is a vote-made parliamentary god: one being or a thousand, the hysteroplasm of universal suffrage. Atheism is a not unreasonable escape from such a ridiculous issue, though the cure is worse than the disorder.

Of course the immediate answer to this is, that the Word alleged to be the voice of God is full of contradictions, and inhumane and unsatisfactory. It attributes to God acts and qualities undivine; and therefore disproves its pretensions,.

THE DIVINE CYCLE. 313

or the claims men make for it. We have already discussed this question, and do not re-open it. But let the reader who is able study the spiritual sense and its modification of "the letter which killeth." Few can do this as yet. But the number will increase; and will be sufficient in a time of waiting to be a light on the hills for those who are in the valleys. If I may use the phrase reverently when I think of this lover of so many great truths, it is a "suspicious circumstance" against the Theist,—seeing that an authentic Word would be a divine proof of love from the Allfather to His offspring, as a father's voice is a human proof of love to the young and inexperienced,—that there is what professes to be a revelation at present in command in the world; in short, what calls itself The Word; and that it is not investigated in the new light brought by Swedenborg. It would seem that it ought to be a subject of much painstaking, nay of devout theist prayer, to consider whether under any of the new conditions it fills the gap between God and Man; and in reality, against some appearances, can have God for its Author.

But the Lord has not only vouchsafed a Word with a future state omnipresent as a visible doctrine in the New Testament; but He has commissioned the same Emanuel Swedenborg to make known the future state of that Word itself, in the world and in the heavens, by revealing through him the spiritual sense which is for the New Jerusalem. And furthermore, by the same instrumentality, he has furnished to mankind a complete and therefore a rational account, of the life after death; adding full experience of all that is needful to be known for the dwellers upon earth. He has also again revealed Himself and His perfections, unknowable otherwise, to all coming generations. He has brought his Heaven of Angels to the doors of knowledge, and made it evident that they are not without a function, but like the good men they were on earth, they are active, working, industrial angels, and our brethren more than ever;

and that they carry the human form with all its marriages and supremest functions; and moreover that as "the heavens are not pure in His sight," and "He charges them with folly," that they are under the correction of divine judicial light, and obedient to this that they are ever advancing and perfecting. See on these subjects Swedenborg's *Heaven and Hell* before cited.

The subject of a spiritual world and a future state is therefore in a series. It was communion of angels with men, in the Most Ancient Church; universal personal experience. It was taught in the Ancient Word to the Ancient Church, and the memory and tradition of the most ancient days were also preserved in it. Doubtless spiritual openings and communications where needed and possible concurred for the strengthening of faith. It was covert in the Jews, and this world was enough for them when they rightly used it. In both the lives of Christ, natural and divine natural, it was His commanding doctrine and most comfortable assurance. In these days, of the initiation of His New Christian Church, it is a revealed unique personal fact. And thus a divine cycle is completed from Revelation to Revelation, and from experience to experience.

THE END.

ROBERT R. SUTHERLAND, PRINTER, EDINBURGH.

WORKS BY THE SAME AUTHOR.

Crown 8vo, cloth, 5s. nett,
Epidemic Man and His Visitations.

Crown 8vo, cloth, 6s. nett,
The African and the True Christian Religion.
His Magna Charta.

Crown 8vo, cloth, 6s.,
The Soul is Form and doth the Body Make. A Chapter in Psychology.

Crown 8vo, cloth, 6s.,
Oannes according to Berosus. A Study in the Church of the Ancients.

Crown 8vo, cloth, 6s.,
Revelation, Mythology, Correspondences.

Second Edition, Foolscap 8vo, cloth, 2s.,
Emanuel Swedenborg : A Biographical Sketch.

Crown 8vo, cloth, 9s.,
The Greater Origins and Issues of Life and Death.

8vo, cloth, 8s.,
Human Science, Good and Evil, and its Works; and Divine Revelation, and its Works and Sciences.

Second Edition, Crown 8vo, cloth,
The Human Body, and its Connection with Man.

Post 8vo, cloth, 2s. 6d.,
War, Cholera, and the Ministry of Health. An Appeal to the British People.

18mo, cloth,
Improvisations.

WORKS BY THE SAME AUTHOR—*Continued.*

8vo, sewed, 1s.,
Our Social Health. A Paper read before the Ladies' Sanitary Association.

8vo, sewed, 1s.,
Painting with Both Hands; or, the Adoption of the Principle of the Stereoscope in Art, as a means to Binocular Pictures.

TRANSLATIONS BY THE SAME AUTHOR.

Foolscap 8vo, cloth, 1s. 6d.,
Angelic Wisdom concerning the Divine Love and concerning the Divine Wisdom.
By EMANUEL SWEDENBORG.

Two vols. 8vo,
The Animal Kingdom, considered Anatomically, Physically, and Philosophically.
By EMANUEL SWEDENBORG.

One vol. 8vo,
Outlines of a Philosophical Argument on the Infinite, and the Final Cause of Creation; and on the Intercourse between the Soul and the Body.
By EMANUEL SWEDENBORG.

8vo, 2s. 6d.,
Posthumous Tracts on Philosophical Subjects.
By EMANUEL SWEDENBORG.

8vo,
A Hieroglyphic Key to Natural and Spiritual Mysteries by way of Representations and Correspondences.
By EMANUEL SWEDENBORG.

LONDON: JAMES SPEIRS, 36 Bloomsbury Street.

www.ingramcontent.com/pod-product-compliance
Lightning Source LLC
Chambersburg PA
CBHW030003240426
43672CB00007B/813